CONVERSATIONS WITH RICK VEITCH

Conversations with Comic Artists M. Thomas Inge, General Editor

Conversations with Rick Veitch

Edited by Brannon Costello

University Press of Mississippi / Jackson

The University Press of Mississippi is the scholarly publishing agency of the Mississippi Institutions of Higher Learning: Alcorn State University, Delta State University, Jackson State University, Mississippi State University, Mississippi University for Women, Mississippi Valley State University, University of Mississippi, and University of Southern Mississippi.

www.upress.state.ms.us

The University Press of Mississippi is a member of the Association of University Presses.

Any discriminatory or derogatory language or hate speech regarding race, ethnicity, religion, sex, gender, class, national origin, age, or disability that has been retained or appears in elided form is in no way an endorsement of the use of such language outside a scholarly context.

Copyright © 2025 by University Press of Mississippi
All rights reserved
Manufactured in the United States of America

∞

Publisher: University Press of Mississippi, Jackson, USA
Authorised GPSR Safety Representative: Easy Access System Europe -
Mustamäe tee 50, 10621 Tallinn, Estonia, *gpsr.requests@easproject.com*

Library of Congress Cataloging-in-Publication Data

Names: Costello, Brannon, 1975– editor.
Title: Conversations with Rick Veitch / edited by Brannon Costello.
Description: Jackson : University Press of Mississippi, 2025. |
  Series: Conversations with comic artists series |
  Includes bibliographical references and index.
Identifiers: LCCN 2025412011 (print) | LCCN 2025412012 (ebook) |
  ISBN 9781496857804 (hardback) | ISBN 9781496857811 (trade paperback) |
  ISBN 9781496857828 (epub) | ISBN 9781496857835 (epub) |
  ISBN 9781496857842 (pdf) | ISBN 9781496857798 (pdf)
Subjects: LCSH: Veitch, Rick—Interviews. | Comics artists—United States—Interviews. |
  Comic books, strips, etc.—United States—History and criticism. | LCGFT: Interviews.
Classification: LCC PN6727.V45 Z46 2025 (print) | LCC PN6727.V45 (ebook) |
  DDC 741.5/973 [B]—dc23/eng/20250211
LC record available at https://lccn.loc.gov/2025412011
LC ebook record available at https://lccn.loc.gov/2025412012

British Library Cataloging-in-Publication Data available

Major Works by Rick Veitch

(AS WRITER/ARTIST UNLESS OTHERWISE NOTED)

Two-Fisted Zombies (Last Gasp, 1973); with cowriter Tom Veitch
1941: The Illustrated Story (HM Communications/Pocket Books, 1979); adaption of a screenplay with collaborator Stephen R. Bissette
Abraxas and the Earthman (Marvel/Epic, 1982–1983)
Heartburst (Marvel/Epic, 1984)
The One (Marvel/Epic, 1985–1986)
Swamp Thing #65–76, 79–87 (DC, 1987–1989); writer and primary penciller, with contributions from other artists
"The River," *Teenage Mutant Ninja Turtles* #24–26 (Mirage, 1989)
Brat Pack (King Hell, 1990–1991)
The Maximortal (Tundra, 1992–1993)
1963 (Image, 1993); with collaborators Alan Moore, Stephen R. Bissette, and others
Roarin' Rick's Rare Bit Fiends #1–25 (King Hell/Sun, 1994–)
Teknophage #1–6 (Tekno Comix, 1995); with artist Bryan Talbot
"Greyshirt," in *Tomorrow Stories* (WildStorm/ABC, 1999–2001); with writer Alan Moore
Greyshirt: Indigo Sunset (WildStorm/ABC, 2001–2002); with various artists
Can't Get No (DC/Vertigo, 2006)
Shiny Beasts (2007); with various collaborators
Army@Love (DC/Vertigo, 2007–2009); with inker Gary Erskine
The Big Lie (Image, 2011); with inker Gary Erskine
Super Catchy (Sun, 2016)
The Spotted Stone (Sun, 2017)
Otzi (Sun, 2018)
Redemption (Sun, 2019)
Tombstone Hand (Sun, 2021)
BONG! Comix: Underground Classix (Sun, 2022); with various collaborators
Boy Maximortal (King Hell/Sun, 2017–2023)
True-Man: The Maximortal (King Hell/Sun, 2024–)

Rare Bit Fiends Collections
Rabid Eye (King Hell, 1995)
Pocket Universe (King Hell, 1996)
Crypto Zoo (King Hell, 2004)
Azoth (Sun, 2022)

CONTENTS

Introduction   ix

Chronology   xvii

Rick Veitch: A Talk with Swamp Thing's New Writer   3
Mark Waid / 1987

Veitch Speaks: From Swamp to Sewer   7
Darwin McPherson / 1989

Lacking Proper Adult Supervision   28
Daniel A. Dickholtz / 1990

Rick Veitch: The New Breed of Hero   34
Stanley Wiater and Stephen R. Bissette / 1992

Maximum Myths   47
Harley Jebens / 1994

Can't Get No Aquaman? Rick Veitch   55
Jennifer M. Contino / 2003

The Comics Reporter Sunday Interview: Rick Veitch   61
Tom Spurgeon / 2007

Dream a Deeper Dream: A How-To Conversation
with Cartoonist Rick Veitch   70
Jay Babcock / 2009

viii CONTENTS

Rick Veitch: A Vermonter's Life in Comics   85
Andy Kolovos / 2016

Rick Veitch Interview: *1963*   117
Duy Tano / 2020

Rick Veitch Interview: Panel Vision and Greyshirt   135
Duy Tano / 2021

Here Comes the Sun: The Twenty-First-Century Rick Veitch Universe   157
Stephen R. Bissette / 2023

The Form of the Future   193
Brannon Costello / 2023

Index   217

INTRODUCTION

In a metafictional moment in issue #23 of his autobiographical dream comic *Roarin' Rick's Rare Bit Fiends* (2018), artist and writer Rick Veitch pauses to clarify an important distinction between imagination and fantasy. Turning to address the reader directly, he explains, "Fantasy is all about generating wish fulfillment scenarios for our fears and desires, but imagination tackles reality head on. We use our imaginations to build things. Solve problems. Make art." Veitch's explanation offers a useful framework for thinking about a central theme of his long, varied, and distinguished career: the tension between the potential of comics as an imaginative form capable of expanding our capacity to recognize reality's depth and complexity and the all-too-frequent actuality of comics as an exhausted consumer product peddling vapid fantasies that starve and diminish our imaginations. A comics creator since childhood, Veitch knows all too well the many persistent obstacles to making comics that challenge readers instead of condescending to them. Yet throughout a career that has survived speculator-driven booms and busts, the narrowing of publishing and distribution channels, and the rampant success of works that pander to the audience's worst instincts, Veitch remains optimistic about the potential of comics. As he remarked to me in the interview that closes this volume, because of comics' capacity for "syncing word and image" and thus "syncing the mind," comics "might be the form of the future."

If so, Rick Veitch's comics are a map to that future. From his earliest underground publications to his work for corporate publishers to his intensely personal self-published projects, Veitch has created a body of work unlike anyone else's. Employing a style that synthesizes Jack Kirby at his most cosmic, the mind-bending graphic sensibility of European innovators such as Jean (Moebius) Giraud and Philippe Druillet, and the brass-tacks realism of classic war cartoonists such as John Severin and Russ Heath, Veitch infuses popular genres—especially superheroes, war stories, and science fiction—with his personal, idiosyncratic philosophical musings and pointedly satirical, productively askew political perspective. Yet Veitch's capacious mind reaches beyond these familiar genres, too, as the long-running *Rare Bit Fiends* attests. Creating provocative, ambitious work, often within the so-called mainstream comics market, Veitch has earned a reputation as a fierce advocate for creators' rights, a commitment that is evident in his comics' unflinching critique of the corporate publishers' unscrupulous business practices and cynical commercialism. Unsurprisingly, Veitch has had a complex and sometimes contentious relationship with some of the major publishers, especially DC Comics, and he has been an enthusiastic and influential booster of independent publishers and self-publishing—while also being painfully aware of the ways those models have not always realized their full potential. As the interviews collected here make plain, Veitch is both a shrewd observer of the pitfalls of the marketplace and an eloquent spokesman for the boundless potential of creativity. Taken together, these conversations offer profound insights not only into the development of Veitch's graphic innovations and philosophical explorations but also into the upheavals and transformations of American comics from the 1970s to today.

Drawn to cartooning at a young age—despite discouragement from his parents and narrow-minded neighbors in Bellows Falls, Vermont—Veitch found a mentor and kindred spirit in his older brother, Tom. Though perhaps best known for his work on *Star Wars* comics, Tom Veitch began his comics career in the freewheeling world of the undergrounds in the early 1970s, and Rick followed him there as soon as he could. Their early collaborations included *Crazymouse*, published in the University of Vermont's student newspaper and in a scattering of underground titles beginning in 1968, and *Two-Fisted Zombies* (1973), a science-fiction/horror comic that recalls both Jack Kirby and "Spain" Rodriguez. Although his early comics are, as one would expect, relatively crude compared to his mature work, Veitch's underground roots remain vital to his identity and approach to his work, regardless of publisher. As he told me, "[I]n my heart of hearts, I'm really an underground cartoonist." Indeed, the iconoclastic, boundary-pushing sensibility of his underground work also characterizes his subversive take on everything from Swamp Thing to superheroes.

Looking for ways to make a living with his art, Veitch became a member of the inaugural class of the Joe Kubert School of Cartoon and Graphic Art, where he met lifelong friends and collaborators Stephen R. Bissette, Tom Yeates, and John Totleben. More than just a means to improve his drawing and advance his career, the Kubert School also inculcated in him a spirit of collaboration and community. In our interview, he recalled being a student working with Kubert as an equal in the service of a larger goal: "We would sit, and I'd pitch an idea to him, and the two of us would start playing with it. That's when I first really learned the pleasures of collaboration, where two people kind of surrender their egos to the story itself." Veitch began his professional career with journeyman efforts, often working with his Kubert School classmates, on titles such as *Sgt. Rock* and *G. I. Combat*. However, his aesthetic aspirations were irrevocably transformed in the late 1970s when he encountered borderline surreal tales serialized in the slick French science-fiction magazine *Metal Hurlant* and its English-language companion, *Heavy Metal*. Taking advantage of the high production values of Marvel's *Heavy Metal*–inspired *Epic Illustrated* magazine—as well as of *Epic's* unusual creative license and creator-friendly rights agreements—Veitch produced several visually stunning short pieces and serialized his first long-form work, the *Moby-Dick*–inspired outer-space adventure *Abraxas and the Earthman* (1982–1983), in its pages. Veitch's next major work, *Heartburst* (1984), originally intended for serialization in *Epic Illustrated* before being switched to the Marvel Graphic Novel line, reflects the development of Veitch's visual style and the emergence of his thematic preoccupations, including the pernicious similarities between religious devotion and the worship of popular culture. Veitch's next work for Marvel/Epic, a six-issues series called *The One* (1985–1986), is also the first entry in his mature phase. In this early revisionist superhero tale, Veitch weaves together a penetrating critique of the fascist aspects of the superhero myth with a trippy, psychedelic vision of the spiritual possibilities of the superhero archetype, possibilities only attainable if readers and artists can reimagine the superhero as something other than a nationalist icon or corporate property. Though overshadowed by later works of superhero revisionism, *The One* remains an original and powerful investigation into the limitations and affordances of the superhero.

During the 1980s, Veitch collaborated with rising star Alan Moore on a variety of projects, including the controversial graphic childbirth issue of *Miracleman* (#9, 1986). Veitch also pitched in to assist Bissette and Totleben when deadlines were looming on the Moore-penned *Swamp Thing*, an act of friendly generosity that led to Veitch's commercial breakthrough, first as a regular artist on *Swamp Thing* and then as Moore's chosen successor to write the series beginning in 1987. Although his tenure on *Swamp Thing* was justly celebrated in its time for its originality and ambition, it is best remembered now for its notoriously abrupt conclusion. As part of a lengthy time-travel epic, Veitch planned a story in which Swamp Thing would meet Jesus Christ during his meditations in the Garden of Gethsemane. Though originally approved by DC editorial as a respectful treatment of the subject, the company got cold feet at the last minute and refused to publish it, and the understandably indignant Veitch resigned. DC's behavior ignited a controversy in the comics press, as many commentators praised Veitch's integrity and pointed out the hypocrisy of the company's skittish handling of sensitive subject matter in a series that it promoted as a beacon of artistic sophistication and maturity.

Veitch channeled his rage at the narrow-mindedness and cynicism of corporate comics into his next two major works. *Brat Pack* (1990–1991) explores the scuzzy underside of the "kid sidekick" figure to expose the authoritarian and psychosexual subtext of the superhero genre and jab at the exploitation of young comics readers who are sold heroic fantasies by cynical publishers. Although the series' fiercely barbed satire of caped crusaders is consistent with the attitudes of his later work, Veitch has expressed regret for the ways in which his depiction of the predatory relationship between Midnight Mink and Chippy, a pair of Batman and Robin stand-ins, relied on homophobic caricature.[1] *The Maximortal* (1992–1993), set in the same universe as *Brat Pack*, builds on the ideas in *The One* to provide a shadow history of twentieth-century popular culture as a contest between the sublime potential of the superhero archetype and the social and political forces that can only understand the superhero as a commodity or a weapon. These works form the foundation of what he calls the King Hell Heroica, an elaborate superhero metafiction that is still ongoing.

During this period, Veitch embraced self-publishing, which gave him the freedom to produce titles such as the idiosyncratic dream comic *Roarin' Rick's Rare Bit Fiends*, launched in 1994. Remarkably long-lived for such a personal project, *Rare Bit Fiends* draws inspiration from classic newspaper cartoonists such as Winsor McCay and contemporary comics surrealists such as Jim Woodring, exploring the philosophical and psychological nature of dreams by documenting Veitch's own dreaming life. Moreover, each issue of *Rare Bit Fiends* typically features a lively letters column along with reader-submitted dream comics and suggested resources for those interested in dreamwork. In this way, *Rare Bit Fiends* functions not simply as a vehicle for Veitch's own dream explorations but also as a site of connection and collaboration for fellow dreamworkers. This approach is typical of Veitch's view of himself not as an alienated individualistic genius but as a member of a thriving community. In his interview with Andy Kolovos published for the first time in this volume, Veitch connects this sensibility to his identity as a Vermonter. Describing how he and Bissette approach the world of comics, he explains, "as Vermonters, we have a sense of community. We want everybody to succeed; we want the art form to grow."

This generous, collaborative spirit is also apparent in Veitch's exploration of the new possibilities of the internet in the 1990s with his virtual comic convention website Comicon.com, an online space for independent creators to connect with each other and to hawk their wares directly to customers.

Although this incarnation of Comicon.com has ended—it lives on as a pop culture news site—Veitch's comments on the experience are invaluable for understanding the evolving relationship between comics culture and the internet. Around this time, Veitch also worked with upstart publisher Image Comics on 1963 (1993), a collaboration with Alan Moore, Stephen R. Bissette, and others that replicated the visual and narrative style of early Marvel Comics and drew an implicit contrast between Silver Age and modern comics. He and Moore collaborated again on *Supreme*, which also blended and contrasted modern and retro comics sensibilities, and on stories featuring Greyshirt, a trilby-sporting crimefighter inspired by Will Eisner's the Spirit, in *Tomorrow Stories*, part of Moore's America's Best Comics (ABC) line for WildStorm Productions. In *Greyshirt: Indigo Sunset* (2001–2002), written and primarily drawn by Veitch along with an all-star cast of guest artists including Dave Gibbons, Russ Heath, and David Lloyd, Veitch reveals the character's origins in a rewardingly complex tale that brings a fresh perspective to some of the themes that it shares with the King Hell Heroica by engaging with the history and popularity of crime narratives in American culture. Only in a Rick Veitch comic would the final villain turn out to be the avatar of an ancient cosmic horror who is *also* a cutthroat television producer playing fast and loose with the intellectual property rights to his latest project.

When WildStorm head Jim Lee unexpectedly sold the company to DC Comics in 1999, Veitch and Moore found themselves producing comics for a company that had put them both through the wringer. Moore moved on after bringing his ABC stories to a close, but Veitch cautiously reconciled with DC, writing comics starring the Question and Aquaman and, more significantly, creating two projects for DC's Vertigo imprint. The first, *Can't Get No* (2006), is a luminous, hallucinatory fable about America in the aftermath of 9/11; here, Veitch brings his interest in Jungian thought to bear on his investigation of the collective psyche of a nation. The other, *Army@Love* (2007–2009), is a skewed take on classic DC war comics such as *Our Army at War* and *Sgt. Rock*. *Army@Love* satirizes the all-too-cozy relationship between the US military and the American entertainment industry that shaped how Americans understood the invasions of Afghanistan and Iraq during the George W. Bush era. Veitch's skepticism about the Bush administration also informs *The Big Lie* (2011), a controversial one-shot comic that gives voice to conspiracy theories about the collapse of the World Trade Center on 9/11.

In 2020, Veitch was named Cartoonist Laureate of Vermont, a position previously held by Alison Bechdel. However, now at age seventy-four, he shows no inclination to rest on his laurels. In addition to publishing educational comics

xiv INTRODUCTION

with his partner, Steve Conley, through their company Eureka Comics, Veitch has produced some of the most vital, boundary-smashing work of his career in recent years, including the long-delayed next installment of his King Hell Heroica in *Boy Maximortal* (2017–2023), further explorations into the dream-world in *Rare Bit Fiends*, and his experimental Panel Vision comics such as the downbeat multiversal media critique *Otzi* (2018) and the eerie Western *Tombstone Hand* (2021). His engagement with the politics, psychology, and spirituality of the superhero is a clear influence on works as different as *The Boys* (both the comic and the TV show) and *All-Star Superman*. Moreover, his incisive critique of how the corporate death-grip on superheroes impover-ishes our ability to recognize the genre's potential to radically reimagine the future is especially salient, given the overpowering dominance of the Mar-vel Cinematic Universe over our popular culture. In an era when the direct market seems to be perennially on the verge of collapse and cartoonists and publishers look for new publication and distribution avenues, Veitch's inter-views provide a valuable historical perspective on the evolution and strug-gles of self-publishing, independent publishers, and the use of the internet to sell, promote, and distribute comics. Always willing to consider a familiar idea from a fresh angle, Veitch is tremendously insightful about the connections between his work and the broader historical, social, and commercial contexts from which it emerges.

The interviews in this volume are arranged chronologically by the date they were originally conducted, to the extent that this could be determined. They have been reprinted as they were originally published, aside from minor corrections. Although some repetition across interviews is inevitable, the recurrence of particular subjects provides a valuable opportunity to consider how Veitch's perspective has evolved over the course of his career. No book can be completed in isolation, and that is doubly true for a collection like this one. Lisa McMurtray at the University Press of Mississippi is due great thanks for acquiring this project and seeing it to completion. Thanks also to Norman Ware for his careful and keen-eyed copyediting and to Corley Long-mire for ably shepherding the book through production. I extend particular gratitude to Tyler Sheldon, who provided invaluable transcription and editing assistance. Thanks to Rick Veitch for his patient and thorough assistance in compiling the chronology and pointing me toward interviews of which I was unaware as well as for permission to use the images included here. I am grate-ful to all the contributors who allowed their pieces to be included, with spe-cial thanks to Andy Kolovos and Stephen R. Bissette for allowing their pieces to appear here for the first time. Readers interested in further reading about

Veitch and the historical, aesthetic, and commercial contexts from which his work emerges would do well to read Bissette's *Teen Angels and New Mutants: Rick Veitch's Brat Pack and the Art, Karma, and Commerce of Killing Sidekicks* (2011). My appreciation to Brian Cremins for his encouragement about this project as it was taking shape and to Qiana Whitted for her insightful feedback on this introduction. My gratitude also to Gil Roth and Rebecca Damsen for putting me in touch with Jordan Raphael to secure permission for the piece from the late Tom Spurgeon included here. Finally, my thanks to Gina Costello, for nearly three decades (and counting) of inspiration and support.

BC

Note

1. See, for instance, Veitch's interview with Josephine Riesman, "Comics Creator Rick Veitch on Superhero Fascism and His Doubts about 9/11," *Vulture*, February 28, 2018, https://www.vulture.com/2018/02/the-one-creator-rick-veitch-talks-superheroes-and-9-11.html.

CHRONOLOGY

1951   Richard Ian Veitch is born on May 7 to Robert Veitch Jr. and Margaret MacDonald Veitch. He is the fourth of an eventual six children, including his older brother Tom, an important early influence on Rick, who would go on to become a poet, novelist, and well-known comics writer. Though born at Bellows Falls Hospital in Vermont, Veitch's earliest years were spent in Walpole, New Hampshire.

1956   The Veitch family moves to Bellows Falls when Veitch's father is hired at Robertson Paper.

1957   At age six, Veitch begins creating his own comics under the Sun Comics banner, including a series called *Hero Comics* starring his character Radioactive Man.

1963   In seventh grade, Veitch receives an honorable mention for a monster illustration submitted to a contest for *Drag Cartoons* magazine, a recognition that cements his ambition to become an artist.

1968   Veitch encounters underground comics, including *Zap Comix* #1, after his brother Tom moves to California. Rick and Tom's first published collaboration, the underground strip *Crazymouse*, runs in the University of Vermont newspaper the *Vermont Cynic*.

1969   Veitch graduates from Bellows Falls High School.

1970   Veitch moves to Stinson Beach, California. Crashing in the barn of underground cartoonist Greg Irons, Veitch begins working on *Two-Fisted Zombies* with Tom. A selection of short Crazymouse stories appears in the underground comic *Hee Hee*. Veitch's father dies.

1971   Veitch moves back to Vermont and continues working on *Two-Fisted Zombies*. "Old Magik," a Crazymouse story by Tom and Rick originally drawn in 1969, appears in *Tom Veitch Magazine* #4.

1973   *Two-Fisted Zombies* is published by Last Gasp. Veitch moves back to California.

1974   Veitch meets various figures associated with the underground comics scene at a *Rolling Stone* release party for *The History of Underground*

xvii

xviii CHRONOLOGY

Comics. Veitch begins keeping a dream journal and delves into the philosophy of Carl Jung. He returns to Vermont, where he marries his girlfriend, Kristen Keefe.

1975 Veitch's first son, Ezra, is born in February.

1976 Veitch enrolls in the Joe Kubert School of Cartoon and Graphic Art with the assistance of a Comprehensive Employment and Training Act (CETA) grant. A member of the school's inaugural class, he meets lifelong friends and collaborators there including Stephen R. Bissette and Tom Yeates. Veitch contributes "The White House Horror" to issue #2 of the underground series *Dr. Wirtham's Comix and Stories*.

1977 Veitch publishes his first work for DC Comics, collaborating with Stephen Bissette on "A Song for Saigon Sally!" for *Sgt. Rock* #311. Future Veitch collaborator John Totleben enrolls in the Kubert School.

1978 Veitch graduates from the Kubert School. He continues contributing to *Sgt. Rock*, including his first professional writing credit for "Welcome to the Machine" in issue #316. Veitch and Kristen divorce.

1979 Veitch collaborates with Steve Bissette on *1941: The Illustrated Story*, an adaptation of the Steven Spielberg film, as well as on "The Tell-Tale Fart!" for *Dr. Wirtham's Comix and Stories* #4. He also contributes his first story to *Heavy Metal* magazine, "Alien Comix Presents" (published in the January 1980 issue of the magazine, which appeared on newsstands in late 1979) and collaborates with writer Bill Kelley on "Momma's Bwah" for Kitchen Sink Press's *50's Funnies* #1. Veitch meets his future wife, Cindy Leszczak.

1980 Veitch's recurring "Li'l Tiny Comics" feature makes its debut in the July issue of *Heavy Metal*. Veitch begins a long and prolific relationship with Marvel's *Epic Illustrated* magazine with painted colors for a Stan Lee/John Buscema Silver Surfer story in the debut issue. *Epic Illustrated* #2 includes the Veitch/Bissette collaboration "Monkey See," and issue #4 features Veitch's "Solar Plexus." Veitch and Bissette also team up for "Cell Food" in *Dr. Wirtham's Comix and Stories* #5/6. Veitch contributes colors to Al Williamson's adaptation of the *Flash Gordon* film for Western Publishing. His collaboration with Williamson continues on Marvel's *Star Wars* series beginning with issue #39, providing lettering and assisting Williamson with backgrounds.

1981 Veitch continues to find work at DC Comics, including collaborating with Tom Yeates on art for backup features beginning in *Jonah Hex* #53 and providing art for his brother Tom's short story "Guts" in *Sgt. Rock* #356. Veitch's contributions to *Epic Illustrated* include "Conquest of the

CHRONOLOGY **xix**

Banana Planet!" in #5, "Shipmates" in #6, "Shiny Beast" in #8, and the launch of the serialized epic *Abraxas and the Earthman* in #10. Veitch visits Lucca, Italy, for the International Congress of Comics, where he meets Jean "Moebius" Giraud.

1982   Veitch collaborates with future *Goosebumps* author R. L. Stine on "A Day to Remember" in *Bananas* #54.

1983   Bissette and Totleben begin as the regular art team for *Saga of the Swamp Thing*, with Veitch providing initially uncredited art assistance. Veitch's "Bossy" appears in *Epic Illustrated* #19.

1984   *Heartburst*, originally intended as a serial for *Epic Illustrated*, is published as part of the Marvel Graphic Novel line. Veitch's "Landmass" appears in *Epic Illustrated* #25, and "The Everlasting Tag" appears in issue #28. Veitch pencils a backup feature for *Grimjack* #2, and he and Bissette team for a short feature, "War Wind," in Archie Publications' *Mighty Crusaders* #10.

1985   Veitch pencils *Swamp Thing* #37, his first full issue of the series and the first appearance of John Constantine. Veitch launches his six-issue *The One* miniseries for Marvel's Epic Comics. *Epic Illustrated* #29 features Veitch's "Ghosts in the Machine," and Veitch and Alan Moore's "Love Doesn't Last Forever" follows in issue #34. Veitch and Moore also collaborate on "The Jungle Line" for *DC Comics Presents* #85. Veitch illustrates a short feature in *Timespirits* #4. Veitch and Bissette publish two issues of *Bedlam* through Eclipse, collecting a selection of short pieces.

1986   After sharing art duties with Bissette and Totleben for *Swamp Thing* #50, Veitch becomes the regular *Swamp Thing* penciller with issue #51. He also pencils two issues of Moore's *Miracleman*, most notably the controversial "Scenes from the Nativity" in issue #9, as well as *DC Comics Presents* #97 and *Nexus* #29.

1987   Veitch marries Cindy Leszczak and takes over *Swamp Thing* as writer/penciller with issue #65. Veitch pencils the lead story in *Scout* #15 and writes a Floronic Man origin story for *Secret Origins* #23.

1988   Veitch, Bissette, and Moore collaborate on "The Mirror of Love" for the pro–gay rights anthology *AARGH!* #1. Veitch and Bissette's "The Brain Zoo" appears in *The Puma Blues* #20. Veitch meets *Cerebus* auteur and self-publishing advocate Dave Sim at a symposium on comics at Greenfield Community College in Massachusetts. Veitch joins Sim, Bissette, Scott McCloud, Kevin Eastman, Peter Laird, and many others at a summit in Northampton, Massachusetts, to draft the Creator's Bill of Rights.

xx CHRONOLOGY

1989 Veitch's second son, Kirby, is born in March. Veitch resigns from *Swamp Thing* after #87 in protest of DC's abrupt refusal to publish his story intended for #88, "The Morning of the Magician," in which Swamp Thing would have met Jesus Christ. Veitch writes and draws a three-part story for *Teenage Mutant Ninja Turtles* #24–26 and writes "A Touch of Vinyl" for *Taboo* #3. Veitch launches his self-publishing imprint King Hell Press, which debuts with the first trade paperback collection of *The One*.

1990 Veitch launches his five-issue *Brat Pack* series, published by Kevin Eastman's Tundra under the King Hell imprint. *Brat Pack* is the first entry in the King Hell Heroica, Veitch's revisionist superhero epic. He also contributes a *Drag Cartoons*–inspired story to *Teenage Mutant Ninja Turtles* #30.

1991 Veitch begins drawing comics based on his dreams in response to Scott McCloud's 24-Hour Comic Challenge.

1992 *The Maximortal*, a seven-issue Heroica series, debuts from Tundra/King Hell. Veitch also publishes the first collected edition of *Brat Pack*, featuring a revised conclusion, among other changes. Veitch's "Try to Remember" appears in *Images of Omaha* #2, and his collaboration with Kevin Eastman, "Casey Jones: North by Downeast," begins its run in *Plastron Café* #1.

1993 Veitch spearheads the Image Comics miniseries *1963* along with Moore, Bissette, and other collaborators. Denis Kitchen's Kitchen Sink Press takes over Tundra, and all rights to *Brat Pack* and *Maximortal* revert to Veitch.

1994 Veitch launches his dream comic *Roarin' Rick's Rare Bit Fiends*, self-published under the King Hell banner.

1995 Veitch begins a six-issue run as writer on the series *Teknophage*, with artist Bryan Talbot, for Neil Gaiman's Tekno Comix line. He releases the *Rare Bit Fiends* collection *Rabid Eye: The Dream Art of Rick Veitch*. *Rare Bit Fiends* is an Eisner nominee for Best New Series, and the series also earns Veitch a nomination for Best Cover Artist.

1996 Veitch becomes a regular collaborator on the Moore-penned *Supreme* for Rob Liefeld's Extreme Studios (later Awesome Entertainment), drawing flashback sequences. Veitch publishes the *Brat Pack/Maximortal Super Special* #1, and *Rare Bit Fiends* enters an extended hiatus with issue #21. Veitch publishes the second collection of his dream comics, *Pocket Universe*.

CHRONOLOGY **xxi**

1997 Veitch publishes the *Brat Pack/Maximortal Super Special* #2. He also writes and draws *Cabbot: Bloodhunter* #1 for Maximum Press.

1998 Veitch and Steve Conley found Comicon.com, a website that functions as a virtual comics convention and hosts the comics journalism column the *Splash*. Veitch's mother dies.

1999 Veitch collaborates with Alan Moore on the third issue of *Supreme: The Return*, and he and Moore create the recurring "Greyshirt" feature in *Tomorrow Stories* for Moore's America's Best Comics (ABC) imprint. He also writes six issues of *Cy-Gor* for Image Comics and teams with writer Peter Hogan for "Mr. Bigfoot Goes to Washington" in *Unknown Quantities*, an anthology benefiting the Kensington Welfare Rights Union.

2000 The final issues of Veitch's collaboration with Moore on *Supreme: The Return* appear, including the Jack Kirby homage "New Jack City" in issue #6. His autobiographical piece "Underpass" appears in the anthology *Streetwise* from TwoMorrows. Veitch and Paul Jenkins cowrite two issues of *Witchblade* and cocreate the Sentry for Marvel.

2001 Veitch debuts the six-issue miniseries *Greyshirt: Indigo Sunset*. Veitch both writes and draws this series, which also features contributions from artists including Russ Heath, David Lloyd, John Severin, Dave Gibbons, and Frank Cho. Veitch's "Subtleman" is included in the Renaissance Press anthology *The Forbidden Book* #1.

2002 Veitch and artist Sergio Aragonés contribute a short story to DC's benefit anthology *9–11*.

2003 Veitch begins a stint as writer on DC Comics' *Aquaman*, launches his six-issue *Question* series, drawn by Tommy Lee Edwards, and writes *JLA* #77.

2004 Veitch releases his third dream comics collection, *Crypto Zoo*.

2005 Veitch cocurates the Amadora International Comic Festival in Portugal, which features the special theme "Dreamcomics." He reteams with Tommy Lee Edwards for *What If? Daredevil* #1.

2006 DC's Vertigo Comics imprint publishes Veitch's graphic novel *Can't Get No*. Veitch also publishes a collected edition of his serialized *Epic Illustrated* graphic novel *Abraxas and the Earthman* and contributes to two issues of *ABC A to Z*. Veitch illustrates "The Secret Life of the Brain" to accompany the PBS television series.

2007 Veitch launches the Vertigo series *Army@Love*, which he writes and pencils with Gary Erskine on inks. His short stories for *Epic Illustrated* are collected in the King Hell book *Shiny Beasts*, and he contributes

xxii CHRONOLOGY

the short piece "Sounds in the Silence" to the first issue of PBS/WNET's *Nature Comics*.

2008 The first volume of *Army@Love* concludes; the second volume begins with a new #1 a few months later. Veitch republishes *Heartburst* along with a selection of short pieces under the King Hell banner as *Heartburst and Other Pleasures*. Veitch contributes short pieces to *Nature Comics* #2 and #3.

2010 Veitch teams with writer Joshua Dysart for "The Guns of Africa" in *Unknown Soldier* #21. Veitch begins work on "S'équiper pour la vie" for the University of Quebec. He provides illustrations for Erich Origen and Gan Golan's *The Adventures of Unemployed Man*.

2011 Image Comics publishes Veitch's *The Big Lie*. "The Guns of Africa" is an Eisner Award finalist in the "Best Single Issue/One-Shot" category.

2012 Dynamic Forces purchases Comicon.com.

2013 With Steve Conley, Veitch launches Eureka Comics, an educational comics publisher with a wide range of clients including McGraw-Hill Education, PBS, and the University of Quebec.

2015 Veitch contributes illustrations to Ed Sanders's *Sharon Tate: A Life*.

2016 Veitch debuts Sun Comics, his new print-on-demand imprint, with his first Panel Vision title, *Super Catchy*. Veitch brings *Rare Bit Fiends* back from hiatus with #22.

2017 Veitch continues his Panel Vision project with *The Spotted Stone* and publishes the first issue of his King Hell Heroica series *Boy Maximortal*. Eureka Comics begins work on two series of graphic novel math workbooks, *The Remainders* and *The Outliers*, for McGraw-Hill Education.

2018 Veitch publishes *Otzi*, a Panel Vision book, and *The Spotted Stone* is an Eisner Award finalist in the "Best Single Issue/One-Shot" category. *Rare Bit Fiends* #23 is published, along with poet Ed Sanders's collaboration with Veitch, *Broken Glory: The Final Years of Robert F. Kennedy*. IDW publishes a hardcover edition of the newly recolored *The One*. The International Monetary Fund publishes the Eureka title *Nepal: Into and Out of the Grey*.

2019 Veitch publishes *Redemption*, a Panel Vision book. IDW releases a hardcover edition of *Brat Pack*.

2020 Veitch is named Cartoonist Laureate of Vermont, succeeding Alison Bechdel. He publishes the second issue of *Boy Maximortal* and *Rare Bit Fiends* #24. Meadows Bee releases the Eureka title *Revisioning Food, Farm, and Forest*.

CHRONOLOGY **xxiii**

2021 The third issue of *Boy Maximortal* and the Panel Vision book *Tombstone Hand* are published. Veitch contributes "Tiny Dancer" to the anthology *Slow Death Zero* and "One Suffers to Provide for the Family" to *The Most Costly Journey*, published by the Vermont Folklife Center.

2022 Tom Veitch dies on February 14. Rick Veitch publishes a selection of his underground comics work as *BONG! Comix: Underground Classix*. He also publishes *Rare Bit Fiends* #25 and his fourth *Rare Bit Fiends* collection, *Azoth*. *The Most Costly Journey* is a 2022 Excellence in Graphic Literature finalist and a Library of Congress 2022 National Book Festival selection, and is shortlisted for the Graphic Medicine Award; the anthology is also selected as the Vermont Reads 2022 Book of the Year. The University of Vermont releases the Eureka title *Who Farms? Oral Histories from Vermont's Diverse Community of Farmers*.

2023 Veitch releases the fourth and final issue of *Boy Maximortal* as well as the collected edition of the series. He also publishes a hardcover edition of *Pocket Universe*. Eureka Comics produces *Cracking the Codex* for McGraw-Hill Education.

2024 Veitch provides illustrations for *The Moon and Serpent Bumper Book of Magic* by Alan Moore and Steve Moore from Top Shelf/Knockabout. Veitch contributes a short comic to the online *Stop Project 2025* anthology and publishes the first issue of *True-Man: The Maximortal*. Columbia University Libraries acquires Veitch's archives for their Comics and Cartoons Collection.

Note: Whenever possible, periodical publications are listed by their on-sale date instead of cover date.

CONVERSATIONS WITH RICK VEITCH

Rick Veitch: A Talk with Swamp Thing's New Writer

MARK WAID / 1987

From *Comics Buyer's Guide*, no. 712, July 10, 1987. Reprinted by permission.

Question: Beginning with issue #65, you'll be taking over the scriptwriting and penciling on *Swamp Thing*. I'm sure this isn't the first time you've heard this, but following an act like Alan Moore's isn't the most enviable position to be in. You're really on the hot spot. How'd you stumble into this assignment?

Answer: I'm the only one stupid enough to really take it on, I think. [*Laughs*] Plus, I was the obvious one to do it. Not only was I working with Alan as a penciller, but I'm good friends with Steve Bissette and John Totleben, who were the artists. Even before that, Tom Yeates was doing the art, and he was another one of my good friends. It was just a matter of time before it slipped into my hands.

The problem is, of course, that Alan knocked everybody on their seat with what he did.

Q: On a scale of, say, one to ten—how intimidated are you?

A: Really. But once I actually started rolling and slid into the "*Swamp Thing* style of writing," it picked right up.

Q: And what is the "*Swamp Thing* style of writing"?

A: For starters, there's a lot with the transitions between panels and between scenes. Alan had a real knack for using these little verbal and visual hooks to ride between the scenes. Once you get into that, it's a lot of fun to play with. I'm seeing it cropping up more and more in other comics, especially DC comics, because other writers are picking up on it.

I started to really look at Alan's work. Of course, when you're penciling from his script, you can really study what the guy's doing. I started running with the ball, and I'm having a lot of fun. I just finished writing this year's *Annual*, which is the All-DC Gorilla Issue.

Q: Excuse me?

A: The original idea came from Alan, who wanted to do a Congorilla/Congo Bill story. When he came to his end of the run, he offered me the plot. And, of course, he had his own vicious little take on it—what had happened to Congo Bill over the years. All of a sudden the *Annual* came up, and we needed a good idea. I said, "Well, hey. We can start with Congo Bill and we can bring in all these other gorillas, too." And before you know it, we had a gigundo cast of characters.

Q: Chock Full o' Apes, I guess. You got Grodd.

A: Yeah, we got Grodd.

Q: Detective Chimp, I guess.

A: Well, we didn't get him because he wasn't an actual gorilla.

Q: Oh. Of *course*.

A: We got Angel and the Ape. We even got the Mod Gorilla Boss.

Q: No!

A: However, we've turned him into the Mod Gorilla Couch Potato. Anyway, we included just about everybody except Titano, whom [John] Byrne had already taken care of in *Superman*.

Q: In regard to the regular book, did Moore leave you anything to work with?

A: Sure. His run ends quite nicely. I think he tied it up as well or better as anyone's done on a series—and it still left me with plenty of room to move. Maybe a year ago, when we first talked about me taking over the book, I sat down and typed up some sort of overview of what I wanted to do, so he knew where I would want to take it, and he segued right into that.

Q: How is your approach to the series different from Moore's?

A: Immediately, I just don't have the verbal skills that that guy had. I think I can compete with him on the storytelling level and maybe pretty closely on a characterization level but, when it comes to the actual use of words, he's a poet. He's really got it. Words are more of a struggle for me because I came to comics through my art and got into writing after the fact.

Q: So Moore's poetry will not be there. But that's okay. The important thing is to tell the story.

A: Yeah. And also to come up with new and fresh ideas and takes on Swamp Thing and the other characters, which I'm just having a lot of fun with.

Q: I assume that all the supporting characters will still be around.

A: Oh, yeah. I don't know if I want to get in too deeply on what I'm planning, but Constantine is going to be there. Of course, he's going to be getting his own series—*Hellblazer*.

Q: Are you handling that as well?

A: No, but I'm probably going to be working closely with [British author] Jamie Delano, who's writing it. Constantine is a man of mystery who appears out of the woodwork all the time. He knows everybody, and he's had relationships with all the women—he really gets around in the DC Universe.

It actually works having him appear in two books at the same time. I'm probably going to use him for five or six issues, have him appear somewhat regularly, then sort of move him out of the book, except for guest appearances. Then I'll let Delano take over the character. He wrote up a character sheet on Constantine that DC sent me, which I thought was right on. He told Constantine's whole history, from birth right through today.

Q: What about other supporting characters?

A: Well, there's Abby, of course. She's really the heart and soul of the whole book, and one of the hardest characters to write because she's a natural woman. She's not a sexpot, she doesn't carry a grudge, or anything like that. She's just a really natural person. I'm counting on [editor] Karen Berger to help steer me in the right direction on that character, because I think that Karen herself has a good understanding of Abby and her speech patterns and how she would react to certain situations. We're working really closely on that to make sure that Abby fits in with what we're doing.

Q: How about Liz?

A: Liz and Chester will still be around. The eco group will still be active, and all those supporting characters will be playing small parts in what's coming up.

Q: What about Swamp Thing himself? How do you see that character?

A: Well, he wants to retire to the swamps with Abby, and that's the main thrust of the next year's worth of plotline. He's just had it. He doesn't want to be an earth elemental anymore. He doesn't want to be a violent thing and beat up on bad guys, and he doesn't want to be manipulated by Constantine. He just wants to hang out in the swamps with Abby. Unfortunately, it's not that easy. He is an earth elemental, and that means that there are certain—I don't know if I want to call them "duties"—certain things that are going to involve someone of that status and power. The Parliament of Trees is going to get involved. When Swamp Thing left Earth, they thought he was dead and began preparing for his successor, which is what you're going to see in #65, my first issue as a regular writer-penciller.

Q: Let's talk a little about DC's new guidelines. You've got the mature readers label on your book.

A: I'm sort of partial to that. That's the kind of book that I want to do. If DC had said all of a sudden, "Hey, it's for a universal audience," I would have lost interest really quickly. I definitely believe there's a place for comics for kids and comics for teenagers, but, personally, I just want to work on a more mature level and do comics for people my age. It's the only way I can work right now.

Q: How long do you plan on being on the book? Any idea?

A: I would imagine at least two years if they'll have me. [*Laughs*] But you never know. There might be some insane critical reaction.

Q: Are you under contract for a year?

A: No, I'm not under contract at all. But two years is how far ahead Karen and I have talked.

Q: At what point are you going to be satisfied with your work on the book?

A: That's a tough question. When folks can enjoy the book at least sometimes as much as I know I enjoyed it when Alan was on it, I suppose. I hope I can have at least some of the effect he had. I doubt *Swamp Thing* could ever again have that amazing impact it had with "Anatomy Lesson." No one expected that. Now they're demanding it. [*Laughter*] It's all in catching the characters—making sure they're still Swamp Thing and Abby even now that Alan is gone. That, I think, is the real crux of the book.

Veitch Speaks: From Swamp to Sewer

DARWIN McPHERSON / 1989

From *Amazing Heroes*, no. 171, September 1989, Fantagraphics Books. © 1989 Darwin McPherson. Reprinted by permission.

Rick Veitch hasn't sought the limelight overmuch. What most people know about him boils down to three facts: (1) he was a graduate of Joe Kubert's school, (2) he was a frequent contributor to the late, lamented *Epic Illustrated* magazine, and (3) he was the artist on *Swamp Thing* for three years and began to write the title when Alan Moore departed.

Veitch came into the forefront big time in March [1989] when it was announced that he was resigning from *Swamp Thing* because of DC's decision not to publish his version of *Swamp Thing* #88. The story, which would've included Jesus Christ in a pivotal role, was initially approved by the DC hierarchy. The art, by guest artist Michael Zulli, was almost complete when DC suddenly decided that it would be offensive to associate Christ with a monster and withdrew their assent. Already in conflict with DC over a contractual dispute, Veitch decided to leave for greener pastures.

This interview covers the span of Veitch's career—from his underground comics start in 1973 with his brother Tom (of *Light and Darkness War* fame), to his future plans, which include not only a stint on *Teenage Mutant Ninja Turtles* but the implementation of his own publishing company, King Hell Press.

This interview took place in April [1989] and was conducted and transcribed by Darwin McPherson and copyedited by McPherson and Rick Veitch.

Amazing Heroes: You've been in comics a lot longer than I thought you were.

Rick Veitch: Yeah, I've been kicking around for a number of years.

AH: How old were you in 1973?

From *Two-Fisted Zombies* by Tom and Rick Veitch (Last Gasp, 1973). © Rick Veitch and Tom Veitch Estate.

RV: I think I was about twenty-one when *Two-Fisted Zombies* came out, but I had done it when I was nineteen or twenty. It took that long from the time I actually did the work 'til it actually saw print.

AH: How long was your brother into underground comics when you got into them?

RV: Just about a year or so. He's about ten years older than I am. We both always liked comics while living in Vermont. As soon as we saw the first *Zap Comix* we started to create our own weird little comics, too.

Then in '67–'68, he headed out to San Francisco to do the hippie thing. He met Greg Irons and a number of other underground cartoonists and started to work in the underground. So as soon as I graduated from high school, I zipped right out there. My stuff really wasn't very good at the time; I was still learning.

AH: I noticed your style had a bit of a Kirbyish lean to it then.

RV: Oh yeah, definitely Kirbyish. Kirby was my hero, he still is.

I went out there and Tom showed the first six or seven pages of *Two-Fisted Zombies* to Ron Turner at Last Gasp. Ron was just starting a line called *All New Underground Comix*, giving young people a chance, and he thought I'd fit right in. He accepted it and I spent the next year, year and a half doing the comic. I'd moved back to Vermont at that point, and it came out in '73.

AH: Did you do a series of *Two-Fisted Zombies* stories?

RV: No, but I had done a number of other underground stories that never saw print because my stuff was kind of lame. *Two-Fisted Zombies* was really my first professional publication.

AH: How'd you go from there to Joe Kubert?

RV: Well, basically, I stalled for three or four years. I lived in Vermont and I got married and had a little kid and I was working a regular job. The underground comics scene had fallen apart because the Supreme Court ruling against obscenity closed down a lot of the sex shops, which sold underground comics. They went through a big bust and there wasn't any work for young guys starting out. Only people like [R.] Crumb and [Gilbert] Shelton and those guys were getting any regular work. Everyone else was scrambling.

So I was working at a wood stove company building furnaces. In the evenings I would still draw my comics. At that point in my life, I loved comics and I was doing comics, but I didn't really believe I could become a cartoonist. Then I got to be about twenty-five and I said to myself, "Well, gee, I would like to do this. What I need is art school."

I started exploring schools like the School of Visual Arts [in New York] and different art schools in the New England and New York area. Then I was looking in the *New York Times* one day, and—boom—there was this little ad saying, "Opening next year, Joe Kubert School of Cartoon and Graphic Art." I sent him a card and he sent me back some fliers. I went down, saw him, and showed him the stuff I had done. He said, "This school is just for you!"

I was very fortunate; I got a grant from CETA [the Comprehensive Employment and Training Act] to go to school, and it paid my way for two years and made it all possible. It really changed my life to go to the Kubert School because it wasn't until that point that I really thought it was possible. It was like wanting to be a cartoonist was like wanting to be a movie star.

When I went to the school, it was like this revelation. Not only studying under really great cartoonists like Kubert, Dick Giordano, Rick Estrada, Hy Eisman, and people like that, but meeting other people just like myself. Steve Bissette, Tom Yeates, Ken Feduniewicz, Sam Kujava, and John Totleben, and a slew of other people—Tim Truman, too. We were all young and eager and very serious about doing comics. We were all from the hinterlands; we didn't live in New York. It wasn't until that time that I thought, "Hey, I can do this, I can be a cartoonist."

AH: What was it like at the school, a class of comic book students? Back then, there wasn't anything like it.

RV: It was really interesting. It tended to break down into different levels of seriousness. It seemed like in every class there'd be like 10 or 20 percent of the people who were *really* serious, and you could tell they were going to make it because they really wanted it. Then about 30 or 50 percent of them were sort of serious, but maybe they were going to have some other art career in advertising or something else. And then, there'd be like 10 or 15 percent on the other end who were just marking time, just doing something, going to some school.

AH: Professional student.

RV: Yeah, they'd just gotten out of high school and it sounded like a good idea to go to art school and they went. It was an interesting mix, it definitely was. I had a ball going there, it was a lot of fun.

AH: Did you think this would land you a job as a professional cartoonist?

RV: It wasn't that *it* would land me a job, but I could see that it would give me the skills so I could land my own job. There *were* jobs at the school. Joe set up this deal with DC Comics to do a bunch of short war stories for the backups in *Sgt. Rock* books.

By our second year, a lot of the kids who were serious about comics were working in comics doing these little two- and four-page backups and "Battle Albums" in *Sgt. Rock*. Joe was really smart; he wouldn't let us sign our names or anything like that, which I'm thankful for today. [*Laughs*]

But it really grounded us and gave us a taste of working in the confines of the business.

AH: What happened when you graduated? When did you start getting professional work?

RV: Well, I'll tell you. . . . The weird thing that happened when we graduated was the DC Implosion. DC really hit the skids . . . I think it was '78. A few months before, they had announced the DC Explosion with all of these new titles. Somebody, somewhere, pulled the rug out from under them, and there was no work for anybody.

We thought we had an "in" because we had done these *Sgt. Rock* stories. But there was no work for even a lot of established professionals at DC. So we all ended up going over to Marvel, where most of us got gigs right off the bat.

Epic Illustrated was just beginning, and they were looking for new, interesting, off-the-wall, highly illustrative stuff. We were able to adapt to that, and a lot of us got gigs there.

AH: You were in virtually every issue of *Epic*; how did you manage that?

RV: I was just there all the time with a new story idea. I think one of the reasons I got in is because I had the airbrush. One of the things I'd taken on my own to learn while I was at the Kubert School—it wasn't taught at that point although I think he does have a course now—was to learn how to operate an airbrush and incorporate it into illustration . . . comics illustration. There weren't that many people doing it.

The look of the airbrush was something all the art directors who had high-quality printing wanted. I was able to go in there and show them airbrushed, high-finished illustrations and say, "Hey, listen, I can do comics with an airbrush!" And they'd go, "Yeah!" So I found a ready market for my stuff at *Epic*. I did a slew of short pieces, then spent a year painting *Abraxas and the Earthman* for them.

AH: You just did stories for them until the *Heartburst* graphic novel?

RV: *Heartburst* originally was designed as a three-part *Epic* story, but by then, their inventory had grown so large that they decided to put it out as a single graphic novel.

AH: How'd you feel about that?

RV: I felt really good because there's a slightly better deal with the royalty plan doing a Marvel Graphic Novel. To this day, I still get royalty checks once or twice a year—it's still selling copies out there somewhere—so I have no complaints at all.

AH: Did you own everything you did for *Epic*?

RV: The *Epic* magazine deal was excellent. It was very simple; I kept the copyright and trademarks and they kept anthology rights for a period of five years or something like that. It was very minor, the things they kept. So now I own a whole backlog of fully illustrated *Epic* material, which includes *Abraxas and the Earthman* and tons of short stories and stuff that ultimately I will print under my own imprint of King Hell Press.

AH: When did *The One* come in? Were you still working for *Epic Illustrated* or had the magazine stopped by then?

RV: It was still going strong. In fact, it was going so strong they were spinning it off into a line of creator-owned comics. After I finished *Heartburst*, I had all of these ideas, and I just sat down and talked to Archie [Goodwin] about them.

From "Love Doesn't Last Forever" by Alan Moore and Rick Veitch, originally published in *Epic Illustrated* #34 (Marvel, February 1986). © Rick Veitch and Alan Moore.

He said, "Why don't you do a proposal for a series for Epic Comics?" I didn't want to get into a monthly series that would go on infinitely; I wanted to do it as a limited thing. I proposed *The One*, he went for it and I did it. It was in the middle of *The One* that *Epic Illustrated* finally went under.

AH: You'll be collecting *The One* in trade paperback form?

RV: That'll be my first trade paperback for King Hell Press.

AH: Can you tell everyone unfamiliar with it a little about it?

RV: *The One* was my attempt at the revisionist superhero. This was in 1984–85, I believe. Alan Moore's *Marvelman* had just come out, and we were getting it in the States in *Warrior* magazine. I read it and it hit me while reading it that the superhero was a viable idea. It was a viable vehicle with which to express yourself.

Even in the early eighties a lot of people were down on superheroes because there were just so many of them. It's like the person who eats too many McDonald's hamburgers never wants to eat another hamburger no matter who cooks it. But you can look at superheroes from a different point of view. Not from the point of view of somebody who's consumed too many of them, but like a child! We have a lot going on there in terms of archetype and meaningfulness to society.

The thing that was going through my mind at the time I did *The One* was World War III. I don't know if you remember back then; Reagan was in the White House and everything had become quite confrontational between the United States and Russia.

AH: When Reagan first became president, I was certain we were talking war here.

RV: Everybody was. It just seemed like they were pushing it too far with this insane brinksmanship. If you read *The One*, you'll see that the bomb is like this underlying character in the whole thing. In fact, World War III is what creates the One out of the collective unconscious of the human race. And that's only the first issue; [*laughs*] it gets even bigger from there.

I'm really happy to report all those tensions between Russia and America have evaporated and people aren't as worried about it anymore. At the time, it seemed very real and it definitely became part of the mix that was *The One*.

AH: From there, where did you go? I'm a little blank on exactly where you were between your last *Epic* and when you went on to DC.

RV: Well, in the middle of *The One*, *Epic* magazine was going to have its last issue. I had this script from Alan Moore called "Love Doesn't Last Forever," which was to be a full-color, eight-page science fiction thing that I had promised to do for Archie. So I had to put *The One* aside and take three or four weeks to fully illustrate it because this was airbrush color stuff. That was the first Alan Moore job that I ever did. It was really fun to work on.

Then I went back and finished *The One*. As soon as I finished it, I started doing fill-ins for *Swamp Thing* to help out Bissette, who couldn't quite keep

14 CONVERSATIONS WITH RICK VEITCH

up the monthly grind of doing a book. I was also doing fill-ins all over the place. I did a *Scout* fill-in, a *Nexus* fill-in, a couple of *Miraclemans*; I was a jack-of-all-trades.

I was also working in television. I worked on the bible for the initial setup on *ThunderCats* with Rankin/Bass and a couple other things. It wasn't that great of an experience, but it was interesting learning that stuff.

AH: When you went to DC, the Rick Veitch everyone knew was kind of lost. Suddenly, you were inked by other people.

RV: I had always wanted to work for *Heavy Metal* and *Epic* because I wanted to get away from the superhero, cookie-cutter idea of comics, but it ended up attracting me back. The thing that attracted me was working with Alan, there's no two ways about it. I was able to read his scripts when Steve and John [Totleben] started working on *Swamp Thing*, and I had been really taken by them. His scripts just blew me away, they were so great.

It was like he took this quantum jump in what a comic script could be. He gave all these silly superheroes and silly characters these real, very tangible reasons to exist, so you cared about them again. I definitely wanted to be a part of that. I wanted to work with him again.

AH: So, except for Alan Moore, there was no big reason for switching from Marvel to DC?

RV: Well, I guess in the other part of my mind, there was also . . . I worked doing this *Epic* stuff for four or five years, and people still really didn't know who Rick Veitch was. It almost seems like you have to go in there and work inside the mainstream to get any kind of reputation or a certain "box office appeal," if you will, among the people who buy comics. That definitely worked; I can see that more people know who I am now that I've done *Swamp Thing* for a couple of years than they did when I worked for Epic.

AH: When you were doing fill-ins for *Swamp Thing*, did you ever think you would become the regular artist on the book?

RV: Not really. Seeing the problems that Steve and John and Alan had in doing the book . . . the deadline problems, and the fact that the book was so advanced in terms of content—they were fighting with DC all the time. They were always pushing the envelope about what the comic could be. I could see that those guys were suffering a lot just getting their stuff printed. I couldn't really imagine subjecting myself to that.

But it seemed that right about the time I took over as penciller, there was a revolution at DC in terms of how they saw their books and their characters. This new flush of freedom of what you could do and where you could go with these characters helped. The two books that everyone points to—actually the three books including *Swamp Thing*—would be *Watchmen* and *Dark Knight*. It's like those books couldn't have happened in 1980 or 1982, but there was something that happened at DC that allowed the creators to really work fresh with the material rather than to align themselves with what had gone before.

AH: What was Alan Moore like?

RV: Alan was constantly evolving. The marvelous thing about working with Alan is reading his scripts. It's like I've got this whole other dimension to *Swamp Thing* because I got to read his scripts. There's so much information he puts in his scripts that regular comic book readers just don't see that you cry [*laughs*] if you read them.

His design sense was just expanding every issue. He would often design the whole issue for me. He'd say, "Let's do all the panels in this certain shape," or something. And then he'd work his script around those shapes in this really elegant fashion. I think most people think I designed those issues, but I didn't. Some of them I did—I've filled that role—but most of them are Alan Moore–designed issues.

AH: Did he approach *Swamp Thing* differently with you than with Steve Bissette and John Totleben?

RV: I think so; simply because Bissette and Totleben are horror fanatics. They love doing horror; that's all they want to do. They always used to resist bringing in the superheroes, and they didn't want science fiction.

I like horror, but I also like doing science fiction and I definitely have an appreciation for the superhero. It seemed Alan sensed that, and the plot took off into outer space to the point where every issue was kind of science fictiony. With "My Blue Heaven," Swamp Thing is way out in outer space and creates a whole new civilization on a planet. Then he goes and meets what's-his-name there?

AH: Adam Strange?

RV: Yeah, Adam Strange and all that stuff. I don't know if it was Alan's interest or because he was working with me, but he was definitely focusing a little bit more on science fiction, although there were really nice horror elements in each of those stories.

AH: How much input did you have in Alan's stories when he was writing it?

RV: We used to talk on the phone a lot, because by the time I became penciller, he was running really late on his scripts. He assumed a huge amount of work with *Watchmen*, *Swamp Thing*, *Miracleman*, and a lot of other things he was carrying. It's a wonder he didn't burn out with the amount he was doing.

But the upshot of that is he used to phone in the scripts from England, so we used to get to shoot the shit and talk and bounce ideas back and forth. I did suggest things, but anytime I would suggest something, he would always take it and give it that Alan Moore spin, which was so satisfying as a reader. He would move off in a way with it that you could never imagine. That's what I found so wonderful about working with him.

AH: How much input did he have in your stories, at least at the beginning?

RV: He had some, definitely. To this day, because we'll chat on the phone sometimes and I'll talk about what I'm doing, he'll pump in ideas and stuff like that. He's really selfless in that sense where he just loves to spin ideas out and doesn't want credit or anything like that.

He was a lot of fun to work with on that level, and, of course, his ideas were always brilliant. I think he originally came up with the B'wana Beast idea that we did for the annual—the all-monkey annual.

AH: Why did you take on the role of writer of the book? It wasn't exactly the easiest job in comics.

RV: It was the impossible job in comics at the time. Alan and I used to kick around a lot of gallows humor that I was committing career suicide [*laughs*] taking it on. But literally, I think he and Karen Berger were the only people in the whole world who believed that I could pull it off to any degree. It just seemed that no one felt that anyone could follow in Alan's shoes, as they say.

AH: Did that worry you?

RV: It did. It definitely did, but at the same time, I was the logical person to write the character. I was an experienced writer; I'd done *The One*. I worked on *Swamp Thing* for a year and a half at that point; I was immersed in the character. I also had some very strong ideas about what I wanted to do with him. So when they asked me about writing it, I was able to sit down and do a projection on which direction I'd like to go with the character, which involved the Sprout, Abby, Constantine, and all that. Both Karen and Alan liked it so I took the jump.

It was tough at first, but it seemed to work out . . . it seemed to be accepted. The letters we got were very, very strong. People seemed to be happy with the direction of the book. Most of the letters expressed the same thing; they never believed that any poor schmuck could follow in Alan's footsteps, but somehow I managed to cobble enough of it together so it continued as a decent-reading book.

AH: I noticed in your *Swamp Thing* there seemed to be a very strong presence of the DC Universe, and you often acknowledge the pre-*Crisis* DC Universe. This was really apparent when you had Swamp Thing going back in time. Why did you always draw these little DC things in?

RV: Because they're fun and that's it. I grew up reading those DC books, so it's part of my personal mythology. [*Laughs*] I was ten or eleven years old when Carmine Infantino shocked the world with the Flash and Adam Strange. I read all those issues and they were really important to me.

I learned to draw [by] copying, laboriously copying, panels and stuff like that. As I went on and Kirby ended up over at DC with that whole Fourth World thing that he invented . . . I always loved that stuff. When you get the chance to utilize them in your mix as you create stories . . . you'd do the same thing, I'm sure.

AH: Yeah, I probably would. I also noticed in your *Swamp Thing* you used innovative storytelling techniques. Circular stories and stuff.

RV: I'll tell you, one of the most fun things when taking over the book was DC starting this thing called the New Format, which put all the ads in the back of the book so there were none in the middle of the story. That opened up a lot of new horizons for me as a storyteller because I could use double-page spreads anytime I wanted.

As soon as I figured that out, I was doing it. In this story, "Gargles in the Rat Race Choir," it's a virtual maze on each double-page spread. You're led around in all these weird directions where you're not used to. In the story where Abby and Swamp Thing make love across the center of the spread, "The Secret Life of Plants," we got some help. Brett Ewins did the top and bottom tiers while I did the center tier of the page.

It worked really well, but unfortunately, after about five or six issues of that, DC all of a sudden changed their minds and put the ads back in the stories. They weren't even paying ads, they were just house ads for other comics. That took a lot of fun out of it right there.

AH: If the *Swamp Thing* #88 controversy and that contract problem didn't come up, do you think you'd still be writing *Swamp Thing* now?

RV: Probably, yeah. I was originally planning to have the baby born in #92. Then I'd stick around for another year after that to establish the baby's powers, which I had a wild idea for.

But when I ran into the contractual problem I said, "Okay, I'll just have the baby born and then you take it from there." Then with the *Swamp Thing* #88 problem, I said, "I'm quitting immediately," because it was the only tool to defend myself at that point.

AH: Can you explain to everyone what the contract problem was?

RV: The problem with the contract was that it didn't exist unless I signed a *second* contract. The original deal was I was [going] to do a mature comics crossover, which would involve *Swamp Thing*, *Green Arrow*, *Hellblazer*, and I guess *The Question*—all the mature comics and characters in the DC Universe. I created a title and a character called King Hell. That was going to be it. I

18 CONVERSATIONS WITH RICK VEITCH

was going to rearrange the DC Hell Universe, the demonic side of it and the angelic side of Paradise and stuff like that.

But right at the time I was proposing it, they had come out with new contracts that supposedly gave the artists and writers equity in the characters they created. I thought I was getting that contract. But I was really surprised to learn when contracts finally came through that the only way I could get equity in my own character was to sign a second contract for a *second* twelve-issue series involving the character.

I just felt it wasn't really an honest approach to deal like that. At that point, I said, "Well, I'm not doing the mature crossover now and I'm leaving *Swamp Thing* after #92," because I just couldn't stomach negotiating with them anymore.

AH: Why'd you go public with the *Swamp Thing* controversy to begin with?

RV: Because it transcended my problems with DC. Yes, I was peeved. Yes, I was hurt. Yes, I felt like I'd been wronged. But deeper than that, it seemed like an issue that the readers of DC comics, the readers of *all* comics, should be aware of . . . that this kind of thing happens. Especially right now.

A lot of people, I was one of them, felt there was freedom at DC to experiment with new ideas. Ideas that had never been done before in comics, to approach taboo issues, to do all kinds of stuff like that. They ripped the blinders off me when they chickened out of *Swamp Thing* #88—especially that late in the production of the book.

I think it was a big mistake on DC's part to do that, and I think it sends a signal to everybody—readers and creators alike—that the freedom that DC offered the last three or four years is a thing of the past.

AH: Do you think the Salman Rushdie/*Satanic Verses* thing had anything to do with it?

RV: I'll tell you, I've sat around and speculated on what their true reasons are for doing what they did, and I could spin ten different scenarios on why it might've happened. But to be honest with you, unless they come out and talk about it, I don't know. All I got from Jenette [Kahn] was, she felt it would be offensive to have a monster appear with a religious icon. Later on, trying to negotiate some solution to the problem with Karen, I was told it was all political. I don't know what that meant.

I didn't even know that Jenette was no longer the publisher because that was announced in the same *Comics Buyer's Guide* that the *Swamp Thing* #88 story broke. I thought she was publisher. I didn't know she was editor in chief and Paul [Levitz] had become publisher. It was all news to me. Maybe it was a part of that. Maybe it was part of the hassles that happened with *The Last*

Temptation of Christ. Maybe it was the Warner/Time merger. I really don't know; I wish I did.

AH: You said in the *CBG* that you could understand how difficult it would be for DC to publish this stuff in the market, where people still perceive comics to be kid stuff . . .

RV: Well, I didn't think my story was offensive, but I do understand that DC has a problem publishing offensive material in a kid's market. The truth is, they publish a *lot* of offensive material in their comics. The one I pointed out in my letter to the *Buyer's Guide* just happened to be on the stands the day I was battling with DC over my story.

It involved this prostitute being slashed and crucified [while] wearing a chain-link chastity belt in a full-page spread. Plus, they used it on the cover. There's been a lot of stuff like that in DC comics, and I find that really irresponsible.

AH: If it's irresponsible, do you think maybe DC realized they did that with *Green Arrow* and, incidentally, with *Dr. Fate* #5, where a vampire drinks Christ's blood . . .

RV: [*Laughs*]

AH: . . . do you think because of all that, DC realized they were getting out of hand and when it came up to you, they decided, "We'd better draw the line now"?

RV: I doubt it. I mean, I just read in the paper they're going to collect *The Longbow Hunters* in trade paperback. That contains another sequence of a woman tied up, slashed, brutalized, and raped. It's just gruesome, it's absolutely gruesome. I think the problem is they have *no* policy and it's like a spot check thing happens where every once in a while Jenette actually looks at one of the comics. If it doesn't fit in with whatever problems she's dealing with at the moment, she pulls it out.

I think that what I was referring to about the problems I see they're facing is that most people in America don't understand that comics have gone through this evolutionary phase in the last few years. Most people think that comics are still blando, little kid's fare. And when they pick up something that tries to deal with a mature issue, or a taboo issue, they think of it as exploitation. They think that greedy publishers are putting out this material just so kids can sneak this stuff home and be aroused by it.

That's why I see something like *Green Arrow* as irresponsible. Because in that climate, a parent could really be incensed if their kid brought that home. We're on a cusp right now with comics where we're suffering intense growing pains. I think the big companies, DC and Marvel, need to get out there and

20 CONVERSATIONS WITH RICK VEITCH

do promotion and let people know that everything has changed. I don't know *how* they should do it, but it's gotta be done.

AH: Now on mature comics, do you think there should be a limit on what Marvel or DC does? Some kind of line that the companies express that they won't cross?

RV: No, I'm not asking for censorship. Really, censorship is the last thing I want. I think what I'm looking for is a raising of consciousness of the creators and editors themselves and an attitude of responsibility to this art form, which is obviously evolving and just emerging into a world where people don't understand what we're doing.

And responsibility also to children who obviously *do* pick up these books. I guess one of my big problems with a book like *Green Arrow* is that it looks and reads just like a superhero comic. Even though the little tag up in the corner says "Mature Readers," it looks like all the rest of 'em.

AH: Most of the time, those books are being read by older readers. Even the "Mature Readers" doesn't apply to just adults. They won't be sold to an eight-year-old, but if you're a mature fourteen-year-old with a brain in your head, you can still buy it. Most of the time, *Green Arrow* is available for general public consumption, but that particular issue of *Green Arrow* crossed the line that comic stores have to watch out for.

RV: But I'll tell you, there's another aspect to extremity in a mature comic. There was an issue of *V for Vendetta* that Alan did where the female lead, Evey, is subjected to this concentration camp environment. She's humiliated and her head is shaved. She's put through all this awful stuff; it's very degrading. But you read it and you never once think of it as exploitative because there's a strong point of view. It's obviously done to evolve her character, as well as the story, not just for simple shock value. It's a valid literary device.

AH: I don't know. I read that issue of *V* and it bothered me. V tells Evey that she went through that, now her character is stronger. But if I grabbed you in the middle of the night, put you in prison, tortured you, and I let you out a year later and said, "Hey look, you're a stronger person now," would you really *thank* me for it?

RV: Well, the thing is, Evey is a character. You can't think of that sequence without thinking of it in terms of its part in Evey's evolution and as you read her in those issues. In the *Green Arrow* book, the character is an anonymous prostitute. She's murdered and mutilated for sheer shock value. There's no other reason for her existence in the story. You don't know who she is, you'll never know who she is. The only other time you see her is next issue when she's nude on the autopsy table. That's irresponsible. It's immoral. It's exploitation.

AH: Well . . . okay. You said in your memo to DC: "I believe the decision not to publish *Swamp Thing* #88 to be the death knell of a period in mainstream comics that started with *Swamp Thing* #21." Do you really think that's true? Isn't that a bit of an extreme statement?

RV: It was true for me. That's all I can really speak for. I worked at DC Comics for all those years thinking that there was more freedom than, say, doing a book at Marvel Comics. On a lot of levels, that was true. I ran into very few problems there.

This came from left field—not being able to do this issue. We had gone through channels. We told them what we were going to do, and still this "imperial order" came down. What it does is, it brings up the specter of the DC standards that Jenette tried to institute and that caused Alan, Frank [Miller], Howie [Chaykin], and a bunch of other guys to quit DC.

AH: If DC objected to the story early enough, would you have changed it?

RV: Yeah. If they told me it was impossible to do, I wouldn't have done it. When I finished the script and turned it over to Karen, she thought I'd pulled it off and didn't expect there would be any changes. It took her as much by surprise as it did me.

AH: Say DC felt that something could happen but they published it anyway and then they were attacked by Preacher Bob or someone. Do you really think it's fair to have DC take the heat for that when they had some objections to it?

RV: If they're going to ask their creators to do mature comics and to bring comics to a new level, the publisher has to stand up and have the courage to publish the comic that the writers and artists come up with.

If it was a regular magazine or a film or a paperback book or a regular book of poetry, no publisher worth its salt would chicken out and not publish something because it dealt with a sensitive religious issue. No way.

AH: Once you left, obviously you'd be replaced. How do you feel about someone being called in to take your place on *Swamp Thing*?

RV: Well, first off, I'd have to publicly thank Neil Gaiman and Jamie Delano, who exhibited real solidarity. They were destined to take over the book when I left and they refused to because they felt that what had happened wasn't right.

Saying that, I also feel a certain amount of guilt at the mess I left poor Karen Berger with. She didn't deserve any of this, and she's being the good soldier by cleaning it all up. I also feel really close to the characters themselves, and I want Swamp Thing and Abby and Chester and all those people to go on. Even more than that, the real victims of something like this are the readers, the people who bought the comic faithfully for months and years. I secretly hope that someone will be able to pick up *Swamp Thing* again.

AH: Someone named Doug Wheeler is supposed to do it. Do you feel he's a scab or anything?

RV: No, not at all. I wish him the best.

AH: Why did you reveal what you were going to do in *Swamp Thing* #92 in the *CBG*?

RV: One thing is, Don Thompson [coeditor of *Comics Buyer's Guide*—D.McP.] asked me to, because he'd been following the book and he was real interested. Another thing is, why not? They're my ideas; DC doesn't own them. At that point, I felt no loyalty to DC, obviously. They did a number on me, so I felt, "Well, why not tell everybody what I was going to do?" It made me feel better to get it out because I had planned the whole story like a year ago so I knew a lot of what I was going to do.

AH: Do you see yourself working for DC again?

RV: Not in the next couple of days. [*Laughs*] The thing is, things change in this business. I've seen that enough in my ten years. I know I'm going to be cartooning for the rest of my life, and I betcha that the people I've been in conflict with up there will be gone at some point. They'll go on to other jobs and other things, and DC Comics will be a different place a few years from now.

Never say never, that's what I say.

AH: When you decided to quit, what did you decide to do next?

RV: Kevin Eastman and Peter Laird had been asking me for a long time to do *Turtles*. In fact, we had already planned a series that I was going to do as soon as I quit *Swamp Thing*. I just stepped in and started working on it.

The first issue is done. I'm working on the second issue right now. It's going to be a three-issue story line entitled "The River." It'll run . . . I think it starts in *Turtles* #23 or #24 . . . sometime this summer anyway. I'm writing, drawing, and inking it and I'm having a lot of fun.

AH: It's been a while since you inked your own stuff.

RV: Yeah, but also with the Turtles, you use that Craftint paper where you put the chemicals on and you get those halftones. That's a gas playing around with that.

AH: Have you always been a Turtles fan?

RV: Not always. When I first read it, I was like everyone else, I didn't understand it. But I have a fifteen-year-old son, Ezra, who's followed the Turtles since he was ten or eleven. He's helped me understand the appeal the characters have.

AH: Well, it's very real.

RV: One of the things that's really strong that I see in it is a strong family unit bonding thing among the characters of *Turtles*. That's one of the things I've played with in my story.

It involved Raphael starting to de-evolve, and he actually de-evolves all the way back down into a little pet-shop-size turtle. The others have to go out and find a cure for him. It's a real heart-tugger.

AH: Are you doing anything else for Mirage?

RV: I'm going to do another *Turtles* story after that with, I think, Al Williamson, who's going to ink it. That one's going to involve another dimension, which is sort of like the "Kirby Zoomway" or something where there's this war going on and this giant superhighway spans the whole planet. The people who are at war are like "Road Warrior" types. They come to our dimension to get classic cars so they can take them to their dimension and trash 'em and fight in 'em and stuff. They get ahold of Casey Jones's '57 Chevy. They steal it, and the Turtles have to follow them. So it'll be like *Super Car Chase Comics*. Something I've always wanted to do.

AH: How long will you be working with the Turtles then?

RV: Beats me, probably a lot . . . I hope a lot. They have one of the fairest deals in comics. Actually, it might be *the* fairest deal in comics. It's so far ahead of the work-for-hire rip-off that the big companies foist on creators. They seem to like what I do, and I'm just going to do as many as I can.

AH: From there you're going to move to the wacky world of self-publishing?

RV: Actually, I'm going to mix the two. I'll probably be doing the Turtles to make money until my wacky world of self-publishing also begins to make money. Of course, when that'll be, I can't tell you. In 1989, I will have two projects from King Hell Publishing. One, of course, will be the trade paperback edition of *The One*, which should come out in the fall of '89. And probably in late '89, maybe in early '90, I'll be doing a new comic book series called *Brat Pack*.

AH: Why did you decide to go into self-publishing?

RV: Because it seems like the only place where I can get the freedom to do the kind of work I want to do. Also, after working in this industry for ten years, I can see that I'm getting ripped off. It's really hard to get any kind of equity in your creations. You end up slogging work-for-hire and you get a paycheck and that's it. You have nothing.

I was fortunate to attend the self-publishers summit with Kevin and Peter, Dave Sim, Steve Bissette, and a bunch of other really good people. I was able to see the numbers involved in self-publishing. How much of a profit goes to the publishers. How much of the cartoonist's labors go just to support the

24   CONVERSATIONS WITH RICK VEITCH

lifestyle and offices and all that crap that are superfluous to what we're really trying to do.

AH: Have you explored the publishing world in any great deal?

RV: Not a great depth, but I've watched Steve Bissette. He's one of my best friends in the world, and he just started SpiderBaby Graphix, his own publishing thing. I've watched the birthing process of that, and I've seen the numbers generated by the books. I know that's not easy, but I also know that it can be lucrative when it works.

I've sat down and talked with Dave Sim, who was a really strong self-publisher advocate at one point. He's probably more successful at it than anyone, not counting the licensing that Kevin and Peter do, and all he does is his comic. He's been doing it so long that he can start reprinting the earliest issues for a whole new readership. People want to read those books and for only the word of him getting the damn thing printed and distributed, he makes a good living just from that. He can also keep on doing *Cerebus* monthly and turning that out.

One of the things that really killed me doing *Swamp Thing* was every once in a while, I would get a book in the mail from England. It would be this edition of *Swamp Thing* that's being published in trade paperback in England. Here's my work in this nice edition and I wouldn't be getting one penny for it. Not one red cent; can you imagine how that feels?

AH: What problems do you anticipate being a self-publisher?

RV: I think the biggest problem facing self-publishers is the distribution end of it. Distributors are obviously going through a big shakedown, and the small distributors are being eaten up by the bigger distributors. What worries me, the self-publisher who wants to do mature and adult comics, is that those distributors might not agree with that approach and might not order the books because of content. I saw what happened with the Diamond/*Puma Blues* controversy and how Michael Zulli and Stephen Murphy were so badly served.

If the distribution boils down to one or two big distributors, the people who run those outfits can dictate the content of comics. We'll be right back where we were fifteen years ago when there was only DC and Marvel running the comic book world and everything was blando. That's the problem I see in the future.

AH: Okay now, your first all-new project for King Hell is going to be *Brat Pack*?

RV: Yeah, it'll be a four- or five-issue miniseries in fully illustrated gray tones. It will focus on a real-world approach to the kid sidekick phenomenon in superheroes. As I said before, I still see a lot of stuff I want to do with superheroes. I know it's trendy now to put superheroes down and say they've been done to death, but I think there's a lot of neat stuff that can be done. I intend to have a whole King Hell universe of superheroes before I'm done.

The way I'm going to do them is in different miniseries. There'll be a four- or five-issue miniseries of this superhero, then a second miniseries of another superhero, and then another. They'll all interlock in a universe of King Hell superheroes.

Veitch superheroes aren't like regular superheroes. [*Laughs*] That was one of the things I was always running into problems with at DC—that my superheroes were just too off the wall for them. My approach to *their* superheroes was just too off the wall. I did an issue where Superman appeared with Swamp Thing, and I had to redraw and rewrite five pages because they didn't like my treatment of Superman. Anyway, I'm fascinated with superheroes, but I can't look at them without seeing the obvious holes in who and what they are. And that's going to be my approach.

Brat Pack is going to look in excruciating detail at what would happen if there really were kid sidekicks. How would society react? What would the pressures be upon those kids who became sidekicks to extremely powerful super-people? I think it's going to be a series that's really going to shock people, and it might blow the lid off mainstream comics, I hope. [*Laughs*]

AH: I know you submitted it to DC at one point . . .

RV: Yeah, it bounced right out of DC. They considered it much too hot of a potato even though it doesn't utilize Batman and Robin, Green Arrow and Speedy, or any other of the familiar costumes and faces. It does create characters who are obviously of the same mold as Batman and Robin. I have these characters called the Midnight Mink and Chippy. Instead of Superman and Jimmy Olsen, there's Bulldada and Jack Cricket. I intend to use those kinds of surrogates, if you will, or archetypal forms to explore these relationships. It will be a type of thing that could never be done in a mainstream comic because it would just be scandalous.

AH: I notice that your characters tend to be more excessive than the counterparts that they're based on. Is it fair to cast some kind of aspersion on the kid sidekick genre when Captain America and Batman and Green Arrow aren't as bad as the characters you're portraying?

RV: Well, my feeling is that it's an illusion that Batman and Robin and Green Arrow and Superman are as noble as the mainstream comics try to make them. It's always given that a person receives superpowers, and he either becomes totally noble and goes out and fights crime and saves the world or he becomes totally evil and tries to enact crime and destroy the world. In a real-life situation, I don't think it would be that cut and dried or black and white.

I think people who possess great power tend to become corrupted in some senses. I mean, the idea of having powers is power over someone else. It's like saying you're above it, you're not equal. Once you even begin to think along those lines, a lot of possibilities begin to unravel.

AH: I was just wondering . . . I mean . . . I hate this question, but . . .

RV: That's okay.

AH: If you and your son received superpowers, do you think the first thing you'd do is take over the world? Or would you try and do good?

RV: The thing is, if I took the law in my hands, is that good? Basically, most superheroes take the law into their own hands. It's kind of accepted that's good. I don't think that's good. I think the law is something civilization has to deal with; it's for everybody. It's not for someone who's superior, who can physically beat up everybody to subvert the law for their own ends. These are the kinds of issues I want to approach with superheroes. Because then, all of a sudden, things get really complicated, like what's good and what's bad. At that point, it approaches the problem of real life more succinctly than regular superhero comics do.

AH: Are you going to publish anything other than your own stuff? It seems that so far, King Hell is "Rick Veitch presents Rick Veitch."

RV: Yes, that's its only reason for its existence. I don't want to be a big publisher or amass an empire or anything like that. I want to create comics, and my only reason for becoming a publisher is to give myself freedom and fair equity in what I'm doing. So tell everybody not to send samples. [*Laughs*] I also intend to collaborate with other people so it won't just be Rick Veitch, it'll be Rick Veitch working with, say, Steve Bissette or other people.

AH: Anything else from King Hell?

RV: There's *Bedlam*. *Bedlam* is going to be two trade paperbacks; one is going to be published by Steve Bissette's SpiderBaby Graphix and the second by King Hell Press. They'll comprise a history of Steve's and my collaborations over the last ten or twelve years. We've got a lot of material that's never seen print or only seen print in weird places that most comics fans have never seen. A lot of it is kind of extreme and strange and weird, and we think it's time to get it out there.

Along with the actual comics, we hope to do an oral history of the comics scene that we experienced. Breaking in all the way from the Kubert School to *Heavy Metal* and *Epic* and DC and all that stuff. Just to give a flavor and a feeling of the weird stuff and weird dealing that goes down in the back of a store that readers aren't really privy to.

AH: Any closing comments that you'd like to say to the comics world?

RV: To the readers of *Swamp Thing*, I'm really sorry about the way it all worked out. I wish that things could've been done the way they should've. I hope you all understood the position I had to take, as much as it hurt. I think Swampy himself would have approved.

Lacking Proper Adult Supervision

DANIEL A. DICKHOLTZ / 1990

From *Comics Scene* 2, no. 14, August 1990. Reprinted by permission.

Once Batman took Robin under his wing, few of the 1940s costumed crime-busters saw anything wrong in letting their young wards join them on their danger-ridden exploits. Bucky and Toro dared Axis bullets as they invaded enemy nations with Captain America and the original Human Torch, Speedy and Pinky cheerfully challenged the mobs with Green Arrow and Mr. Scarlet, and hundreds of other adolescent adventurers happily donned masks and tights to seek out excitement at their more mature partners' sides.

Now, though, while there seem to be just as many teenage heroes around, hardly any operate under an adult's "guidance." After all, Bucky perished on his last war mission with Captain America, Speedy turned to drugs when Green Arrow preferred crimefighting to parenting, and Jason Todd met his end at the hands of Batman's worst enemy. And as the pages of Rick Veitch's first King Hell project, the five-issue *Brat Pack*, reveal, even more dire fates can await the unsuspecting youth who still feels the need to aid a cloaked champion.

"What I'm intending to do with this series is to explore the relationship between kid sidekicks and their superhero adults in ways that have never been done before but have often *begged* to be done," says the self-publishing writer/artist. "One of the problems I've run into working in mainstream comics is that I feel that there are certain artificial limits set on how far or how deeply you can explore characters. What I'm hoping to do with all my King Hell stuff is to head in those forbidden directions.

"Look at Batman and Robin; half the people on the planet wonder about the sexual relationship between them. Of course, DC could *never* do a book that would really explore that, but I can. Kids are taking steroid drugs to build up their muscles and look like superheroes, and if there really were superheroes and kid sidekicks, the kids would be taking these drugs so that they could compete. I also wanted to deal with the 'Peter Pan Syndrome' of adults who never grow up and the effect that would have on a kid in a relationship with [that kind of] adult. These are things real people face. What I'm trying to do is explore some of the negative aspects of adult/adolescent relationships that I've observed in our society, and superheroes are a good way to do it."

The masked avengers of Veitch's world stalk the streets of Slumburg, a somber, wretched city, its former majesty corroded by years of unchecked lawlessness. For the last decade, these self-appointed, self-righteous champions have struggled with the underworld, often striking as much fear into the hearts of ordinary citizens as into those of criminals, accompanied always by their ever-youthful proteges.

"When we meet the existing Brat Pack, these are kids who have been doing this for three or four years, and you feel bad for them, because they're all screwed up and neurotic. And they're all *killed* at the first issue's end. In the next four issues, we follow their replacements as they're culled from civilian life and brought into superherodom, and we slowly watch these new kids become corrupted in the process so that at the end, they're almost in the same position as the original Brat Pack. And the finale of it all is that they must come in conflict with the adults to find out who and what they really are and to save themselves."

Among the fiercest of Slumburg's sentinels, Veitch details, are "the Midnight Mink and Chippy, the Boy Sensation. The Mink is an aging homosexual, and he's not above using his position as a crimefighter to fulfill certain fantasies. He has had quite a few partners over the years who have worn the Chippy costume, and they've all been brought in to fill a void left by the first Chippy, who is someone the Mink just can't get over. The Chippy that we follow through the series is caught between doing his duty as a superhero and dealing with his sexual identity being dictated by an adult. With his costume and the history of the Chippies, he's always encountering derision from people wherever he goes. But there *won't* be any overt sex scenes. Since Chippy's a kid, it's not so much the actual relationship that's a problem, but the *threat* of such a relationship. There's a lot of baggage that the superhero/sidekick phenomenon carries with it, and the Midnight Mink and Chippy will address that directly."

Considering the way he darts through the city's smog-drenched skies on his jet-propelled board, it seems as though Wild Boy must always be on the verge of grazing the walls of skyscrapers, the roofs of cars, the heads of pedestrians. But if he's too reckless, he is only following the example set for him by his mentor. Outrageously irresponsible and rarely troubled by mature

From *Brat Pack* #1 by Rick Veitch (King Hell, August 1990).

matters, yet armed with deadly technology better off in other hands, it's easy for the graying King Rad to convince his young comrades to follow him on his freewheeling escapades. Those who join him, however, only have so long to enjoy their costumed, carefree lives. "In reality, King Rad is leading them into life-threatening situations they're not prepared for," Veitch notes. "He's like the biggest kid around, and he often leaves his partners in the lurch.

"Now, Judge Jury and Kid Vicious are the superpatriots. Judge Jury is a racist, really hardcore vigilante." A savage disciplinarian who demands nothing short of perfection from his sidekicks, "his strategy is to completely poison the minds of his young charges with his own ridiculous version of politics and world events and use that to release their more violent instincts. What I'm going to explore with Kid Vicious is how a nice, adolescent kid can have his personality changed and shaped by an adult and how a kid can become a tool of an adult to commit virtual crimes."

At press time, Slumburg's distaff defenders were known as Moon Goddess and Luna, "but I think I'm going to change those before it sees print," Veitch confesses. "Here, I'm going to be dealing with the problem of the creation of a sex object. One of the things that people put down superheroes for is that they're so obviously sex objects. They dress in these skimpy dresses, especially the women; they all have these high-heeled boots. At one time, Moon Goddess was the typical sex bomb crimefighter, so what I also plan to play with is the neurotic competition that develops between this middle-aged woman and this nubile young girl. There's a great deal of unvoiced suspicion in their relationship.

"There is one last set of characters. There's an omnipotent superhero who's actually never seen in the book but he's talked about a lot, True-Man. He has a little chum, Jack Cricket, whose problem is hero worship and the negative effects this creates in his life and in the lives of people around him." And although they're not as directly involved in the events of *Brat Pack* as the rest, Veitch does plan to feature them more prominently in their own forthcoming miniseries. "Superman just doesn't work for me anymore; I look at him and say, 'Why doesn't this happen? Why doesn't that happen?' This is the strongest person on the planet, and no one seems to care. So, I've incorporated a character who *might* be equated with Superman, and I'll get to explore all that and bring it to a conclusion [in a way] that a company more involved in the licensing process than in good fiction cannot do."

While the adventures of True-Man may begin even as his junior colleagues' exploits reach their end, *Brat Pack* should *not* be considered the cornerstone of what the writer/artist calls "the King Hell Heroica." Unlike the tightly knit universes of both Marvel and DC (where Veitch once tried to have *Brat Pack* published, but "of course, it just bounced right out of there"), his Heroica is held together only tenuously, relying on fleeting appearances of characters from his other projects to provide its structure. In fact, the True-Man miniseries will not even immediately follow *Brat Pack*. Instead, another resident of Veitch's world will be featured in *The Ironic Man*, a graphic novel written by Veitch and painted by John Totleben.

"Basically, it's a story about a man's quest for his identity through the costume itself," Veitch relates. "It begins with a little kid seeing this little toy mask in a store window, and it builds from there. He tries many different ways to be a superhero, from being a simple, sort of Batman-type vigilante to being an Iron Man, where the mask at the beginning creates a full costume that's filled with all kinds of weaponry. And by the book's end, the mask and costume come alive, and he finds himself in conflict with this identity he has created."

In the mid-eighties, admittedly "inspired by *Miracleman*" then still running in the British magazine *Warrior*, Veitch crafted *The One*, a tale of superbeings sent by the superpowers to fight World War III who are all but oblivious to a real apocalypse taking place around them. Since then, *Watchmen* and *The Dark Knight Returns* have appeared, and others have displayed their own skewed visions of superheroics, and until his falling out with DC over the original contents of *Swamp Thing* #88, Veitch frequently used that title to show sides of familiar characters usually kept hidden. Still, as enthusiastic as he is now about his own and others' work in this area, there was a time when garishly garbed adventurers couldn't hold the slightest fascination for him.

"For years, I had been pondering on superheroes and whether they were worth doing or not. And a couple of weird things happened to me," he recalls. "In 1980, I went to Italy, and at that point, I was *completely* down on superheroes. I thought it had all been done, and I didn't want to have anything to do with it. But at this comic convention in Italy, I met Moebius very briefly.

"We were having a little chat about comics in America, and I gave him my spiel: 'Oh, there are too many superheroes, they've all been done to death, it's ruining comics.' And he just looked at me very intensely and said, 'No. They're beautiful.' I tried to repeat my thing, and he looked at me again and said, '*No. They're very* beautiful.' And the experience haunted me for a while, because I respected Moebius's work a great deal and he was the last person I ever would have thought would like superheroes. But the more I thought about it, the more I began to understand that he was able to look at them like a child. Those of us who have grown up on them, we've read so many superhero comics we're just like the guy who has eaten too many McDonald's hamburgers—we *never* want to see another one. But that and reading what Alan Moore did with *Miracleman* . . . Alan was the first one who was able to break through all that cynicism that most of us carried within us about these stupid costumed heroes and to treat them with the respect and dignity of any other fictional character. Both of those experiences inspired me greatly to go on, and I'm really happy that there is the revisionist superhero movement now. I hope there's more of it. I think the future of comics is in treating these heroes and their relationships and problems as if they were real.

"You know, if you look at popular culture today, superheroes aren't just a comic book phenomenon; they're everywhere. People *want* to explore the ideas of superhumans. People are really interested in it. Sure, on the one hand, it's a stupid little children's fantasy, but on the other hand," says Veitch, "it's much more than that."

Rick Veitch: The New Breed of Hero

STANLEY WIATER AND STEPHEN R. BISSETTE / 1992

From *Comic Book Rebels: Conversations with the Creators of the New Comics*, edited by Stanley Wiater and Stephen R. Bissette (Donald I. Fine, 1993): 243–55. Reprinted by permission.

Rick Veitch's thirty years in the comic book industry have spanned everything from underground comix and *Heavy Metal* to *Swamp Thing* and *Teenage Mutant Ninja Turtles*.

He was first enticed into the underground fold by his older brother Tom, whose own collaborations with artist Greg Irons remain seminal works. The two brothers did complete one rough-and-ready masterwork, *Two-Fisted Zombies* (Last Gasp, 1973), before leaving the underground comix scene to go their own separate creative ways. Veitch subsequently enrolled in the Joe Kubert School of Cartoon and Graphic Art in Dover, New Jersey, and was a member of the school's very first graduating class. He then quickly established himself as a low-profile but highly accomplished writer-artist.

Veitch's fertile relationship with Marvel Comics' *Epic Illustrated* magazine and the Epic Comics line had him working with legendary editor Archie Goodwin, who offered Veitch the blend of guidance and creative freedom he craved. This period yielded the serialized novel *Abraxas and the Earthman* (1982–1983), an ambitious fantasy drawn in part from Herman Melville's *Moby-Dick*, and the subtly complex series *The One* (1985–1986; later collected by King Hell Press). Notably, both *Abraxas* and *The One* laid significant groundwork for his eventual "Heroica" line of revisionist superheroes.

In 1986, Veitch left the pastures of creator-owned independence to till the soil broken by Alan Moore, Stephen R. Bissette, and John Totleben with their

From *Abraxas and the Earthman* by Rick Veitch, originally serialized from 1981 to 1983 in *Epic Illustrated* (King Hell, 2006). © Rick Veitch.

reinvention of DC Comics' Swamp Thing (a character originally created by Len Wein and Bernie Wrightson in 1971). Initially assisting on, and then penciling, various issues, Veitch eventually took over the art chores for the final year of writer Moore's tenure on the title. Though filling Moore's shoes seemed a

36 CONVERSATIONS WITH RICK VEITCH

Herculean task, Veitch later did just that—becoming the writer-penciller for *Swamp Thing* and admirably extending and reinterpreting the spirit and specifics of Moore's seminal work. However, DC Comics' policies and nefarious business practices took their toll on Veitch as they had with the others before him on the title, and he left the series in 1989 due to management's refusal to publish *Swamp Thing* #88 (after the script had been accepted, and guest penciller Michael Zulli had completed all but the last three pages of the issue).

Disgusted with the industry's work-for-hire practices, Veitch returned to creator-owned and controlled projects, launching his own publishing company, King Hell Press. In association with Tundra Publishing, King Hell launched the "Heroica Universe" with the controversial *Brat Pack* (1990–1991), which gleefully exposes, lambasts, and deflates the terrifying subtexts of the superhero "teenage sidekick" conventions. First in a number of interlocking miniseries, *Brat Pack* successfully led to *The Maximortal* (1992–1993), and in collaboration with John Totleben, *Hellhead* [never completed—B.C.]. Like the rugged, take-no-bullshit superheroes in his cutting-edge Heroica Universe, Rick Veitch is not what most people expect a talented and successful comic book artist to be like, either.

Comic Book Rebels: What started this almost obsessive, lifelong romance with the medium?

Rick Veitch: I know that comics were read to me as a very small child; I actually learned to read from memorizing what words looked like that were told to me in comic books. As I grew older, and was in the first or second grade, I noticed my older brother Tom—who is ten years older than me—was drawing his own comic book. This was absolutely *enthralling* to me. You know how it is when you have an older brother: everything they do is really cool! [*Laughs*] I tried to emulate him, and the passion just stuck.

Comics became part of my life in a very organic way. Instead of sitting in front of a television set, I'd go up to my room with a clipboard and a piece of white paper and draw out my fantasy stories in my own comics. I put out monthly comics all through grade school and through high school until the underground scene hit.

CBR: Your professional career goes back to the underground comix, with the collaborations you did with your brother Tom on *Crazymouse* and *Two-Fisted Zombies*. What brought you from that era into working for the major mainstream publishers?

RV: Probably the Joe Kubert School. I had always read mainstream comics as a kid, and if you look at a lot of my underground work, the Jack Kirby influence is pretty obvious. But after doing *Two-Fisted Zombies*—and watching the whole San Francisco publishing scene collapse—I moved back into the woods. I got married, had a kid, and gave up trying to have a career in cartooning. I was still drawing comics for myself, but I just couldn't make the business end of it work, either through the undergrounds or through the mainstream. After two or three years of that, I realized that I still really wanted to draw comic books and that I needed to go to art school. Basically I was running on the energy of an adolescent, in terms of my art, and I needed to reformulate it, and to learn new things.

Completely penniless, I somehow got the money together to go to Joe Kubert's cartooning school, and that, more than anything else, allowed me to break into mainstream cartooning. For one thing, it put me into the New York metropolitan area, which was where mainstream cartooning was happening in the late seventies. I also got to work on a day-to-day basis with professional cartoonists, people who had been doing this for twenty or thirty years. Up to that point, drawing had been something I did whenever I felt like it, or was bored. But when you hang around a human dynamo like Joe Kubert, some of that energy rubs off on you! Drawing then became much more integral to my life, and I started drawing *continually*.

CBR: After graduation from the Joe Kubert School, you first attempted to break into DC Comics during the great implosion of the early seventies. Your career almost ended before it began.

RV: While in school, I had done a number of stories for DC under the tutelage of Kubert, and the feeling was that we were kind of being groomed to start our careers there. But it was just at the time of graduation that the implosion happened, and I believe they canceled anywhere from a third to nearly half of their titles. So I went up to DC and basically got the door shut in my face. It was traumatic at the time, but it actually turned out to be a wonderful twist of fate. Because of course, where do you go when DC shuts the door in your face? You go to Marvel. And in fact the door was wide open there, and it was doing much more progressive types of comics, such as *Epic*.

CBR: You worked for Marvel Comics throughout the eighties while still maintaining creative autonomy and even ownership over most of your material. Simply put, how did you "get away with it" for so long with one of the major companies?

RV: I was just in the right place at the right time, when Marvel began their Epic imprint, apparently responding to the brand-new direct sales market and the then just-being-born independent comics such as *Cerebus* and *Elfquest*.

I had taught myself how to run an airbrush and was working with Steve Bissette on a number of color projects. Together we evolved an interesting

From *The One* #1 by Rick Veitch (Marvel/Epic, July 1985). © Rick Veitch.

illustration style using colored pencils, Dr. Martin dyes, and collage, which worked really well with the new reproduction techniques that *Heavy Metal* and *Epic* magazine were kind of pioneering in the comics. Their contract was terrific; they only purchased one-time North American rights, which was unheard of in those days. And Archie Goodwin was the editor. Just about everyone in the business would crawl over broken glass to work with Archie! So it was great while it lasted, and it left me with a really large body of work that I'm very proud of, and which someday I hope to reprint.

CBR: It was at Marvel you began your first series of revisionist superheroes, especially with *The One*, your final series for Epic. How did *The One* come about?

RV: What led to *The One* was my belief that there was a depth and an importance to the genre of superheroes that had never been plumbed.

I can remember talking to others at the Kubert School about superheroes and saying, "If only a more literary and honest approach was taken, then something *really* interesting might be created." I had a feeling this could be done, but I didn't have the skills at that point to do it—or even to see what had to be done. But reading Alan Moore's work on *Miracleman* brought it all into focus for me. I was definitely still developing my writing skills on *The One*. But I felt then and still feel today that there are many layers of depth to be explored. And possibly our own generation won't even understand the levels. It might take twenty or thirty years before people fully understand what we've been doing.

The One was the first step for me in that direction.

CBR: Why did you eventually leave *Epic* magazine?

RV: Well, for various reasons *Epic* magazine died and was replaced by the Epic Comics line. Which was a slightly different animal—though I must say my experience with Epic Comics was terrific as well.

But what really took me away from them was the work that John Totleben and Steve Bissette were doing on *Swamp Thing*. Up to that point, I wouldn't have *touched* the idea of doing a monthly comic book until I saw how that trio [including Alan Moore] shook up the comic book world with *Swamp Thing*. Along with what Frank Miller was doing with *Daredevil* at the time, those guys really showed how a mainstream comic could be really good and creatively fulfilling. It could also be a real hotbed of ideas, and a very exciting thing to do. And once I saw that happening, I gravitated over in that direction.

CBR: Eventually you came on board to lend your talents, and after the above-named trio left the title, you were working full time as both artist and writer on *Swamp Thing*.

RV: Yes, I started with a few fill-in issues and then took over the penciling after Steve and John left the book. I worked with Alan for a couple of years, and when he left the book as writer, I took over the writing as well. This went on for a couple more years. It was working out pretty well even though it was very hectic, and was probably more work than I cared to do all at once.

CBR: What we're leading to, of course, are the events dealing with the infamous issue #88 of *Swamp Thing*, which was killed by DC and to this day remains unpublished. What's your view of what happened?

RV: I was working on a long-term story line, over the course of a year, in which Swamp Thing went back in time. And each issue went progressively further and further back, with our hero meeting characters in the DC Universe who were from the past, such as Tomahawk, as well as real people out of world history, such as Hitler. I then got the great idea of doing an issue in which Swamp Thing witnessed Christ's passion in the Garden of Gethsemane. I knew it was a tricky subject to deal with in comics, so I discussed it with my editor, Karen Berger. And under her direction, I did a proposal, which we then showed to the powers that be at DC Comics, and they okayed it. I went ahead and wrote the complete script, which was then approved by my editor and, I assumed, by the powers that be above her.

It wasn't until a few months later, when the book was just being finished in pencils by Michael Zulli—who did a gorgeous job—that our problems began. Anyway, I think the first few pages were beginning to be inked, and somehow Jenette Kahn saw it, and she stopped the whole project—dead. Refused to publish it. I got a call from Karen, who was quite distraught, telling me that the book had been canceled and that I had to write a new script within three days to replace it.

Which I wasn't going to do; as soon as I heard that they had stopped publication of the book, I resigned. Immediately.

CBR: The *Swamp Thing* #88 incident received a noticeable degree of media coverage, both inside and outside of the industry. Did it change anything for you in terms of effectively dealing with DC?

RV: I first got a call from somebody at MTV News, and they ran a small news segment on it. Then I got a call from the *Wall Street Journal*. Then *Time* magazine. Then the AP wire service, and Scripps-Howard, and several other media organizations ran news items. The incident sailed around the country for a couple of weeks, which I must admit was kind of fun. But that was it for me, in terms of DC Comics, because I'd broken the Mafia-like "code of silence" that all freelancers are expected to abide by. Every once in a while I get a call from an editor at DC saying they want me to work with them again, and I always go, "Only if you publish *Swamp Thing* #88." And they never call back.

But I do have a feeling that someday, somehow, the book will get published. That DC will come to its senses and realize they made a terrible mistake. I suspect if that ever happens, people will read the story and wonder, "Hey, what was the fuss all about?"

CBR: What's your personal assessment of why the issue was killed?

RV: On the surface, I think it had to do with Kahn's battle with Alan Moore and Frank Miller and a couple of other guys who had resigned—or threatened to—over her "standards of practice." About six or eight months earlier she had, just out of the blue, handed down a set of standards that the DC comic books were going to adhere to. And these standards drove just about everybody out. One of the points in the standards was that "there shall be no religious figures in DC Comics." She was later forced to publicly back down, even though Miller and Moore never went back to DC. So it was all part of that previous mess.

I think it also became tied up with the release of the *Batman* movie, and the corporate merger of Warner and Time, which was all going on at this time. I think there was this general feeling at DC Comics that everything had to be "safe"—they didn't want a bunch of right-wing Christians showing up at the Warner Building protesting Christ's appearance in *Swamp Thing*. Unfortunately, I've never had the opportunity to sit down with Jenette or any of the other powers that be and discuss why they did it. But in terms of my career at that point, when I left DC I was able to call Kevin Eastman and Peter Laird, and I was offered a job doing *Teenage Mutant Ninja Turtles* comics right off the bat. So, thinking back, it was really the best thing that could have happened to me, to get out of the clutches of DC Comics.

CBR: Was the DC experience what led to the formation of your own imprint, King Hell Press?

RV: Self-publishing was in my mind from the very beginning, but what clicked it for me was *Swamp Thing* #88. That just moved up my own timetable by about a year. Right now I still don't have the capital I need to make King Hell Press work entirely on its own, and I'm currently publishing my work in association with Tundra Publishing. I worked out a deal with them where I use their infrastructure and capital to get my projects off the ground and get them out into the marketplace. So far it's worked out really well for both of us.

I would like to see a lot more creators start up their own imprints. I think it would help our art form expand in new and exciting ways.

CBR: Would you ever consider working for a major mainstream publisher like Marvel or DC again? Or are they simply no longer necessary to make your career continue and succeed?

RV: I don't want to say I'll never work for them again, yet I don't want to work for them under the terms that existed when I was working for them in the seventies and eighties. I don't want to sign work-for-hire contracts to barely make a living wage and work until I drop, which I've seen happen to a number of individuals. But things *are* changing. I think you're going to see a big change in how Marvel and DC do business over this next decade. Their primacy in the sales arena is going to start to erode, if it hasn't already. And even though they own the great characters, I think that to retain the best and most bankable creators they're going to have to change their ways because there're going to be too many attractive alternatives out there.

To take just one example from 1992: Image Comics, which changed the whole balance of power in the direct sales market. And if Image can continue to succeed, and continue to hold together without flying apart from centrifugal forces, it will change forever how publishers are seen. People won't approach publishers as if they are crime families anymore. They'll be seen as service organizations. Or in the cases of Marvel and DC, service organizations that happen to own a lot of great characters. I think we're at a real turning point in our industry—and our art form—and that maybe the lid is going to blow off what's been bottled up by the monied interests.

CBR: So you're optimistic that, the more small publishers there are, the better off everyone working in the field will be? Assuming the industry giants are going to change their business practices if they're to thrive in the coming years as well.

RV: It's my gut feeling that it's going to work, and that the people out there are ready for us. There's too much lingering resentment against the business policies of companies like Marvel and DC, and even they are beginning to realize you just can't go back to the way things were for the previous generations of creators.

But the major companies will always have the ability to attract young people who just haven't had the experience yet to understand how they screw themselves. *And I've been there.* I can see how certain decisions I made starting out are now causing problems for me, much later on. Or circumstances that happened in my career early on might somehow later lead me to stifle my creativity. Surely signing over ownership of a large body of work to a huge, amoral company was a major mistake.

But you can get hooked on the kind of money you make doing a successful mainstream title. You start out as a starving artist. All of a sudden you're making good, middle-class money, so it's really hard to just jump off and do something else on your own. Especially if by then you've got a family to support, and a mortgage to pay, and everything else. If there was a way of getting to the younger creators, and pointing all this out to them before they sign onto the slave ship, things would change in the industry a lot quicker.

CBR: Why your continued fascination with superheroes? Many creators who have been working in the industry as long as you have eventually burned out on this subject.

RV: I think one reason why other people get burned out is because they don't get to do the type of superheroes that they might really want to do. When I established the King Hell imprint, it was to do *my* version of superheroes. Which are slightly more demented than anything anyone else is doing! [*Laughs*] But I tend to fly in the face of conventional wisdom because I see the superhero archetype as central to twentieth-century American culture. To me, superheroes symbolize the American Dream itself. Certainly they're the foundation of comic books as a medium. Comic books didn't really happen as a mass phenomenon until Superman.

It's much more than comics . . . heroes in film are much closer to "superheroes" than they are to ordinary human beings. People in twentieth-century America live, eat, breathe, and defecate superheroes. All the time. Without even thinking about it. But the only problem with that is that nearly all the superheroes are owned—lock, stock, and work-for-hire—by a few major companies who have no reason to evolve their characters beyond a certain adolescent level. And if this archetype is as vital and important as I think it is to our culture, then it has to grow. To keep it stifled is in a way to keep our whole *culture* stifled.

We have to break it out of the form it's been stuck in for so long. I think in the eighties a great step was made in that direction, but we've got a long way to go. There's a depth to this genre that hasn't even been tapped yet. And it won't be tapped by companies who have a greater stake in licensing their characters—forever as is—than in allowing them to grow and develop in the way that they should.

CBR: Describe your master plan for developing your own vision of a superhero mythos. Clearly *Brat Pack* and *The Maximortal* are parts of an even larger whole of still-developing themes and concepts.

RV: Right now I'm in the middle of the biggest part of the "master plan," which is the story of True-Man, being published in the series known as *The Maximortal*. That series will probably run about fifty issues, if not more. It's going to be broken up into four novels. This cycle of novels will detail, more than anything, where I'm going with this whole "King Hell Heroica" idea. A lot of it's still wide open, and forming even as we speak.

From *The Maximortal* #5 by Rick Veitch (King Hell/Tundra, May 1993). © Rick Veitch.

To begin with, I want to peel back the stratified layers that have grown over the real core of the genre. Some of that's nostalgia, some is adolescent addiction. Some of it is all the ridiculous marketing that goes with the pop culture territory. I want to get to the real human instincts that are at the heart and soul of this thing. I'll tell you, working on it—it's almost too easy. [*Chuckles*] Because so much of this stuff has been kept just under the surface, even used subliminally to sell the superhero comics for all these years.

CBR: *The Maximortal* also tells the story of the comic book industry through the fictionalized experiences of the Maximortal's creators.

RV: It goes back to the idea of art being an organic life process that comes out of people. And the industry has always tended to crush that spirit, and to see creators as interchangeable cogs that can be taken in and out of any project. That it's the fictional characters themselves who make the "machine" go.

It's my feeling that you can't separate a creator from the characters that he or she creates. It's a *crime* to do so, unless it's done under the auspices and with the blessings of the original creator. The obvious parallel that I'm working with here is the [Jerry] Siegel and [Joe] Shuster tragedy. What happened to the creators of Superman kind of sets the tone for all creator-publisher relationships in comics in this century. I've fictionalized some real events that have been documented. I've also created some characters that aren't Siegel or Shuster, but definitely embody certain aspects of those pioneers.

It was done in the hope of enlightening current and future generations of comic book readers about what's been going on in "the backroom of the store."

CBR: Do you feel that you have total creative freedom at this point in your career? Apparently Tundra has never asked you to censor your work to meet their needs as a publisher?

RV: Naah! They just egg me on! I'm sure there are areas I could touch upon that might cause Tundra problems, but I don't see any need to at this point. Nothing I've done with my current work is "X-rated," although an X-rated superhero comic might be interesting, and at some point I might pursue doing one. But I've been plying my art long enough to know how to get what I want, with the effect that I want, without having to resort to the type of material that would put the comic "behind the shelf" or in the "Adults Only" section. And by "X-rated" I mean showing actual sexual penetration, which, when I started my career in the underground comix, was de rigueur.

CBR: Any negative response from fans with *Brat Pack*, in terms of your blasting away the once rock-hard concept that superhero comics should just be "good, clean, harmless entertainment"?

RV: Oh, I'm sure I gored some people's oxes! [*Laughs*] But I think I've discovered a niche, which the major companies don't dare to exploit. My audience is that reader who has been reading *X-Men* and all these other superhero comic books for a long time, and who might not be ready to pick up something like *Love & Rockets* or *Cages* or *Big Numbers* or *From Hell*. But *Brat Pack* and *The Maximortal* are like a step between the tired mainstream superhero books and some of the most mature material being produced right now.

I believe that niche is created by the addictive quality of superhero comics. Kids get addicted on these comics, and they read thousands of them. And at some point they just burn out and it's usually for a good reason: because they picked up the latest issue of, say, *X-Men*, and they realize it's virtually the same story they first read from forty issues ago. They're still interested in superheroes—but they're kind of fried from reading too many comics with the same old ingredients. It's like eating too many hamburgers at McDonald's: you eventually never want to see another hamburger again! When they reach that point I believe they'll enjoy reading comics that conceptually deconstruct what superheroics supposedly are.

That's where I'm at, and that's where my niche audience exists.

Maximum Myths

HARLEY JEBENS / 1994

From *Comics Scene* 2, no. 44, July 1994. Reprinted by permission of the author.

Rick Veitch is a dreamer, which is a good thing, because the project the writer/artist is about to embark on is a chronicle, in comic book form, of his own dreams.

Rare Bit Fiends first appeared as a backup strip running along the bottom third of Veitch's *Maximortal* miniseries, the first graphic novel in Veitch's projected five-novel King Hell Heroica project. *Maximortal,* and *Brat Pack* before it (King Hell Heroica part 4, for those keeping score at home), take a hard-edged look at the Superman mythos and the faded icons and stale conventions of the superhero genre. It also retells the history of the comic book industry—as filtered through Veitch's consciousness.

Rare Bit Fiends, however, is Veitch's recounting of his own dreams. He's preparing to release *Roarin' Rick's Rare Bit Fiends* (capitalizing on the sobriquet he gave himself for Image Comics' 1963 project) as a monthly black-and-white book.

Veitch says, "Going back to when I was a kid, I always had interesting dreams, and sometimes I would have what I would call 'big dreams,' which would seem to have depths of meaning associated with them or would be very powerful experiences to me as a child. When I got into my early twenties, I went through the crisis that most people go through when they're coming out of adolescence. And I was *real* confused. I was kind of a mess at that point. I took up dream work, read a lot of Carl Jung, and started writing down my dreams.

"Since then, on and off, I've written them down and created prose diaries of my dreams. I've always paid attention to them, even if I wasn't writing them down. I always tried to remember them for a while, and understand them the best I could.

"*Rare Bit Fiends* started in 1991 when Scott McCloud [creator of *Zot!* and author of *Understanding Comics*] issued a challenge to a number of his fellow cartoonists to draw a twenty-four-page comic in twenty-four hours. He did one, Steve Bissette did one, Dave Sim did one, and Kevin Eastman did one. I was gonna do one, but I had this other idea, one that I had wanted to do for many years: a dream diary in comic book form. But, I had never been able to get it together. And, I just thought, 'Well, this is the way to do it. Except instead of doing twenty-four pages in twenty-four hours, I'll do it in ten minutes a day.' So, I would wake up in the morning and jot down notes of what I had dreamed. Sometime during the day, I would sit down with a marker and a sketchbook and draw my dreams into comic book form. I must have turned 150 dreams into comic books, which I published as these little black-and-white ashcans and gave to friends.

"When I did, virtually all my friends came back and said, 'This is the greatest thing you've ever done.' I would reply, 'Yeah, but look at it, it's all sketchy and crummy. It looks awful.' And they said, 'It's just fascinating to read. We love it.' I got a lot out of doing it. I was totally hooked on it. Even when I was just completely exhausted from working on my other jobs, I would somehow find the time every day to do it."

With *Maximortal* ending, Veitch decided to do *Rare Bit Fiends* before going on to the next King Hell Heroica volume.

"I started doing it, and I just couldn't believe the speed with which I was turning out pages. I'm literally scripting, penciling, and inking six pages a week, which is just fantastic for me. I'm feeling as close or closer to my art than I've felt in a long time. The nature of the work is much like a painter working—you're in a deep dialogue with yourself. More so than when you're doing a commercial superhero comic, which is probably more craft oriented than fine-art oriented. *Rare Bit Fiends* definitely is that for me. It's a very organic art form. To me, it comes from the deepest depths that there are."

Veitch intends to publish his dreams in a monthly, black-and-white, *Cerebus*-type format, possibly for summer [1994] release. "I just want to do it for as long and as well as I can, and hope that I can find an audience that appreciates it.

"Every Monday, I take my notes from the week before and I pick five or six dreams that seem like they would make interesting comics. Certain dreams are very private, and I'm not gonna share them with a huge audience, but with most of the stuff, I try to be as completely honest and straightforward as I can be.

"I've tried to focus on the dreams I've had about comics and their creators. That's a pretty tight-knit community, and those are the people I work with, so it's only natural that I should dream about those people. For instance, I've had powerful dreams that had Alan Moore and Steve Bissette in them—especially when we were working on *1963*. Those dreams reflect, I think, the hopes and aspirations we had for that series, what we were trying to do with it. In that sense, *Rare Bit Fiends* is a useful *1963* artifact."

Veitch says, "What's interesting about *Rare Bit Fiends*, and what's different about my dream comic when compared to other dream comics—what Jim Woodring is doing, what Moebius has done, and what Neil Gaiman is doing with *Sandman*—is that I try to offer representations of the serial phenomena of dreaming. I give you a month's dreams all strung together, so you begin to see a much larger cross section of what's going on in my mind than *any* single dream might give you. The serial nature of dreams has much to teach us about how ideas and concepts and emotions are . . . digested by the human psyche. Friends of mine say it has kind of an addictive quality to it, which is exactly what I'm hoping."

Each issue of *Rare Bit Fiends* will contain several of Veitch's illustrated dreams as well as a "celebrity dream corner," where other comics creators will illustrate their dreams. Already on tap is Dave Sim's "Zelda Café" and Bissette's "Jurassic Parking Lot." Gaiman has submitted a one-page dream comic to Veitch, and the *Sandman* scribe is working on another piece.

Veitch has put a great deal of thinking into his dreaming. He says, "Dreams are very much an art form that we all create. We all share in it. Every night we go to sleep and spend two or three hours creating these little stories in our heads. On one level, it seems chaotic and crazy. But as you come to understand how symbolism works, and how the human psyche is structured, you can correlate how the chaotic, symbolic nature of the stories tends to give you a holistic picture of the human psyche dreaming them."

It's easy to see that Rick Veitch is a dreamer. But he also has his feet planted firmly on terra firma. He learned the business of comics publishing during his work-for-hire days as a writer/artist with Marvel and DC; his *Brat Pack* and *Maximortal* copublishing efforts with first Tundra and later Kitchen Sink; and Image's *1963* project assembled by Veitch, Moore, and Bissette. With all this experience, Veitch now feels he can take on all the duties of running King Hell, the company he formed to publish his own work. Or, as he puts it, "take King Hell *completely* self-publishing!"

Maximortal and the upcoming chapters in the King Hell Heroica deal directly with the myths of superheroism. Though you have ambisexual giants from outer space coming to Earth and raping Russian trappers to produce the Maximortal offspring who will be named Wesley Winston but come to be known as True-Man (*The Maximortal* #1), there's also the story of Jerry Spiegal and Joe Schumacher.

Spiegal and Schumacher's comic book creation, True-Man, is stolen from them by failed Hollywood stuntman-turned-unscrupulous-comic-book-mogul Sidney "Ball-less" Wallace. (Wallace earned that nasty nickname during an encounter with the Maximortal that put an end to his Hollywood career and robbed him of his manhood.) Schumacher and Spiegal's situation parallels that of Superman's creators, Jerry Siegel and Joe Shuster, while Wallace's rise mirrors that of one Walt Disney.

It seems the Maximortal is brought to life by "the collective unconscious mind of mankind," as one reader put it, and the belief that people such as El Guano (who seeks to capture True-Man's power) and Spiegal (who seeks to capture True-Man's essence in comic book form) bestow upon him. No less an authority than Albert Einstein (himself a character in Veitch's chronicle) scribbles on a blackboard, "Reality equals Belief times Consciousness squared."

The fantastic career of the Maximortal (it was he, and *not* the atomic bomb, that destroyed Hiroshima) contrasts with the harsh existence that Spiegal and Schumacher must endure once their creation is taken from them.

Veitch says, "I fictionalize and slightly exaggerate some of the scenes to make it work as a comic book, and especially a satirical, black-humor comic book, but just about everything [that happens to Spiegal and Schumacher] is based on things that really happened.

"Siegel and Shuster got really screwed, as bad as anyone could get screwed. In so doing, they established the whole history of creators being screwed in comics. It's now so endemic to the structure of these corporations that they can't change it. The only way they can change it is to throw Siegel and Shuster like $20,000 a year and get them to sign nondisclosure forms so that the *real* truth gets squashed. Definitely, one of my reasons for doing this kind of stuff is to try to bring this story into the consciousness of comics readers again, so they'll at least start discussing it. If anybody out there is actually planning a book on Superman's creators, I hope that some of these aspects will get thought about and put in there, before history is re-created in the form of DC Comics rather than in reality."

Veitch, it seems, might still burn with some of the anger that caused him to exit DC over the well-known Swamp Thing–meets–Jesus controversy. Then again, maybe it was just an instance of the scales falling from his eyes.

"What happened to those guys [Siegel and Shuster] was so bad and so unfair, and it was based upon one of the great characters of the twentieth century—Superman—who actually kicked comics as an industry into gear. This is *history*. This is the *truth*. So, what you've got is the biggest comic book publisher in America for four or five decades—its whole expansion and profits are based on a character that was literally stolen from a couple of teenage kids. So, they have to build into their business dealings this same sort of ethic, where everybody, every creator that goes through there, gets screwed. Marvel did the same thing with Jack Kirby and Steve Ditko. Every comic book company, right through until the late seventies, early eighties, operated along these same principles.

"This is what I faced, coming into comics as a young guy. You had to sign lifetime work-for-hire contracts to get your first paycheck. Or, when you got a check, there would be a little paragraph on the back saying that you signed away all rights forever for these stories that you were doing. They had the whole thing worded so that you weren't even the author of the work. The *company* was the author."

Veitch says, "Many of the creative geniuses of the twentieth century literally had their pockets picked by this kind of system. Surely, the latest and best example of this has to be Marvel, which recently went public and pulled in something like $400 million on the strength of these characters. I can guarantee you that Kirby didn't get a penny of [that $400 million].

"This is one of the things I want to bring into the spotlight. By using the history of cartoonists as the backdrop to a superhero story, I want people to realize what was happening in the back of the store while the puppet show was going on out front."

Veitch concedes that conditions for creators are getting better. "It mirrors what happened in sports over the last few decades, where you're seeing creators actually owning larger and larger pieces of these characters that they create. You have what happened with the Teenage Mutant Ninja Turtles phenomenon, the Image phenomenon. You have very successful self-publishing entrepreneurs now like Dave Sim, Jeff Smith, and Wendy and Richard Pini's WaRP Graphics. You're seeing the rise of creators who are getting an equitable share."

In the final issue of *Maximortal*, Jerry Spiegal dresses himself in a True-Man uniform, climbs atop the Cosmo Publication Building ("The Home of True-Man by Sidney Wallace"), and is ready to jump. His suicide attempt is thwarted by the arrival of the Maximortal, whom Spiegal had always assumed to be fictional. At the miniseries' end, Spiegal and Wesley have disappeared, leaving a fuming Sidney Wallace behind.

There are three more books planned in the Maximortal saga. "The second one will be the Maximortal's teenage years," Veitch explains. "There will be a little town like Smallville, and he'll live there. One of the interesting things is that Spiegal will end up playing the Pa Kent role. I'm going to try to explore, as fully as I can, the Maximortal's emerging sexuality, enhanced with superpowers and seen through the prism of his own alien mentality. He really doesn't relate as a human being yet. But with Spiegal playing the Pa Kent role, what I'm hoping to do is see that relationship between those two characters help form the Maximortal into the person who will become a real adult superhero. That will be the third book in the sequence. Of course, the fourth is *Brat Pack*. The fifth would be the ending, the Maximortal back on Earth, aware of who and what he is, and what he would do to the planet and all the people on it."

Veitch says, "I see Sidney Wallace and J. Edgar Hoover working together. It's funny, Walt Disney never had anything to do with Superman [eventually animated by Disney's rivals, Max and Dave Fleischer], but, because he became this big-time cartoon magnate and owned one of the other great cartoon archetypes of the twentieth century, I used him as my template for my comic book publisher. And I was always planning this thing about him meeting up with the FBI. Then this book, *Walt Disney: Hollywood's Dark Prince* [by Marc Eliot], came out, claiming that Disney *had* been a secret agent for the FBI and actually allowed Disneyland to be used as a base of operations. And [Eliot] reported on other Hollywood figures during the Red Scare of the fifties. I'm moving in that direction with the Wallace character."

Neil Gaiman wrote, in his introduction to the *Brat Pack* collected edition: "Rick Veitch cares deeply about superheroes. He thinks they matter. That they're important. That they tell us things about ourselves."

Veitch doesn't disagree with that statement. "I think the reason that people enjoy superheroes so much is because they reflect an important part of our psychological makeup that we might not consciously understand, but that we respond to when we read them.

"On one level, it's very infantile. This very infantile need for total power. Then, there's a heavy, unfortunately mostly subliminal, erotic presence to superheroes. I say unfortunately subliminal because the way comic books have been censored in our country since the fifties has forced one of the most powerful aspects of the superhero mythos, which is its erotic side, into a hidden role. I would like to see that opened up quite a bit. In fact, I play with it as much as I can in *Maximortal* and *Brat Pack*.

"What superheroes point toward, in a modern sense, is the future of man. We're coming very close to a point where it's not going to be completely impossible to have superpowers. There will come a time when there will be ways to change our bodies, or possibly enhance our mental abilities, through technology and genetic manipulation. This is a potential reality that our society is facing, and I think superheroes operate as a barometer of how people are feeling about this approaching historical epoch. It's one of the few art forms today that deals with it in *any* kind of depth at all."

Another of Veitch's explorations of the conventions of the superhero genre is *1963*. "The original idea was to redo something along the lines of *Swamp Thing*, but neither Alan, Steve, nor myself were really interested. Alan wasn't interested in doing *anything* like a modern superhero. But he always had in his head—he talked about it a number of times over the years—to go back and do superheroes when they were almost in a state of grace, where everything was sweet, happy, and wonderful, and it was all *fantastic*. Like comics were when *we* were little children. So, he began to sketch this thing out to us, and Steve and I started to give it form visually. And before you know it, we had this whole imaginary line of comics from the sixties.

"One of the things Alan asked us to do was to approach the art the way Marvel comics probably really were drawn in the sixties, which was to do two to three pages a day, complete, which is a *lot* of work. Either it's a lot of work or you have to find many shortcuts. We did it. It was amazing. In a week, we would have a book done. It was great, seeing it come together so quickly.

"A lot of the fun, even on the production end, was designing the package so that it looked and tasted and *smelled* just like those old pulpy comics. The dot patterns were big, just like in the sixties. We spent a lot of time replicating the tactile feel and look of the books.

"The best part of it was that the book sold like hotcakes, and we all did really well—well enough so that we can go off and work on the projects that really mean a great deal to us now. We don't have to make a living doing commercial comics for a while."

In fact, Moore, Bissette, and Veitch are already brainstorming a post-*1963* project, of which Veitch will say no more than, "It's something a bit larger than *1963*, and a bit more modern."

Then, there's the oft-mentioned *Hellhead* graphic novel, cowritten by Veitch and John Totleben and painted by Totleben. "Probably twenty-five pages are complete at this point," Veitch explains. "It's absolutely knockout stuff. John has really outdone himself with this painted work. It's like he has reinvented painted superhero comics. It might take a couple of years before people see it, though, because work on it has been agonizingly slow due to all the detail he's putting into it.

"The story involves two characters, in the modern age. The Scourge is a cross between Batman and Iron Man. Runamok is like the Hulk to the nth degree. They're having this battle, in Sodom City, literally tearing the city to its foundations. Runamok really does a number on the Scourge, to the point where the Scourge is almost dead. He has a near-death experience and begins to meet people from his past. That begins a series of flashbacks that define who he was, and who Runamok was in the earlier decades of their life, going back to the thirties. By the time you get back to the thirties and the forties, the Scourge is a character like the Spirit, and Runamok is his chauffeur or sidekick. And how they got from that point to the completely over-the-top point that they're in now is what the story is all about."

Rick Veitch confesses, "I'm a sucker for comics on a nostalgic level. I grew up loving comics, reading them and creating many of them from the time I was a little kid, using comics as my own means of self-expression. I lived comics very organically; it was a real part of my life. And I love all that stuff.

"When you look at the things I did in the 1963 series, instead of the cynical, dark, satirical approach, it's the completely-in-love-with, happy, fun-fun approach of superhero comics in their purest form. I tend to see the King Hell stuff as a more pointed satirical tool to make people look at these things much closer, or to break through the simple entertainment value that most people associate with these types of comics."

Can't Get No Aquaman? Rick Veitch

JENNIFER M. CONTINO / 2003

From *Sequential Tart*, February 2003, http://www.sequentialtart.com/archive/feb03/rveitch.shtml. Reprinted by permission of www.sequentialtart.com.

Rick Veitch has been making comics since the 1980s. He's worked on a variety of characters from his own deliciously dark creations to the mainstream superheroes in the DC and ABC Universes. His cult classic limited series *Brat Pack* was just reprinted in TPB [trade paperback] form and will be available this March [2003]. His work on "Greyshirt" in the ABCverse was also featured recently in a collected edition. He's working monthly on DC's Sea King, *Aquaman*, and the first issue sold out in less than three days. He's also working on an upcoming project for Vertigo called *Can't Get No*. Oh yeah, he also writes daily for the *Splash* and is one of my bosses at the *Pulse*. *Sequential Tart* caught up with Veitch to talk all these projects and more.

Sequential Tart: When you first entered the comics scene, what were your goals? What did you want to do with your career?

Rick Veitch: My first and foremost goal was to break in and become established enough so that I could live anywhere and create comics. I also felt that comics (this is circa 1976, remember) had a lot of potential, both in the mainstream, which was pretty lame at the time, and what we called the "underground," which was exciting but still limited in focus.

ST: Now, years later, how have you realized your initial goals?

RV: Yeah, I'm living where I want and I'm making comics, so I guess that part is "mission accomplished." And since my career follows the trajectory of the direct sales market, then it's safe to say that comics have gotten a lot better since the bad old seventies. They've still got more potential to live up to, but the form has grown up a lot in the last twenty-five years. Considering

56 CONVERSATIONS WITH RICK VEITCH

what a mess the business was in the mid-seventies, I think my whole generation (creators, publishers, retailers, readers) deserves to take a bow for collectively working to save the art form from extinction in America.

ST: Many people for one reason or another leave comics. Was there ever a point when you considered ending your comics career? If so . . . what happened? If not, what is it about comics that keeps you creating no matter what?

RV: Actually, there has only been one time that I was thinking of going into something else, and that was back after I had just reached my first goal of establishing myself. I remember moping around and then talking to Joe Kubert saying that maybe I should get into animation or something. Joe flatly told me I was crazy and that I should open my eyes and realize that I had it knocked. It turned me right around (Thanks, Joe!). From the perspective of 2003, I think that one moment of doubt back in 1979 had more to do with some sort of weird aftereffect of reaching the original goal. You know how you chase something for years and you finally catch it, and then you feel empty because you don't have the chase anymore? That was me. Today, I'm even more certain there is something about the challenge of drawing and writing, mixed with the juxtaposition of panels in a graphic narrative and powered by the wildest flights of the imagination possible, that has me hooked; like until they pry the pencil from my cold, clutching fingers.

ST: I first became familiar with your work on *Brat Pack*. What inspired that series? What did you like the best about creating it?

RV: I did that series after coming off a very frustrating time working for the big mainstream companies. I wanted to explore the supervigilante archetype and try to uncover its appeal to readers, but many of the ideas I wanted to play with made the large publishers uncomfortable. Those guys make their money on superheroes, and they don't want anyone to get too close to understanding how or why it works. At the same time, there was a strange atmosphere of hypocrisy that clung to these joints. When you talked to editors in private, they'd acknowledge and poke fun at the sexual subtext of superheroes yet wouldn't allow their characters to be used to tell stories that explored it. I mean, anyone standing outside of our little world of comics looks at what we are doing and sees half-naked vigilantes being peddled to children. So *Brat Pack* came out of that. I turned all my anger and confusion into satire.

ST: Why haven't you ever done a sequel to *Brat Pack*?

RV: I did *The Maximortal* after *Brat Pack*, which is set in the same universe. Even though *Brat Pack* was finished first, it is the fourth novel in a five-novel cycle I call the King Hell Heroica. *The Maximortal* is book 1. They are the only two complete at this point. I'll be releasing a new edition of *Brat*

Pack in March. (It can be preordered in the January *Previews*.) *The Maximortal* has sold out its print run. I'll be doing a new edition of that in late 2003, I hope. Each novel can be read by itself, but when you string them all together, deeper themes become apparent.

ST: Looking back at *Brat Pack*, do you think that series served as an inspiration for some of the more recent satirical looks at superheroes like *The Pro*?

RV: I think the real inspiration for breaking the company mentality of superheroes was *Watchmen* and *Dark Knight*. I think *Brat Pack* might have been the first totally twisted successor to those, and maybe in that light pointed the way to the satirical genre that seems to be selling well these days. But it was really Frank [Miller], Alan [Moore], and Dave [Gibbons] who broke through first.

ST: Who is Greyshirt? What made you want to work on this character?

RV: Alan Moore and I were working on *Supreme* when Awesome went belly up, and Alan found an old list of characters he'd written down in a notebook that roughly paralleled the DC big dogs. He originally saw Greyshirt as a Batman type but then decided to make him more of a modern Spirit. He didn't have much in place when he approached me, and we hashed out a lot of it in a few phone conversations. My son, Kirby, was in fourth grade and having problems with school bullies, and he announced one day he needed a chain mail suit to wear to school as protection. That's where Greyshirt's chain mail came from.

ST: How is Greyshirt different from the average hero? What are some of the biggest challenges to working on his adventures?

RV: Alan was trying to meld Eisner with *Raw*. I think the second "Greyshirt," the one about the building, really brought that into focus. The biggest challenge was coming up with some sort of visual hook for each story. Later, when I wrote and drew the miniseries, Alan acted as story editor, listening to my plot ideas and tossing in concepts and suggestions. I'm very proud of *Greyshirt: Indigo Sunset*. It's some of my most complex and satisfying work, I think.

ST: What other characters in the ABC Universe would you like a chance to work on? What would your story be like?

RV: The only character I like crossing over with is Cobweb, who is a natural partner for Greyshirt. I like the wacky personality Melinda [Gebbie] and Alan gave her. All the other artists doing the ABC stuff are all perfectly suited to the material. No way I could do *Promethea*, *Top Ten*, or *Tom Strong*! They are perfect the way they are.

ST: Aquaman's back and you're working on the Sea King's new series. The character has been the butt of many jokes and gone through lots of trials and tribulations since the Crisis. What made you want to work on this character?

RV: Well, I almost turned it down when Dan Raspler called to offer me the series. But my subconscious started running with the concept, and I began to see a whole bunch of neat stuff that I wanted to do with *Aquaman*. And of course, as a writer, the best place to be is getting handed a project no one thinks can ever be a success. The editors are open to new concepts, and if you pull it off, the fans will love you forever.

ST: How are you hoping your series will establish Aquaman as a major player and not a character to be laughed at?

RV: My goal is to create a successful mainstream series, which will include Aquaman and a lot of other characters and concepts. It's a bit of a challenge for me since it means working as part of a team rather than having the complete control I get when I write, draw, and letter books like *Brat Pack*, *The Maximortal*, or *Rare Bit Fiends*. But I learn a lot and it's interesting and fun in its own right.

ST: What are some of the goals you have with *Aquaman*? When someone gets to the last page of the comic, what are you hoping he or she is left with or left feeling?

RV: I want readers to care about Aquaman. I want readers to be puzzled about what is going to happen next. I want them to think "wow!" a few times every issue. I want the fresh direction in his life to carry them along with it.

ST: What's coming up in the first *Aquaman* story arc?

RV: The first issue essentially wipes the old slate clean and introduces a new scenario for Aquaman to play in. The second, third, and fourth issues introduce more new characters and explore Aquaman's new powers. They also illustrate the change in character of Aquaman, who is being forced out of his "angry king" persona into a more mature, adult way of seeing and acting. Issue #5 introduces a new villain, the Thirst, and sends Aquaman on a quest that should last five or six issues.

ST: Besides working on the Sea King, you're doing a new series for Vertigo called *Can't Get No*. What inspired this comic?

RV: Most people know me for my superhero stuff, but right from the beginning of my career I was doing experimental stuff as well as commercial. I spent three years doing dream comics with *Rare Bit Fiends*. So I'm up for pushing the literate envelope and right now seems like a good time to do it. One of the main inspirations I had early on was a passionate speech Will Eisner gave from a panel at San Diego. It was right during the darkest downturn of the comics industry, and he said, if parts of comics died that was because it was their time. And that creators needed to put their graphic storytelling skills to new types of comics that made sense to a modern world. The whole place stood up and applauded!

From *Can't Get No* by Rick Veitch (DC/Vertigo, 2006). © Rick Veitch.

ST: *Can't Get No* is the story of a guy who while asleep is drawn all over by a marker that can't be erased and is now considered a freak. It seems outrageous that just because someone gets marked with a marker, his whole life would change. . . . What type of society does he live in? Why do these marks make him an outcast?

RV: Because he lives a shallow life that is very surface oriented. When his surface is marred, his whole house of cards comes down on him.

ST: How is working on a series you created different from working on iconic characters?

RV: *Can't Get No* is an attempt to create a real graphic novel, meaning that my aspirations are to use the comics medium to communicate the same depth of humanity that a prose novel is expected to give us. Iconic characters are the tool set of myth. *Can't Get No* is more about what it means to be alive.

ST: How is the process similar?

RV: It's not really, except for the fact that both require access to the imagination.

ST: Why should people check out *Can't Get No*?

RV: Because it's going to read like no other comic book they've ever seen. It's going to deal with things most comics ignore. It's going to deal with things a lot of people try to ignore about themselves. Win, lose, or draw, it's going to be a big jump for Vertigo and Rick Veitch. I hope it will be for readers, too.

ST: What other projects are you working on?

RV: I'm doing all kinds of crazy stuff! I've got contributions to two Alan Moore tribute books on the board right now. Just finished helping organize a career retrospective of Alan's work for the comics festival at Amadora, Portugal. Just finished a dream strip that will be featured and analyzed on *The Dream Team with Annabelle and Michael*, which will be broadcast on the Sci-Fi Channel in late January or February [2003]. And of course, I update the *Splash* every day on Comicon.com. I've got my own self-publishing imprint, King Hell Press, up and running again. We sold out the first print run of *The Maximortal* and are preparing a new edition of *Brat Pack* for March release. And of course, there's the top-secret project for . . . ooops, can't tell you about that, yet!

The Comics Reporter Sunday Interview: Rick Veitch

TOM SPURGEON / 2007

Originally published online at *The Comics Reporter*, November 4, 2007. Reprinted courtesy of Tom Spurgeon.

Rick Veitch came into comics as a member of the Direct Market generation, a group of cartoonists, writers, and artists with an appreciation for old-school craft and the desire of most creative people born from the midcentury on to express themselves through their chosen art. Some folks may remember him through projects at Marvel's Epic like *Abraxas and the Earthman* and *The One*; others may recall his contributions to expressive fantasies like *Swamp Thing* or *1963*; still others satirical projects like *Brat Pack* and *The Maximortal*; and yet another group may know him mostly for his dream comics in the self-published *Rare Bit Fiends*. There's even a small chance that some out there might not think of Veitch as a cartoonist or writer at all as much as they see him as a cofounder of the comics internet anchor site Comicon.com.

Like many past Rick Veitch comics, his latest series, *Army@Love*, stands alone in the marketplace: a long-form satire in fictional form, brutally critical of Western military policy and motivation on several levels while respectful of the emotions and human weaknesses in play. *Army@Love* is set in an immediate future with the United States still at war in the Middle East and beyond while employing, exploiting, and encouraging strategies and behaviors that seem completely absurd and outrageous but that contain within them enough revelatory truth as to the country's state of mind, they would likely surprise very few of us were they to one day become standard procedure. This series not only comes at a point when Vertigo seems sorely lacking in the kind of high-energy titles that brought the imprint its initial success, it arrives in the midst of an ongoing Rick Veitch in-print renaissance in terms

62   CONVERSATIONS WITH RICK VEITCH

of current projects and reprints making it onto the stands. I was pleased that he found the time to answer my questions.

Tom Spurgeon: Rick, can I get a snapshot of what you're working on now, and what you have out? It seems like you've had a ton of material out in the last several months. Can you locate where you are exactly with *Army@Love* and the various King Hell projects?

Rick Veitch: Vertigo-wise, I've just finished the pencils to *Army@Love* #12. I'm writing the outline to what we're calling "Season Two," which is essentially the next six-issue story arc. I think #8 is in stores, and the first trade shipped in October [2007]. I believe the next *Swamp Thing* collected volume is about to be released. Over at King Hell I've been publishing about one book a year, but I'm hoping to pick up the pace a bit. I'll be soliciting *Heartburst and Other Romances* for the spring and I've got *BONG! The Lost Undergrounds* in the pipeline, hopefully for fall. I've also been working on another *Nature* comic for WNET.

TS: Do you feel as busy and productive as all of that looks? Like with *Abraxas and the Earthman* finally being collected, did you make a decision to simply have a lot more work out there?

RV: I wish I could say it was a coherent marketing strategy to position myself as a brand, but it's more a case of just me following my interests. I love to make comics and it's the way I've earned my living, so I'm always productive on the commercial side. In terms of self-publishing, I've planned to put the stuff from my Epic period in print from the moment I launched King Hell. It just took a while to get the equipment and teach myself how to use it so I could achieve the color reproduction that the painted originals demanded. It probably does help to release a small press project like *Shiny Beasts* on the coattails of something "mainstreamy" like *Army@Love*. So maybe there is method to my madness.

TS: I think more than anyone I've spoken to in recent memory, you can remember the fallow period before this latest flush period in terms of attention and sales of some books, but you can also recall participating in the last flush period, with projects at Tundra and Image, and before that DC. What are the differences between comics right now and comics fifteen and then even twenty years ago in terms of functioning as a professional in that world? Do you like it the way it is now? Are there more opportunities from your perspective?

RV: Doesn't matter feast or famine, comics publishing has always been a crazy field. Comics is a place where business and creativity collide head on, so there are a lot of casualties as well as amazing energy and no lack of absurdity. I came in with the direct sales market, and except for a brief period at the

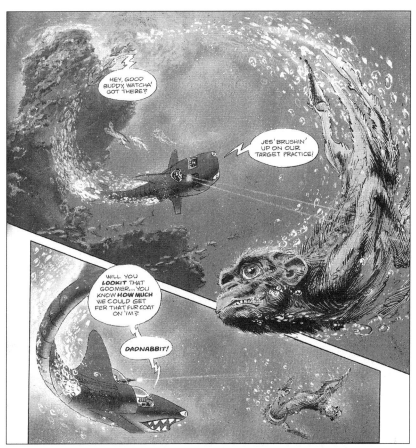

From "Monkey See" by Stephen R. Bissette and Rick Veitch, originally published in *Epic Illustrated* #2 (Marvel, Summer 1980). © S. R. Bissette and Rick Veitch.

very beginning, there's always been too many comics chasing too few readers in the marketplace. Whenever anyone figures out a new angle to sell books, a thousand other guys pig-pile on. It's just the nature of the beast.

The trick, for me at least, has always been to find the right niche where I can follow my own muse and retain some sort of equity. That's why you see me over at Epic doing *The One*, or at Tundra doing *Brat Pack* and *The Maximortal*, or at Image doing *1963*, or self-publishing *Rare Bit Fiends*, or right now at Vertigo doing *Can't Get No* and *Army@Love*. Sure, I had to do a few things like *Aquaman* or *Cy-Gor* now and then to pay the rent, but for the most part I've been really lucky having the opportunity to follow my own vision while retaining either complete ownership or a big piece of most of my projects.

Opportunities are always there for folks who really want (or need) to pursue this form of art. But the business models behind the opportunities seem to rely less and less on selling actual comics and more on creating intellectual properties for other media. And there seem to be a lot of folks making comics out there who aren't getting paid very much for their creative labors. Last year I was approached by a fairly well-known publisher who asked me to pitch a graphic novel. When we started to talk deal, their whole offer was $500 to write and illustrate a complete sixty-four-page color book! On top of that they wanted 51 percent of the rights. Their rationale was that my real payoff would come when they got a movie deal for the property. I can only wonder how many young artists and writers are slaving away under such terms just to get published.

TS: *Army@Love* feels like one of those projects that came together rather than one that came in a bolt out of the blue. Was there a long genesis with the project? Where did you start, and at what point did it cohere into something that resembles what's been published?

RV: The very first thing that came to me was the title, which originally was *Army at Love*. I dug the way it evoked the old war and romance comics, while the impossible grammar made it strangely surreal and subversive.

I let the title roll around in the back of my mind for maybe a year, just giving my intuition free reign to play with what the project wanted to be. The war part came through as a satire of the Iraq mess; that was pretty much a no-brainer. But the romance side was what really caught my interest. Mature Reader titles had evolved to the point where it was okay to show people having sex. But most of those titles used sex in a demented context. Sex is such an important part of being human, I wanted to use it to build character naturally rather than push those horror movie buttons.

At that point I ran the raw concept by Karen [Berger], and she seemed to like the basic premise. We batted it back and forth a little bit, which really helped me zero in on the tone. Then I set about creating the large cast of characters, mapping out who was sleeping with whom and who was stabbing whom in the back. She read the outline and suggested a few additions to the cast to round it out, and pretty soon we had a deal. DC was a little reticent of the *Army at Love* title at first, feeling like it was too much a parody of [DC Comics'] *Our Army at War*. So I substituted the @ sign, which I think sets it apart in a more modern sense.

TS: It's hard for me to think of antecedents in comics form to this project. Was there anything in comics that inspired you? Am I right in thinking it's more the popular satirical antiwar movies and even the more frank-about-sex popular books and movies of the late sixties into the seventies that inform the work?

RV: I'm sure whatever I soaked up in my formative years comes through anything I do. But I'm not overtly copping or vamping that stuff. *Army@Love* has a very distinct soap opera rhythm. The plot unfolds like an origami rather than straightforward like a film or cop show. It isn't as formally challenging as *Can't Get No*, but there's a lot of information packed into each panel, and you need to pay attention to the drawings to get some of the gags and story points. I hope *Army@Love* is its own thing.

TS: Is there anything that informs *Army@Love* that might surprise its readers? Now that you've completed a fair chunk of work, is there anything that you find in the work that surprises you?

RV: The characters aren't heroes or villains, but complicated people acting in their own self-interest. They make unexpected choices, just like we all do in real life. That might be a little difficult for readers who are trained to expect good guy/bad guy setups in comics. What's surprised me is how these characters have come alive in my head, not only when writing them but when I'm drawing, too. They seem to really want to "act" in the panels, rather than stand around looking pretty.

TS: You've mentioned in a couple of interviews a couple of the more serious, cable-ready television shows as a comparison to what you're doing. Is that convenient shorthand for you to describe what you're doing, and did you draw on those shows for your approach as well, say with the ensemble casting?

RV: It kind of contradicts what I said above about not echoing other media, but I really do enjoy shows like *The Sopranos* and *Six Feet Under*. And mentioning them in the course of doing PR helps potential readers get some sort of handle on what I'm trying to do. There are no proverbial three acts in an episode of *The Sopranos*. They drop you down in the middle of a dynamic community of characters, and before you know it you are rooting for career criminals and murderers. I'd love to pull that off in *Army@Love*.

TS: We're a fairly satire-heavy culture, what with the prominence of things like *The Onion* and *The Daily Show*—what can you do with a fictional narrative like *Army@Love* that these more reactive sources can't do? What do you think the strengths in general are to your approach?

RV: *The Daily Show* tends to focus on immediate issues in the news, while *Army@Love* goes after the underlying structures of a society that has allowed something like the war in Iraq to happen. Satire-wise, I think I'm getting at stuff that you're never going to see on commercial TV. Like how the military industrial complex has merged with the entertainment industry. How twenty-first-century people live inside a Skinner Box of media-generated ideas. How deeply marketing permeates our lives, virtually dictating our thoughts and actions. I agree, though, that *The Onion* does a great job of playing with those kinds of ideas.

TS: Can you talk about your decision to fictionalize certain future elements, like Afbaghistan, as opposed to making more elements strictly observant of reality? Is the ambiguity of the term "Afbaghistan" intentional?

RV: The naming is done to give the satire a little room to breathe. After all, hundreds of thousands of people have died over there already and who knows how many have been physically and mentally wounded. In *Army@Love*, it's left ambiguous if "Afbaghistan" is meant to be a fictional country, or if it's a slang term for a much-expanded area of combat operations in the Middle East.

TS: Do you feel like we're headed to an expansion of the Afghani and Iraqi conflicts?

RV: I fervently hope the war is ended immediately, but looking at the strategic situation, I'm really worried it's become such a clusterfuck that it will be impossible for the next president to get out.

TS: Have you heard anything from soldiers?

RV: After *Military Times* did a write-up, I got a bunch of emails from soldiers serving in Iraq who wanted to know how they could buy the book. From what I could glean from their emails, they weren't in the slightest bit offended and seemed to dig the idea. I wasn't able to find any online comics sites that would ship to an APO, though, which was unfortunate. I'd love to get the book over there.

TS: How about magicians or PR people?

RV: Yesterday was Halloween, and I received a coded message from Harry Houdini. Nothing from Funky Flashman yet.

TS: Has there been any backlash, given you're doing this within the publishing efforts of such a big multinational corporation?

RV: Nothing that I've seen beyond a few political kerfuffles on message boards, but you know how that goes. Even though Vertigo is owned by Time Warner, I think comics are perceived as being somehow outside the greater culture wars that have been raging in America for the last few decades. Comics have such small audiences compared to mass media that no one seems worried about their propaganda impact, which makes them attractive to someone subversive like me.

TS: My favorite satirical element in *Army@Love* is the pushing of fighting on the front lines as a peak experience in order to better attract the adrenaline junkie teens. Can you talk about developing that line of satire specifically? For instance, was this something that you extrapolated from the "Army

TOM SPURGEON / 2007   **67**

From *Army@Love* #1 by Rick Veitch and Gary Erskine (DC/Vertigo, May 2007). © Rick Veitch.

of One" advertising, or something you read about, or did it seem like a leap that made sense to you?

RV: I'm not an expert on marketing and advertising, but I'm interested in how it has been refined and how it works on the mind. As a culture, we've had almost a century now of product marketing aimed directly at the subconscious. Did you know that Sigmund Freud's son-in-law is recognized as the founder of modern advertising? Selling something as hideous as a war uses the same techniques of psychological manipulation that keep us buying Pepsi and Twinkies. In Iraq right now we have a professional army fighting a war that most people back home are happy to turn up their iPods and ignore. But if it keeps going badly over there, then the military is going to have to figure out how to sell the idea of a draft, just like they did in World War II. That's when the marketing barrage will really hit, and you can bet it will be perfectly shaped and aimed to get its target audience in the mood to fight.

TS: How do you find the balance between presenting notions that have a strong sense of reality and others that might be more out there?

RV: I'm shooting for something that when first read will come across as comically absurd, but that might begin to make creepy sense with a little consideration. I'm not sure how I zone in on that balance. It just seems to be there for the taking, since modern life is so bizarre to begin with.

TS: In addition to the very strong sex/violence dialectic and the well-portrayed delineation between home front and front line, are there other dichotomies you think are important to note in the story?

RV: One of the subtexts is that the war is essentially a conflict to the death between a religious society, with a medieval vision of God, and a secular civilization, whose god is Mammon.

TS: Have you been green-lit for more than twelve issues yet? When will you know if this is to be an ongoing or a limited series? Do you have an ending in mind?

RV: We've been green-lit through #18. So I'm shaping #13–18 as a distinct arc subtitled "The War That Time Misplaced." From there it will depend on sales of the trades, since sales have been lousy in the floppies. There will be a delay between #12 and #13 to help me catch up on the schedule, with possibly the second trade released in the interim. And yes, I've got an ending in mind, but it can pretty much work anywhere I want to bring it in.

TS: Now that you've had time to step back from what I know was a major project for you, *Can't Get No*, was there anything particularly edifying or even frustrating about the reaction that the book received? How do you look on that project yourself at this point?

RV: The cliché is you write poetry for the echo, and *Can't Get No* got a more intelligent response than anything I've ever put out there. DC did a great job getting review copies out to a broad selection of literary critics, and I was delighted by how many of them really seemed to understand what I was doing with *Can't Get No* and responded favorably.

The way the book uses word and image is challenging, but I think it rewards with a completely original reading experience. In terms of my life's work, it's probably the thing I'm most proud of.

TS: How are things with Comicon.com? I ask only because it's stayed pretty much with its basic functions, which is a really rare thing in the internet world. Do you have plans to do anything different with the site in future years, or are you happy with the way things are right now?

RV: Comicon.com is chugging along happily. There's plenty of online advertising money these days, so we always have our dance card filled. Traffic continues to grow every month, and we're at the top of just about any comics-related Google search. Steve [Conley] and I aren't bloodthirsty business types, so we haven't leveraged what we have to make a killing. We still see it as our way of serving the community of comics. I don't even promote myself with the site, which is kind of crazy when I think about it. We can see that the internet is morphing, and at some point we'll need to reshape Comicon.com to fit that, but right now why fix what ain't broke?

TS: Was it your idea to put all those quotes on the first trade of *Army@Love*? Assuming it's yours, do you have a general approach to design, or do you look at things project to project? The *Army@Love* covers kind of remind me of *Brat Pack* in that a human figure or two tend to be portrayed front and center, but in addition to being a typical character-based comic book cover, the image embodies some sort of satirical point.

RV: It was my idea to try and mimic a *Cosmopolitan* cover for the trade, but I didn't do the actual design. My general approach to cover design on the comic has been to mash up fashion and recruiting advertising. It was one of those approaches that seemed so absurd when we began but now isn't all that far-fetched. In fact, *Vogue Italia* just did a fashion spread in which every photo could be an *Army@Love* cover!

Dream a Deeper Dream: A How-To Conversation with Cartoonist Rick Veitch

JAY BABCOCK / 2009

From *Arthur*, no. 33, January 2013. Text taken from www.arthurmag.com. Reprinted courtesy of editor/publisher Jay Babcock.

Born in 1951 in Bellows Falls, Vermont, Rick Veitch experienced the psychedelic late 1960s as a teenager. After overcoming some profound self-inflicted difficulties as a young adult in the early seventies—detailed in the following Q&A—he got serious about becoming a professional cartoonist. He succeeded. In the last three decades, Veitch has navigated the comics industry's ups and downs while creating a singular, deeply weird and challenging body of work: sometimes raw, rough, and outrageous in an old-school underground comix way, but more often clever and fantastically imaginative, with moments of startling cosmic beauty. My personal Rick Veitch highest highlights are his visionary run as Alan Moore's handpicked writer-artist successor on *Swamp Thing* in the eighties; *The One*, his deeply antisuperhero comics series, somehow published by a Marvel Comics subdivision, which in a better world would have been the final word on the superhero concept; and *Can't Get No*, a daring, dialogue-less graphic novel drawn in landscape format that builds from the story of corporate drone's post-9/11 road trip into something truly poignant and profound. (Not for nothing did Fug/poet/historian Ed Sanders himself salute that work with a rare blurb—as did Neil Gaiman.)

Rick Veitch's most unlikely and enduring triumph, though, has got to be *Roarin' Rick's Rare Bit Fiends*, a black-and-white comic book series he self-published under his King Hell imprint for twenty-two issues starting in 1994. *Rare Bit* featured no continuing characters or stories—its entire subject matter, issue after issue, was Veitch presenting his dreams in comics narrative form. It was a remarkable run that continued to resonate long after it finished due to its enduring, mysterious subject matter.

A few winters ago, suffering from two decades of persistent, distressing nightmares, I visited Roarin' Rick in his rural Vermont home. Here is our after-lunch conversation.

Arthur: So Rick, when did you start dreaming?

Rick Veitch: [*Laughter*] From the time I was a little kid, I was a big dreamer. There were normal everyday dreams, but then were these big dreams that seemed like movies. I think that my fascination with dreaming was kicked off by a series of recurring nightmares. I would wake up in sheer terror from this recurring dream of a little girl trying to pick a flower below a skyscraper that was being built, and something happens, and the whole skyscraper starts collapsing. The girders start landing around the little girl, and the sound is COSMIC. I dreaded that dream. I had it again and again and again. I credit it with making me pay attention to my dreams.

Arthur: Did your parents know what was going on with your recurring nightmares, terror?

Veitch: Not really. I grew up in an odd situation. We were a big Catholic family; I was the fourth kid. My parents had sort of run out of gas running herd on my older siblings. So I pretty much did what I wanted, with not a lot of input from my folks.

I paid attention to dreams in general, just because this terrifying experience kept coming back. I think that's how nightmares work. They want you to pay attention. That's what they're saying: Pay attention to what this phenomenon of dreaming is.

My older brother, Tom Veitch, who also writes comics and is well known as a poet, had an early interest in dreams, and spirituality, too. He was ten years older than me. We grew up very differently. He grew up with a normal family, while our folks were still paying attention. I grew up when no one was paying attention anymore. By the time I started becoming aware, he was out of the house already, living in New York, so it isn't like I saw him a lot, but when I did, I would learn interesting things about the culture, about art, and about dreaming. I was telling him some of my big dreams. He was interested in them. And from listening to him I began to understand that there was a system to analyze the symbolism of dreams, that dreams WERE symbols.

Arthur: Was there a turning point when you started to pay serious attention to your dreams?

Veitch: When I was about twenty years old, I went through a personal crisis. I had just sort of run my life into the ground as twenty-year-olds tend to do. I went into a deep depression. I couldn't even get out of bed in the morning, that's how bad it was. And in those days you didn't go to a psychologist. You just sort of suffered these things. And somebody gave me a copy of *The Portable Jung*, a big, fat paperback that collects a lot of Jung's writings. I read the whole damn thing, kind of obsessively. I didn't really understand it, but I went through the whole seven-hundred-page thing and began to see correlations in the dreams I was having, which were apocalyptic. That's what was going on with me at the time. I couldn't get out of bed. But at night my dreams were just unbelievably strong, really vivid. I began to sense that they were trying to direct me to heal myself. I can't say I sensed all this consciously, but unconsciously, through the assimilation of all of Jung's writings and the focus on the dreams themselves, I began to see a way out of my depression. And it worked.

I started this really detailed dream diary, writing down every damned thing I could, which I've still got, and bit by bit I began to understand the shadow side of my own personality, what was causing me to fail at growing up. I began to see that I had to ally myself with the deeper parts of myself, I had to trust that. I began to understand the nature of the structure of the psyche, which is one of the great things that Jung brought us. And I began to pull myself out of the hole. That was the beginning of my dreamwork.

Arthur: What had happened? What hole were you stuck in?

Veitch: It was a whole bunch of stuff. It was just being a teenage lunatic. I was never a big druggie but I hung out with druggies. Relationship problems with my girlfriend, unable to hold a job, all kinds of stuff.

Focusing on my dreams, looking at them, trying to understand what they meant, I slowly began to heal myself. Got a job, started to make money, pulled my whole life together. Took responsibility for the things I'd screwed up with the people I had alienated. More importantly, I began to realize that the reason I was broken was that I needed to be an artist. I'd known from the time I was a little kid that I was an artist. But except for my brother Tom, the environment around me, my parents, friends, the education system had all basically said, "No, you can't do this." That was a constant growing up. So there was a real deep and dangerous conflict in me.

I began to understand that if I really wanted to spend my life making art and being an artist, I could. But it was up to me to make it happen. That's when my real life began.

This process of dream journaling and study turned me around. I found a school that taught comics, the Joe Kubert School. Even though I was poor, I canvassed the state of Vermont and got a grant to go to school. Within a few years I'd put together a career drawing comic books for the major comic book companies. It really was a case of me making the right moves based on how dreaming was helping me organize my life.

Arthur: Keeping the dream diary, how did that start?

Veitch: First it was a series of indelible dreams, just cataclysmic.

Arthur: The girl with the falling girders?

Veitch: Yeah, they were on that level. But I was older now.

Arthur: So they were uglier . . . ?

Veitch: I think "archetypal" is the best word. They were pointing out both the nature and structure of the psyche. Many were all based upon a borderline, demonstrating how there's this psychological border you cross. On this side, it's your personal stuff you're dealing with, and on the other side things are more archaic and symbolic. The dreams began to map a landscape in my mind of my psychological state. What was extraordinary about this was that the landscape was based on a REAL landscape in my hometown. Naturally you would think of course your psychological landscape is going to be based on where you grew up; what's familiar. But it just so happened that part of this landscape in my hometown, I discovered much later, had been a place where Indian shamans from the Abenaki tribe used to gather and take magic mushrooms. Shamans and shamanism began to come up in the dreams spontaneously.

In my forties I began drawing these very early dreams as comics and began researching the shamanic connection. There are these petroglyphs in my hometown that were left by Abenaki shamans, and they're right on the map in my dreaming! I began to come to understand that information itself had a certain lifelike quality. The information that shamans worked with was ALIVE, and this could all be accessed via our dreaming unconscious. That became a focus of my dreamwork and my art while I was doing my series, *Rare Bit Fiends*.

Arthur: Where did you get the idea to keep a dream diary?

Veitch: I probably got the idea to do it from my brother Tom, because I know he was doing it. And he's the guy who gave me the copy of Jung as well, at that key point. I think he could see what was going on. He handed me the tools I needed, rather than try to teach me himself. He knew that it's something you've got to assimilate on your own.

Arthur: How does keeping a dream diary work?

Veitch: You have a little notebook by the side of your bed and you teach yourself to remember what you've dreamed. In the beginning I'd write every detail I could, nine or ten pages, whatever. Now I don't do it so much. When I wake up in the morning now, even before I open my eyes, I try move the dream imagery from the dreaming part of the brain into the part where there are

From *Roarin' Rick's Rare Bit Fiends* #5 by Rick Veitch (King Hell, November 1994).
© Rick Veitch.

memory cells. That's the key trick. You don't want to open your eyes because once light comes into your eyes, you'll lose a lot of those dream memories. Once they're in the memory side, you got it. So then I'll get up and have breakfast and stuff and then I'll sit down and make little notes. That night, I'll reread the notes, and usually upon rereading the notes, more from the dream comes up.

Arthur: The dreams you present in your comics are not prosaic. They have cosmic stuff happening. You must have a very vivid and supercharged dreamlife.

Veitch: I think that everybody does. It's just a case of paying attention and learning a few tricks. There are different levels of dreaming. One level is the totally cosmic; that seems to happen in the middle of the night. On the other end is the totally mundane, which happens nearer to morning. One trick I learned early on was to drink a couple of glasses of water before I went to bed, so I have to get up and piss, maybe about one, two o'clock in the morning. That's when you're in the deep sleep and the really cosmic stuff happens. Usually we don't remember that because we sleep right through it.

Arthur: The dreams that we tend to remember are the ones we are having as we wake . . .

Veitch: Yeah. They're the ones about having to deal with the postman or the boss and stuff like that. And I had plenty of those. And when doing the dream comics, I tried to mix them in, too. But what really attracts me to dreamwork is that it seems to be a way to get a handle on what's really going on. Dreams are like a dialogue between the ego and the deepest part of the psyche, which Jung calls the Self. What the Self is, no one really knows. You can only see pieces of it. But, using Jung's model of the psyche, the Self is the center, and the ego just sort of floats on it. The ego, our conscious awareness, is maybe like 10 percent of the totality of what we are. So I've come to see dreaming as a dialogue between those two parts: the floating, conscious ego and the deep, unconscious, mystical Self. Once you realize that that dialogue exists, it actually becomes more real, and the characters can actually take on a life of their own. So sometimes you recognize that you're talking to the deepest part of yourself because there's just that certain awareness of the character you're dreaming of.

The "Self" contains the personal unconscious, the collective unconscious . . . and beyond. I think it's a way to understand nature, too. Like say you wanted to get a handle on the quantum, you might be able to do it through dreaming, because on the deepest level, we are made up of quantum bits, so why wouldn't we be able to dream about how we interact in the quantum realm? Or at a deeper, even more mystical level, there is afterlife. Couldn't we contact that? Wouldn't it be through dreams?

So, I approach my dreams with an open mind, in that sense. I'm always like, *Hmm, that dream I had of that guy who's dead—was I VISITING that guy, or was he visiting me in my dreams, trying to give me a message?* You hold that in your mind, after you have the dream, you just try to suss it out. Is that what's really happening, or am I fooling myself, or . . . ?

Arthur: Your journaling technique is necessarily different since you are also a visual artist. You can replicate the visual component of the dream, physically. Your description is a bit richer because you can use text to describe it—and art.

Veitch: Yeah. What happens is, when you create art from your dream, you reinhabit it in a way that you don't do when you write it in a journal. When you write it in a journal, you're using the reasoning, linear side of your mind. When you start drawing, the part of the brain that channels symbolism comes into focus. Your artistic intuition comes into play. Writing the dream, you've got the facts of the action, like: "Here I was on this day, this thing happens, that thing happens." But when you begin drawing them, your intuition starts playing with what they might mean, and it starts juggling the potential: it could be this, it could be that, it could be related to this other thing. As you're drawing the dream, you're waiting for that moment when you go, "Aha!" and your intuition tells you it's right. And so by the time you've drawn something as complicated as a comic book page of a dream, you've got a real handle on what it is your unconscious is talking about.

Arthur: Was there a moment when you realized it was working?

Veitch: I knew a couple months into my first major journal—which I still have!—that this was exactly what I needed, that this was healing me, that I was on the right track in my life. One of the key things I had to learn as a young man was to tell the truth. Part of me wanted to lie about everything. [*Laughs*] In conversation, for some reason, I would make up stories, with the end result being that people didn't trust what I said. Dreaming helped me understand that. As I began to force myself to tell the truth even when I really wanted to lie, my life came together.

Arthur: Were you sharing this with other people?

Veitch: Not really, no. I was a very private person. My friends knew that I worked on dreams but didn't really understand it. To them it probably seemed like one of those odd things some people did back in the hippie days. To me, it's been my ongoing spiritual practice.

Arthur: What happened with the nightmares?

Veitch: Oh, they toned down. I began to realize that nightmares were cool. The material in nightmares just has to be processed. It's scary and it's frightening because it's a part of the unconscious that we haven't dealt with yet. And there's always more in there. It's always gonna keep coming. The repetitive nightmares are the issues that we've GOTTA face, that we've gotta deal with. So I became really adept at that, I think. I would look forward to something that wasn't normal, that was odd and crazy.

Arthur: Were you experiencing lucid dreaming?

Veitch: Lucid dreaming really didn't happen to me until probably 1985. Sometime around then, in the space of a month or so, I had a series of powerful lucid dreams—visionary dreams of waking up and seeing faces actually floating in front of me. Once, I woke up on the ceiling and saw myself and my wife down below. But the biggest one was where I rose out of my body, became aware that I was dreaming and had a body, a dreaming body that was made of energy. As I became aware of that, something started to come out of my chest. [*Chuckles*] The week leading up to this dream, I had been dreaming about going to the gym and building my arms up until they were like the Hulk. And that's what happened in the lucid dream. My Hulk arm grabbed the thing that was coming out of my chest. When that happened, I took off at superspeed down the stairs, out the door and across the landscape at a hundred thousand miles an hour. Visited certain people, saw them in their beds, and came back. I'm sure there might be some odd scientific explanation for it, but to me it was a real experience.

Arthur: The lucid dreaming—once it happened, did that change how you approached dreaming . . . ?

Veitch: No. But I was sharing some of these experiences with some of my friends.

Arthur: So . . . 1985? That would be around the time you were doing . . .

Veitch: *The One*. And *Swamp Thing*. It just seemed like my whole life was accelerating again: not only had I made a career in comics, but I ended up working with Alan [Moore], and the whole nature of what a comic book could be was changing. I was somehow linked to that, to Alan and Steve [Bissette] and John [Totleben]. *Swamp Thing* was really their project, but I was sort of like the side guy, helping Steve out. So I got to read the scripts, and meet Alan when he came to the States, and he and I collaborated on an *Epic* story and then on *Swamp Thing*. Seemed like I was right there on this fulcrum as comics, which pretty much had been left for dead as an art form, all of a sudden was coming back to life.

Around 1990 or 1991, Scott McCloud came up with this comic book challenge called "The 24-Hour Comic." Scott challenged Steve Bissette and me and a few others to do a twenty-four-page comic in twenty-four hours. The reason Steve and Scott came up with the idea is because both of them were sort of perennially blocked. They needed to break through their creative blockage. I didn't need that, I was pumping out comics right and left, so I decided at that point to approach the challenge a little differently. I drew my dreams, one each day, so that over the course of a month, I had a twenty-four-page comic.

I loved what I did so much that I just kept it going in my sketchbooks for I think three months straight. Once I had three months of comics, I began to see the patterns. It was so clear. None of the dreams were a single dream. It was a pattern of dreams, interwoven over time, and there were these extraordinary aspects of it. Sometimes the pattern of a dream came backward in time. You'd see the ending first, and then the middle, and then the beginning of it, over the course of three weeks. It's a thing I had never noticed before, but there it was in the comic strips. I got really excited about it at that point, and as the potential opened up for me to self-publish my own work, I decided, even though it was commercial suicide, [*chuckles*] to focus on dream comics. I knew I was onto something that hadn't been done before.

Arthur: How did you build the narratives for *Rare Bit Fiends*?

Veitch: What I would do is, I would take my little notes from my notepad and Scotch tape them across the top of my board and look at everything I had for that week, or if it was two weeks, whatever. I'd begin to see patterns. The one I had on Monday is REALLY part of the dream I had on Wednesday. And it's also part of the dream that came the next Sunday. And so I'd bring those together into a single dream, continuity-wise. I'd always pull out the most interesting ones. What I learned early on was, there would be dreams that I didn't want to share: I would feel weird, uptight about putting them in the magazine. But I slowly began to realize that if I got beyond that, and got it down, I felt great. It felt great to get it out, it made the work much more authentic, that I wasn't censoring it, I was just laying it all out there as much as I could. There are some things in the dream journals that I didn't share, but 99.9 percent I did.

Arthur: The *Rare Bit Fiends* series was well respected by other cartoonists, but did the general public have any interest in it?

Veitch: Not really. People seemed to relate most to the first twelve issues, which were focused on other cartoonists. I made a point of drawing the dreams I was having of my friends, so I've got Bissette and Alan and Dave Sim and Gerhard and Neil Gaiman and all these people starring in my comic! Those guys were all great about it, too. I was learning how to self-publish

From *Roarin' Rick's Rare Bit Fiends* #4 by Rick Veitch (King Hell, October 1994).
© Rick Veitch.

at that point, and it's difficult, there's a lot of stuff you've gotta learn very quickly, so the dreams reflected that aspect of my daily life. I knew that by drawing comics that were obviously about self-publishing, I would learn more about myself and create this weird infinite loop with my readership, if they were hip enough to figure it out . . .

Arthur: With *Rare Bit*, other people eventually got involved.

Veitch: When I started self-publishing, I swore I wasn't going to publish anyone else. But there was so much material that came my way that was so great. There were so many other artists out there that were doing this kind of stuff that I de facto became the guy. *Rare Bit Fiends* became the only communal dream art magazine in the world. Just extraordinary stuff came in. Also, the guys I was dreaming about, my crew—Steve and Sim and all those guys—they picked up the challenge and started doing their dreams as comics as well. That was extraordinary, because every one of them, to a man, came back to me and went "This is unbelievable!" The experience of drawing their dream as a comic, and they'd all drawn a bazillion comics, somehow stood out as an extraordinary artistic experience.

What also happened while I was out on the road promoting *Rare Bit Fiends* was, everybody would come up to me and go, "Hey man I had the weirdest dream." [*Laughs*]

Arthur: They wanted you to be the interpreter?

Veitch: Or just a sympathetic witness, I guess. Some would want an interpretation if they were going through some kind of life crisis, which I'd do to the best of my ability. But a lot of people just wanted to tell me a wacky dream. I became this weird conduit for the unconscious of comics fandom, where it was all pouring into me. [*Laughs*]

Arthur: You were at the dream switchboard!

Veitch: [*Laughs*] When I did *Rare Bit Fiends*, I was less a professional cartoonist and more like a painter. Even though all my comics are in some sense an allegory of me, the dream stuff is right-in-your-face allegory. I'm laying it all out, as bare as it can be. It's a great feeling to do that. I don't think the worth of it is understood by most people yet, or even by myself yet. I know that, to this day, if I open one of those old comics and read those dreams again, whole new levels of meaning come to me. Or I'll see how they were foretelling the future.

Arthur: What other studies about dreams and dreamwork did you do?

Veitch: I read everything. I got as many of Jung's collected works as I could, and over time, read them all, once or twice. I tried to steep myself in the work. I think it's key to what's going on. Also, all the other modern dream-working guys, like Jeremy Taylor, I love his work. And Robert Moss, too. He really gets the shamanic side of things.

Arthur: What was your experience with the dreamwork community at large like?

Veitch: In trying to market *Rare Bit Fiends*, I would send copies of the comic out to whatever small-press magazines might discuss this. I got a letter back from Jeremy Taylor, who is one of the great dreamwork writers and who was writing a dream column for one of the magazines I hit with my PR package. He loved it. We started corresponding. He seemed to think I was the first person to actually translate dreams into an art form that could be assimilated. I wanted to hear that. [*Laughs*] And so he started to draw me into the Association for the Study of Dreams, of which he was one of the founding members. I attended one of their conventions, '94 or '95, I found it a bit dry and a bit academic and a bit Balkanized. There were very few artists there. There were a few people doing dream paintings. But it wasn't really like it was happening, like there was a real movement there. It was a much more intellectual and literary approach to it.

And scientific, too. They were bringing in all the information that scientists were getting about the dreaming mind. But their approach kind of removed the mystery. The real kick about a dream is that maybe somehow you're plugging into THE mystery. I don't wanna hear from some scientist telling me that my left brain hyperglobulal thing is firing randomly. That doesn't mean anything to me. What's interesting to me is that I'm in touch with the deepest, most secret parts of myself, or even something of a collective nature.

Arthur: Even this landscape you're talking about, that's a collective space . . .

Veitch: Yeah. That's a symbolic space, though. The things that make up the landscape like the river and the mountain are extremely potent collective symbols. I analyze my dreams by what part of the landscape they happen on. You begin to put together a much better psychological picture of yourself by just having that little bit of extra information.

Arthur: Have you drawn an actual map?

Veitch: In the dream journals, I did. In the trade paperback *Crypto Zoo*. It's pretty clear where the basic landmarks are. It still goes on to this day. When I go back to the real landscape that it's based on, it's a lot like walking in a dream. It's not a lucid dream, but it has that magical sense that anything that might happen in reality also has a symbolic weight to it that you wouldn't normally notice. If you assimilate a landscape as your personal dream landscape, then the psychogeography of the actual landscape will start to come up, through the dreams. Because, somehow, this information is all alive and within our reach.

Arthur: Paul McCartney famously got the melody for "Yesterday" from a dream, and Keith Richards apparently got the riff to "Satisfaction" from a dream. What does that say about authorship?

Veitch: It comes from the unconscious. McCartney gets the melody to "Yesterday," it's still his, but he got it in a really interesting, intuitive way. Instead of sitting at a piano and working it out, he heard it in a dream. Now I've heard melodies in dreams, but I'm not a musician enough to write them down. If Keith Richards got the base riff for "Satisfaction" in a dream, he's still the author. Now there are a couple possibilities there. One is, it's something he heard a bazillion years ago and it just sort of surfaced, it came back. The other possibility is that music is a mystic realm, where this stuff all exists. I like to think of it that way. [*Laughs*]

Arthur: So if you're a visual artist, you can work through dreams using your artmaking skills. A musician could . . .

Veitch: I bet if you started talking to them, you'd find that more musicians do get bits from dreams. Maybe not melodies, maybe just thoughts, or couplets, or rhymes, imagery, that end up in their dreams. There are people who do stage plays based in dreams. There are films like [Akira] Kurosawa's *Dreams*. It'd be interesting to know if guys like Mozart, Beethoven, or Bach got their symphonies in dreams.

My theory is that information is somehow alive. I think consciousness is like a dimension, and information inhabits it. When we die and give up our bodies, all we are is information. Maybe that's what the afterlife is, eh?

Arthur: Do you "use" dreams to solve personal problems, work problems . . . ? To break through on something that's proving difficult?

Veitch: Oh yeah. Essentially any kind of personal issue I'm dealing with, I'll start monitoring my dreams, trying to figure it out. I will sometimes just ask myself, before going to bed, "What's going on with this? I don't understand it. I want to know more." And I begin to interpret dream imagery in the context of whatever problem I'm dealing with.

The nature of dreams is that they are healing. They tend to compensate for when you're off kilter. They want to get you back, centered, and, y'know, feeling right with the world. So when you're really screwed up, that's when they start screaming the loudest at you.

That's a great way to approach them—if you have a really scary dream, or a really upsetting dream. . . . Some people, their first response is, "Oh, it's affirmation that I'm crazy, or something terrible is going to happen to me." It's just the opposite. If your own psychology is bringing you these mental pictures, it's because it wants to get you healthy. Pay a little attention, just listen to what it's got to say, and over the course of time those horrible pictures will tone down and get you right back to where you need to be. It's a skill that really should be taught, and something I think that's missing in our culture.

Arthur: How would you teach it?

Veitch: Well, first off you need to get people collecting their dreams, sharing their dreams—and this is something that tribal cultures have always done—but our rational, industrial culture kind of pooh-poohs all this stuff. Or they see it as Freudian mumbo-jumbo, but it's not—it's how we're wired. We should teach people about the structure of their own psyches just like we teach them about their bodies.

Arthur: Dreams really are regarded to consciousness or well-being in the way that "junk DNA" is regarded to DNA . . . they exist, but they are irrelevant.

Veitch: Our society is based on rationalism and scientism, and it downplays intuition. But intuition is GREAT.

Arthur: When did you find out about the local Native Americans?

Veitch: Well, they started to appear in that first important series of dreams that I was telling you about. What I learned later on as I began to research the history of that area in 1994 or '95, when this stuff really began to come together, in ways that astounded me . . . I was getting bits and pieces of it. . . . You know, Indians camped out at this one spot up the river. There was this one bridge downtown—right below this bridge there were these old Indian carvings. What I didn't realize was, those Indian carvings were the classic shaman symbols . . . the circle with two horns, the eyes, and the mouth. There were dozens of them down there. A lot of 'em got destroyed in colonial times.

What I found out when I began to research it in libraries was, this was the place where all the tribes gathered, because the salmon got caught there—there were falls up above—so at certain times of the year the shad and the salmon would come in. All the tribes would come. All the shamans would get together and start doing mushrooms. The carvings they left are records of the visions. [*Chuckles*]

I found this extraordinary . . . I was having cosmic dreams about this area, as all this was coming up . . .

One time in a dream, I was looking down on this place where the carvings are and I raised my line of vision and I saw the globe of Earth floating above it with all the ley lines illuminated on it.

And then I looked up above that and there was a globe of the Cosmos, the whole universe, with more glowing lines connecting stars.

Showing me that there was a connection: the universe—the planet—this one spot.

Special thanks to *Arthur*'s Man in Manchester, John Coulthart.

Rick Veitch: A Vermonter's Life in Comics

ANDY KOLOVOS / 2016

Transcript of an interview recorded on August 25, 2016, by Andy Kolovos of Vermont Folklife for the Vermont Comics and Culture Project. This transcript has been edited for concision and clarity and reviewed by Andy Kolovos and Rick Veitch. Reprinted by permission of Vermont Folklife.

Andy Kolovos: I'd like to start with a little bit of background about your experience growing up.

Rick Veitch: I was born in Bellows Falls and grew up there. From a very early age, I knew I was an artist. I had this inner, intuitive knowledge that I wanted to make art. I remember teaching my little hand to coordinate a pencil at four years old, really struggling and concentrating on it. Everyone around me recognized that I had this artistic talent, but I was fighting these societal headwinds because my parents didn't believe in art as a career. In fact, no adult I ever met said anything other than *You can't make a living at it!* That was the refrain I heard over and over and over again. But I was making art continually from the time I was very young, in all sorts of variations—anything I could try. I would try mural painting, comic books, sign painting—anything I could do. It was my thing and I was really into it. There was no formal art training at school. The closest training I ever got to learning the fundamentals was from *Treasure Chest* comic books, which I got in Catholic school and which had a cartooning course in the back. Up to then, I had been copying panels from the comics I loved, and still love. Since I had no parental or adult supervision or training of any sort, the only art that was available to me was comic books. I came of age right at the time when comic books reignited, with all the Silver Age titles from DC and then with the Marvel explosion. I bought all those off the newsstand. They were like this incredible cornucopia of imagination and graphics, and if I shoveled a few walks or delivered a few papers, I could go and buy them with my own money and bring them home. And I was enthralled with the stories, the art, and the audience participation.

But more than anything, I began to teach myself to draw and make my own comics with my own characters, based a lot on the work of Jack Kirby, Carmine Infantino, and Joe Kubert—just making pencil reproductions of what I saw and what I dug and trying to get to the heart of, like, *What makes a Kirby illustration so powerful? And why can't I do it with a pencil? And those guys do it with ink somehow!* I was trying to figure all this stuff out. By the time I hit high school, it was the same deal. There was an art class, but they essentially sat me in a corner with paper and a pencil and ignored me. There was no training. And then what I drew, they hated. My art teacher didn't teach me a thing; she only complained that I drew monsters. I spent the first year in drawing class making these really tight pencil reproductions of [Frank] Frazetta's covers, which were blowing my young mind. I had to get to the heart of, like, *What is this thing? Why does it speak to me on such a level?* I had an older brother, ten years older. He had gone out ahead of me to San Francisco and made some connections out there in the underground comics market. He and I had been collaborating on a number of different art projects over the years, so after high school, I whipped out there and we were able to sell the concept of *Two-Fisted Zombies* to one of the big underground publishers, Last Gasp. At which point I came back to Vermont, and that photograph I showed you of me and my pals, that's when I was drawing *Two-Fisted Zombies*, living in this crazy crash pad, with a country-bumpkin, hippie thing going on. I finished the book and it was published but then the underground comix economy collapsed. At that point I was kind of lost because I couldn't see how to take my art to the next stage and make a living at it.

I tried to break in at Marvel by mailing in samples, and they told me my stuff wasn't ready. Again I didn't know what to do. And then the planets aligned and my life turned around. Even though I was penniless, I began to think, *Well, I've got to go to art school somewhere and learn the basic stuff*. I started looking around, and I stumbled upon this little ad for the Joe Kubert School in New Jersey. I went down and I met Joe, and he looked at my stuff. I was embarrassed by *Two-Fisted Zombies*, but Joe totally dug it—he said, *Yeah, I want you at this school!* I went back to Vermont and tried to figure out how to get the money. My family didn't have anything, so they couldn't help. The Kubert School pointed me toward a federal jobs training program called the Comprehensive Employment and Training Act. This is back when our government actually would step in and help people when there was unemployment. So, I applied for a CETA grant to go to this cartoon school. And of course, they said no. They wanted me to be a sewage treatment plant operator. But I just kept knocking on their doors and working my way up the CETA hierarchy until I got to the lady who ran the program on the state level. I think her name was Catherine Dragon or something like that. I sent her this whole wad of Xeroxes that I had made from samples of my comics, and I got a phone call. She said to me, *I see a lot of supermen in here but no superwomen!* And thank God I had the gift of gab that day. I said, *That's what I need to learn!* And sure enough, they gave me a grant. They paid for all my tuition and they gave me a stipend. So, I go from having no prospects to finding myself at the Kubert School, training with one of the great Golden and Silver Age artists and the teachers he had hired.

This is where I met [Steve] Bissette and [John] Totleben and [Tom] Yeates, and we formed this really strong group. Ending up in New Jersey in 1976, it was as if you loved folk music and landed in Greenwich Village in 1962. The Kubert School was a bus ride outside of Manhattan, and the whole comic book industry was in a state of complete collapse. Even guys like Joe Kubert were saying it was all over—but as it turned out, the business side of comics publishing was rebooting itself. A whole new distribution and money model was rising out of the ashes. All of a sudden publishers were hungry for the vision of young artists. And I walked right into it.

AK: One thing I'd like to go back to is your early childhood memories of comics. What compelled you as a kid? What inspired you?

RV: Well, at the very beginning, when I'm probably not even four years old yet, my older brothers had the Carl Barks duck books, and they had *Little Lulu* by John Stanley, and even though I couldn't read, they would read them to me, and I would memorize them. I can remember just being really involved. There was one panel from a *Little Lulu* comic, which sometimes told stories that were on this faux–fairy tale level, where there was a Little Lulu who had a mother who was a witch, and she made Little Lulu sleep on this wooden bed with a log for a pillow. I can remember being a little kid and just worrying about Little Lulu, and also being enthralled by what Barks was doing with Uncle Scrooge and Huey, Dewey, and Louie. That was the very beginnings of it, and then I just naturally gravitated to whatever came my way. As I got to be seven and eight, I'd be in a grocery store and there would be a wall of glorious comics. I loved them, and I could often afford to buy one at a dime or twelve cents. I began with the DC titles, *Superman* and then *The Flash, Green Lantern, Hawkman, Our Army at War.* And then right on their heels came the Fantastic Four and Spider-Man and the whole Marvel thing, which kind of made the DC stuff, in my mind anyway, seem a little old and obsolete. I bought every

Marvel, every month. I'd bike down to Karpinski's Economy Market on Tuesdays when the Independent News truck dropped off the bundle. I would help Karpinski open the bundle and put the comics on his rack, just so I knew I could get each comic. Comics became an important focus in life.

AK: Were there other kids or peers around who were as enthusiastic?

RV: Not really. There was one kid I knew, Franny Cozine, who really dug comics, but everybody else—they didn't get it. They might look at one, but they weren't participating in it like I was. Even as a kid, I would try to show my friends my homemade comics, but they just didn't understand why I dug it so much. So, it became much more of an introverted art form for me. It was something I did for myself, or maybe I'd show my brothers. It was a very organic creative process, too. It wasn't like I was trying to sell comics. I was really expressing my little ten-year-old, twelve-year-old self through fantasy characters and trying to learn to draw.

AK: I have a brother who's nine years older than me, and a lot of my interests definitely came from him and his interests. Was there a culture of comics in the family?

RV: My older brother had grown up during the *MAD* years, and he was totally devoted to *MAD*, so much so that he wouldn't let me read his *MAD*s. But we had the little paperbacks, like the *MAD Reader*, and of course you would read those a hundred times because there's so much going on. He had made his own comics when he was ten, and I found them in the attic. That was an inspiration. He was very creative in a lot of different ways. He was pretty good at drawing, but he didn't really focus on that. He went more into writing, but I naturally went into the drawing side of it, and that's why we ended up collaborating. Even with the age difference, he basically dug the concept of making this type of art. He wrote, and I drew, and we did a lot of fun, crazy stuff together.

AK: This is your brother Tom.

RV: Yeah.

AK: Do you remember finding his comics? Is there a story behind them?

RV: Well, he was one of these kids who not only drew his own comics, but he had a local street newspaper, the *Burt Street Bugle*, that he mimeoed. And he had a great mechanical mind. He wired our house for speakers, and he would have his record player upstairs and he'd be the DJ. He had model trains. He was just really creative and a real hands-on doer kind of guy. The story was I probably ruined his collection that he'd carefully packed away. He's probably never forgiven me for that, but it was definitely my inspiration.

AK: Were you just going through boxes?

RV: Yeah, you know, you're up in your childhood attic just looking around, and here's a box, and it's like, *Wow, here's some cool stuff!*

AK: What was he doing comics about?

RV: He was doing the same thing I was. He was inspired by whatever he was soaking up with popular culture. He did a Dick Tracy sort of character—Rip Kirby, or something like that. One of his great talents was, even though his drawing wasn't super excellent, he caught that general weirdness of Chester Gould in his strips, and I was really enthralled with that. He figured out how to do 3D comics with colored pencils. We had the glasses, and he figured out how, if you move the red and the blue either closer or farther apart, it created the illusion of depth. So, we were able to draw comics by hand that worked in 3D.

AK: There were three siblings in the family?

RV: No, six. It was a Catholic family, and it was kind of coming apart as I came of age. My parents were hard working and hard drinking. But by the time I'm becoming aware, there was less hard work and more hard drinking, so my younger brothers and I were kind of neglected. No one was really watching us. We never went to doctors, dentists. A lot of times meals weren't prepared. The whole family structure was kind of collapsing, and that was mirrored in the town, which was a dying mill town. There was this real feeling of failure, and partially it came from my family and partially it came from everybody in the town. People in Bellows Falls just had a real odd idea that you couldn't make it. Nobody understood art. Nobody. The one guy in Bellows Falls whom I knew was a really successful, quality painter, was a guy named Stephen Bulaski, who had been a Depression-era painter. He'd gotten one of those government gigs to do these beautiful murals all around the state. I went and knocked on his door, and I said, *I want to be an artist. What do I do?* And he says, *Don't do it, kid. You'll never make enough money, you'll be scrounging.* So, that was the position I was in. I guess if I had any character trait, it was stubbornness. And again, I had that deep belief that I had to do this, and if I didn't, my life would be a failure.

AK: Your description of the culture of Bellows Falls at the time—how much of that were you aware of when you were a kid?

RV: Well, I was living it, so it was creating my environment. What had been a really well-off town that had a lot of industry and a lot of big houses and beautiful things was deteriorating. And then, by the time I'm doing *Two-Fisted Zombies*, that's when the influx of out-of-state hippies showed up, and all of a sudden, because Bellows Falls was also a big bar town, it became like the Wild West, with drugs and drinking and just the general craziness of young people all over the streets. It was a wild time.

AK: How old were you did *Two-Fisted Zombies*?

RV: Twenty years old.

AK: Let's just talk about that for a second. I'm not trying to say there are connections where there aren't, but I'm curious. The degenerated world of *Two-Fisted Zombies*—where did that inspiration come from?

RV: Well, I was generally plugged into the whole underground sensibility. Another benefit of knowing Tom was a steady stream of underground publications. Poetry and things like the *Realist*, the *East Village Other*, *Rat*, all this stuff. So I became aware of a lot of the questioning concerning the war in Vietnam really early on, like '64 and '65. I was already against the war, and I was just a young guy. We were all living under the threat of the draft and being sent to Vietnam as well. The world seemed like a really dark, violent place, so I brought that sensibility to *Two-Fisted Zombies*. But I was also inspired very much by Jack Kirby's magnum opus, the Fourth World, which had been cut short. He had brought comics to a more brutal, vital level, I thought, and I wanted to take that even further. The whole Kirby style was just something that just kind of poured into and out of me. I can't say I planned any of this. It was really more organic. The scenes in *Two-Fisted Zombies* were mostly drawn unscripted by me. I left the word balloons empty, and Tom added those later. He took a whole bunch of scenes that I had created and he made it flow into a single story, which we then looked at, and then we figured out, *Okay, we're missing this and this, and if we have an ending, we've got a complete book here*. And that's how we built it. Again, a very organic process. I think the general darkness and violence and nihilism of the book is expressing where my little brain was at when I was twenty and the kind of life I was living, which was kind of crazy.

AK: Were you out West when you drew that?

RV: I went out West and got the job, but then I came back to Vermont. I actually drew it in Vermont.

AK: And you were living with the other guys at that point?

RV: Yeah, in Gageville, Vermont.

AK: How old were you when you left your parents' house?

RV: Well, I got kicked out of my house when I was eighteen. My father had passed away, and my mother was just kind of going down the tubes with a drinking problem. I was the oldest child then. Everybody else had fled. I had two younger brothers. They were running wild, and I didn't know enough to try to talk to my mother or to tell her she needed help. What I did was, one day I just took all the liquor out of the house, and she threw me out because of that.

AK: Six kids, so you're in the middle pretty much.

RV: Yeah, I'm the middle guy.

From the *Rare Bit Fiends* collection *Crypto Zoo* by Rick Veitch (King Hell, 2004). © Rick Veitch.

AK: And where does your brother Tom fall in that?

RV: He's the oldest.

AK: Bissette described himself with a term I hadn't heard before, as a "monster kid." Was that part of your interests?

RV: Yep, the Aurora models and the Universal monsters—I was totally fascinated with them, and Rat Fink as well. One of the big moments of my life was when I was in seventh grade. This is 1963, the year Kennedy was shot and the Beatles showed up. I was really getting into Marvel and all this popular culture stuff. Big Daddy Roth, especially. At school they sent around these intelligence tests. Not that I'm a genius or anything, but I'm really intuitive and I can score really high on a multiple-choice test. I had to guess half the answers, but somehow I scored high. Since my marks were kind of going down the tubes, because of what was going on at home more than anything, the school got ahold of my parents, and this was the last time my parents ever tried to do anything. They decided that my fascination with these art forms was the problem, and they got rid of all my stuff. Everybody came down on me. I was getting it from all ends, really feeling it, and in the mail comes a package from Big Daddy Roth Studios. A couple months before, I had entered an art contest for *Drag Cartoons* magazine to draw the monster—and I got an honorable mention. I got my name in the book, and they sent me these prizes. It was like this affirmation—I had parents and school coming down on me, but here was my name in the magazine. And that was it. I never looked back from there. I just figured out how to work my way around their bullshit, and since my parents were having all their problems, it was real easy to get around them.

AK: Did you go through Catholic school your whole life?

RV: Up to eighth grade. St. Charles Catholic School.

AK: And then you went to the town school?

RV: Yeah, Bellows Falls High School.

AK: Were there any religious concerns expressed about the kinds of things you were into?

RV: Not really, although I was at the point in seventh and eighth grade where I was questioning catechism class, the basic logic of it. At one point they sent me in to talk to the priest. In the middle of class, I had questioned the nature of Hell. They were teaching us that Hell is a place for people who hated God. My reasoning was, *Well, if people hate God, then Hell is going to be Heaven, right?* That got the nuns upset. They sent me in to talk to the priest and he said, *You've been reading Nietzsche, haven't you?* I hadn't been reading Nietzsche; it was just logic. None of that stuff really stuck with me that much, I don't think. Some people got corporal punishment, but I didn't. There was the whole weird sensibility of nuns, but I can't say it was really that negative a thing. They really taught us well. I knew my math and all that. I read at a very young age, and I think it was because they really got that going.

AK: Is your family French?

RV: No, Scottish. My dad came over on the boat from Scotland. My mother is from an Irish family that's been around since the 1850s in Vermont.

AK: Did your father go to Catholic church, too?

RV: No, he was Episcopalian or something like that.

AK: I was curious if he converted or something.

RV: Actually, late in life he did convert. As his life became unraveled, it gave him some sort of anchor.

AK: What about the community that you were part of in Bellows Falls, your friendships?

RV: Even though I had this geeky thing that I did on my own, I lived a pretty normal life. I had lots of friends. I was hanging out. I dated. I played sports. I probably got into drinking and cigarettes too early, and then probably got into smoking dope too early, and probably sexual relations too early. That was more a case of having no parental influence, but there were a lot of kids in Bellows Falls who were running loose like I was as well. That picture I showed you is like a group of lost boys all living together, nineteen or twenty years old, because there was no other option.

AK: Did you think about it that way at the time?

RV: No, it just seemed that the society coming up through the sixties was on a really wrong track. We'd experienced the Kennedy assassination, the Martin Luther King assassination, the Robert Kennedy assassination, Vietnam, the Pentagon Papers, all this stuff. So, between that and this feeling of *Live now because you're going to get drafted and go to Vietnam*, there was just this wild child lifestyle. You add to that marijuana and LSD, and then the low drinking age in Vermont at the time—you only had to be eighteen to go into a bar. So, everybody was partying, big time. I didn't party as hard as a lot of these people. I was back home at night, working on *Two-Fisted Zombies*. Most of my crowd would be down at Meatland in Bellows Falls, drinking and dancing and doing speed. Fortunately, I never liked the heavy drugs. I smoked a lot of pot, and I'm kind of glad I did. I think it's actually a benign drug that made a stressful life more bearable.

AK: As a folklorist in the state of Vermont, one of the things I'm really curious about is, you had this sort of indigenous population, then you had these weirdos coming in, and then you had a certain take on the counterculture that emerged from local people.

RV: Parts of it were really good for me, because these kids coming in were well off. They had been at college, they were out for kicks—but they understood creativity and art. They were some of the first people I ever met outside of my brother who looked at what I was trying to do and would go, *Wow! That's cool!* That was an inspiration for me. One of the problems it created for us locals was that all of a sudden there was no housing. When we were in high school, you could rent a little cabin for forty bucks a month, and they were all over the place. We were thinking, *We could rent a cabin, two or three of us, we won't have to work too hard, we'll have everything we need.* But by the time I got out of high school and this wave had arrived, the rents just started to go up and up and up, and you couldn't get a place in the country. So, we were stuck renting these rural ghetto places in Bellows Falls and Gageville, real lousy, expensive places that people called beehives. But it was all we could get, and that made a difference in my lifestyle because I'm the type of person who wants to live in nature, and that's what I really love about Vermont. So, I wasn't happy or settled living in Bellows Falls.

AK: Even as a little kid, you lived in Bellows Falls proper?

RV: Yeah.

AK: It's interesting—these are the countercultural bits that I don't know how much the Historical Society is touching on.

RV: Well, it was the beginning of this whole real estate boom in Vermont, and a lot of the hippies that came in preaching free love and communal ownership ended up being the realtors and owning the properties. So, it's always been a struggle as a local person who has very little opportunity to get a job, because all the industries just disappeared in the seventies. I've been blessed in the sense that I can make money outside of Vermont and live in Vermont.

AK: So, you graduated from high school and left the house that summer, and then you supported yourself?

RV: Yeah, I had already worked all through high school, generally because I wanted music and I wanted comics. My family life was such that if I wanted to go to a dentist, I had to pay for it myself. I had to buy my own clothes; I just had to organize my life at a very young age. I think people would refer to me now as a survivor. The downside of that is I kind of had a really hard shell. I didn't want to feel. I tended to be an asshole. But life kind of helped me through that—I hope!

AK: So, *Two Fisted-Zombies* was your first published comic. How long had you been doing your early, home-drawn comics?

RV: Probably from '62. So, that would put me at eleven years old. But I was making other cartoony drawings from the time I was six. I can remember doing it.

AK: Now a question I have to ask, because it's my particular proclivity. Was your brother an EC reader in addition to *MAD*?

RV: Yeah, but they weren't allowed. My parents still remembered the [Fredric] Wertham stuff that was in the *Saturday Evening Post*—that anticomics attitude was still hanging on. When they got on my case in seventh grade, they were bringing up that whole Wertham thing and how the comic book publishers were evil. The propaganda had hit home.

AK: Can you elaborate about that?

RV: There was a general societal take that comics were real trash put out by irresponsible jerks. A lot of that came from what Wertham had done in the popular press, blaming juvenile delinquency on comics. To be honest, I think some of his points were good, and a lot of the things I ended up exploring in comics were those same points, but in a creative way—you have to explore them if you want to get at the basic building blocks of superheroes. But at the time it was all just a scare, and it ended up destroying the whole comic book industry in the late fifties and bringing in a censorship scheme called the Comics Code Authority, which was that little stamp in the corner of all comic books. The superhero rebirth in the early sixties was a direct response to that. Superheroes had to be squeaky clean, and there was a lot of stuff they couldn't show. But they remained kind of kinky with the skintight costumes, and they glorified vigilantism. It took someone as dynamic as Jack Kirby to make it work without relying on titillation or horror or anything like that. He had to graphically and heroically shape a story to make it enthralling, and he succeeded.

AK: Do you think that's what you were responding to in Kirby as a kid?

RV: Definitely. The sheer power of the graphics—but the stories as well. Every issue had some sort of new mythological thing or science fiction idea. A lot of it was old hat to him, but as a kid, I was getting it all brand new—time travel, superpowers, all that stuff. You just go to Karpinski's Market and you come back with a load of the most amazing, imaginative stuff that would just feed your head.

AK: Were superheroes your thing as a kid or were you more ecumenical?

RV: I was totally focused on superheroes, but I was interested in any form of comics, any form of graphics, any form of art. It's just that all I could dependably get was comics, and the only other kind of art I could find was what was in the local library. I got the first issue of *Creepy*, and so I began to see the EC style, Al Williamson and Roy Krenkel, and Archie Goodwin was writing it. I instantly loved that as well. It wasn't a fight in my mind. I just loved it all. Anything that was great, I loved. I was absolutely addicted to every single one of them. Bought them off the stands from the beginning and copied all the Frazetta covers. I bought all the Tarzans just for the covers, too. Ended up reading them, but it was really for Frazetta. He had some sort of magnetism. I can remember the first moment I saw Frazetta. I was going into Fletcher's Drugstore in Bellows Falls, walking toward the comic rack like usual. You had to walk past the paperback rack, and something just twisted my head—and there was this paperback cover of *Jungle Tales of Tarzan*. I was mesmerized by that painting. Even though I was a total comic book guy, that day I bought that paperback and brought it home and learned who Frazetta was. And not long after that, there he is on *Creepy*. I could never touch what he did artistically, but he became one of my gods.

AK: Do you paint, too?

RV: Not really, no. I'm a penciller, and I've had to learn to ink. But I'm a penciller, a storyteller guy.

AK: When you mentioned Frazetta covers earlier, I wondered if you were talking about paperbacks or *Creepy*.

RV: Anything. Anything I could find by the guy. He was in *MAD* sometimes, and then my brothers had *Playboy*, and he would be working with [Harvey] Kurtzman and [Will] Elder on "Little Annie Fanny." You could see it—all of a sudden Annie would have these incredible butt cheeks, and you'd be like, *That's Frazetta!*

AK: I've got a fondness for the DC superhero revival books, and I'm happy to hear that you were also a fan of those, because most people I've talked to are Marvel people. What do you remember? Do you remember buying those? What was the first one you picked up?

RV: It was probably *Superman*. I think the first Flash was '56, and I don't think I got that. It was in *Showcase*. But *Superman* was really interesting, and it turned out later it was being written by Jerry Siegel, and they were bringing in all this imaginative stuff about Krypton and red kryptonite. I found that fascinating. I loved the way Curt Swan could make a comic book character really real. He had this really great way with faces and figures. I didn't understand that he was swiping his own figures over and over and over again, but there was some charm to that, too—here's Superman, standing in exactly the same pose again and again and again. Somehow that seemed cool. I ended up exploring all that material with Alan Moore on the *Supreme* series where we did a whole bunch of retro *Supreme* stories that were set in that very same milieu. Those were Alan's urtext as well. He told me that the whole mythos and the idealism and Superman's code of ethics is really what informed him as a child and up to today.

AK: That's interesting, because I think about how he writes Superman, and to me, it resonated with Dr. Manhattan. I've wondered, is Alan Moore cynical about Superman?

RV: No, he loved it like I loved it, and it's in my DNA. So, when it comes time to draw it, I don't even have to look at the stuff. It just comes out, and he'll look at it and he'll go, *Whoa! I remember that panel*, but I didn't copy the panel. It's just in me. I drew it in when I was a kid and I exhaled it as an adult.

AK: So, *Superman* was a big early influence.

RV: *Superman*, and then the Carmine Infantino *Flash*. I remember the iconic covers. That's when I really started copying. The Infantino *Flash* was so successful that they immediately relaunched *Green Lantern* and *Hawkman* and *Atom*, and I bought and liked all that stuff. I can't say I was as rabid about it as I was about the Kirby stuff. I wasn't allowed to buy the early Atlas monster mags, but I did see them at the barber shop. Kirby at that point was creating these monsters out of the id that were pretty fantastic. Even though it was the same story over and over and over again, I would check out what he was doing and I would really dig it.

AK: You've hit on something that I've totally forgotten about, which is these other venues for interacting with comics, like the barbershop. Did you have any other barbershop-type comic venues?

RV: Well, the Charltons were in the barbershop. The barbershop, for some reason, didn't have the good comics. They probably had some deal going with Karpinski to get the Charltons where the ink would come off on your fingers. I never warmed up to the Charltons. They just didn't grab me, but I probably read a lot of them, waiting to get my hair cut.

AK: Yeah, my memory of reading Superman as a kid is in the barbershop, because my brother hated DC Comics. That was the only place I ever saw Superman. So, it feels to me like comics provided you with access to this bigger world.

RV: It ultimately did, but in the beginning it was an inner world. It was an imaginary world. Comics are like Silly Putty of the imagination. It can be anything, and you can take it anywhere. As an art form, it's pretty outstanding. I'm kind of glad it happened the way it did. If I'd had a high school art teacher who sent me to Pratt, I would have ended up doing conceptual art or something, which might have been interesting. But here we are today—comic culture has kind of taken over. So, I feel kind of vindicated in that sense. Comics are just the most amazing form. There are so many things you can do with them. As a kid, I went into them in such depth, and it allowed my own mind to play with those concepts in such a creative way that I think was a very good thing. It created a new problem, though. How do I bring this out into the real world? In the beginning, I relied on my brother Tom, who was more worldly. When I was going to the Kubert School, it helped me get out of that hard shell I was talking about. I had to learn to talk to people and to show my stuff and not to argue, and also to collaborate with people like Joe Kubert and Bissette. We started these creative collaborations that were very, very fun, and we continued it into our commercial work.

AK: How do you feel like Vermont—being from here, the cultural experience, the geography—informs your work?

RV: I'm kind of an odd duck. I go back to the fact that I chose this art form, and it was an organic form of expression for me. I had this little clipboard with typing paper on it through my whole growing up, and when other people were watching *Gilligan's Island*, I was drawing my little comic and just pouring myself into it. So, I approach this stuff on that organic, creative level, not as a sharp commercial artist, although I have to play that role sometimes. On the commercial art level, on the macro scale, one of the problems I think Steve Bissette and I have both run up against is that as Vermonters, we have a sense of community. We want everybody to succeed; we want the art form to grow. We want everybody to have a chance at doing it. Manhattan publishing is much more about straight capitalism, selfishness; everybody's in it for themselves. If you can see a way to screw your buddy, you've got to do it. So, we were always clashing with the New York publishing culture. It led to some really great advances in terms of bringing out creator rights and respect for creators who had been thrown away when we first were breaking in. All of us, and I would have to include Alan Moore in this, were the first generation to stand up to the publishers and just say, *You can't do this or we're not going to work for you.* So, I'm kind of proud of that. That was very much a Vermont versus New York sensibility.

AK: Before moving to New Jersey, you'd been out to San Francisco?

RV: Yeah, I've lived there a couple of different times. I was a little more worldly in that sense. I'd been a bicycle messenger in San Francisco, so I knew how a city worked and I was a little better at getting around.

AK: Often, we become aware of cultural experience through contrast, and you just made a great one regarding the comics industry. Were there any other things about living in and around New York City that put in perspective that you were from someplace else?

RV: Well, New York was a mess in those days. It was '76. They were having all kinds of problems. It wasn't safe. One of the neat things, though, was that hip-hop culture was coming up on the streets. Before there was rap, you'd see these Black guys on the streets, singing this stuff and chanting these poems. There was this air of underground creativity that was bubbling up all around. Punk was coming up in a big way as well, and even though we looked like hippies, we had a punk sensibility, and I think I applied that to a lot of my early comics—you know, blow things up, piss everybody off. I also found it invigorating just to be in Manhattan as a young man, because there's so much going on, and you're in the hive. But the real buzz was that we very quickly had jobs at all the biggest companies, Marvel and *Heavy Metal*. DC was a little slow on the uptake because they were kind of behind the curve on the change in attitudes. But we just found ourselves in exactly the right place at the right time.

AK: Did you ever publish in the Warren magazines?

RV: No, I almost did. I did a sample for them, but they turned it down.

AK: Considering some of the crappy stuff that they were publishing at the time, and then they reject people who actually can draw . . .

RV: Well, part of that is the finances. They were operating on stuff they were licensing from Spain for ten bucks a page, and here comes a guy who's got to make at least seventy-five. What's the point? Same with *Heavy Metal*. All their stuff was coming from France, but the people who ran *Heavy Metal* were hip, and so they opened up the back into these little areas where you could do comics. Those were our first gigs. Then Steve and I, of course, got the job doing *1941*, the illustrated graphic novel of the Steven Spielberg film, which was our first big, money-making commercial project.

AK: Can you talk a little more about that?

RV: Sure—we did a sample, and it knocked them out. We got the job because Alex Toth had quit, late in the project, so they were desperate to get someone to work on it. I had trained myself in the airbrush, so Steve and I started doing these samples, he and I working together, and we're just laying on this really bright, powerful color. The reproduction techniques had come up to the point where they could reproduce that. We got the gig, but then we talked to the people from the film, and they were complete jerks. They wouldn't share any preproduction material. They were very stingy with what they would show us, but Steve was great at finding historical references. He had a big library already, and he was able to find all these film books with a lot of the actors in it, so we had material to work from. The shooting script was dumb. It wasn't funny. *Heavy Metal* didn't like the script they had gotten, written by Allan Asherman. They threw it out. So, I rewrote that as I laid out and lettered and penciled and Steve would ink and then we would both color and do the collage on top. The book is completely visually distinctive because of the collage aspect, where we were cutting up old *Life* magazines and sticking World War II–era graphics everywhere, so it had that sort of gags-per-square-inch that *MAD* used to pull off. If there was a problem, it was that the two crazy underground cartoonists went back to Vermont on their own and just ripped a new a-hole through the middle of Steven Spielberg's film. The book has very little to do with the feel of what Spielberg did. I guess he was kind of mad at us, but I'm real proud of the book.

AK: I find it perplexing that Alex Toth was the one who was originally going to do that.

RV: I don't know what the backstory was on that. I just know that they were pressed. They had to get warm bodies. There was one other guy that was trying to do it, but it was one guy, and when they actually added up how many days were left to do a sixty-four-page colored comic, they just thought, *Nah, we'll go with two guys*. But I think our stuff was funnier, too.

AK: I like to use the word "professionalization," which may be the wrong word, but where did your work go from *Two-Fisted Zombies*?

RV: I just continued to make work for myself. The underground economy had collapsed due to a Supreme Court decision on pornography that allowed local communities to define pornography. This put all the head shops out of business, at least in terms of selling any sort of material that might be deemed pornographic. There was no national standard. So, all the underground comics companies just went away, and the only work they had was for people like [R.] Crumb. I was living back in Vermont, I had this great comic that had come out, I was producing new material—but my only option at that point was to try to get in at Marvel or DC. This is before the Kubert School. So, I put together a big portfolio of pencils and I sent them to Marvel and I got a rejection letter back, which crushed me. Just last year, I found a lot of my old mail. I opened it up. There's the rejection letter that crushed me—and underneath is a letter from Marie Severin, saying how much she dug *Two-Fisted Zombies*. She said, *Your stuff's a little rough, the layouts are good, you just need to make it a little tighter*. But I completely ignored that. I never called her. I never sent her anything. I was destroyed by not getting what I wanted, that immediate acceptance from Marvel. But it all worked out in the end because when it came time to apply to the Kubert School, I had all this material to show him. Same with the CETA grant. I showed that I was doing the work and I just needed training. And that sold me to them.

AK: Did you publish at all from *Two-Fisted Zombies* until the Kubert School?

RV: I was in other little undergrounds. Cliff Neal did a book called *Dr. Wirtham's Comix and Stories*, and he published one of my stories. By the time I hit the Kubert School, Steve and I had done some stuff for him as well. There were a lot of little people out in the world putting out their own little underground comics. They didn't have much money, but it was a labor of love. I was trying to connect with them. I connected with a group up in Canada called Orb. They had a government grant to put out a science fiction magazine. Dave Sim was part of that group as well, even though I didn't know it at the time. And I was working as a sign painter for a wood stove manufacturer.

AK: There's a history that's developed around 1980s independent comics that almost ignores the underground. It's like there was *Cerebus*, there was *Elfquest*, and then suddenly there was this boom. As someone who was present there, how do you perceive that?

RV: It was the next extension of the underground, but it was like another generation. At first, I don't think people like Crumb and [Art] Spiegelman understood that there was a new distribution model popping up on the East Coast. This is what became the direct sales market. The people at Marvel were just beginning to see the gleamings of it. *Heavy Metal* still had pretty good newsstand coverage, but the material *Heavy Metal* was running was obviously inspired by what the undergrounds had done, and they upped the ante by making it so much more professional. We were all inspired by that. There wasn't much in regular floppy comic books that was interesting. [Frank] Miller was the only one doing anything interesting at the time. Soon Marvel started *Epic Illustrated* magazine, and I could do these eight-, ten-page stories, these graphic novels, that were real undergroundy. You couldn't actually show penetrating sex or genitalia, but you could do just about anything else, and the general weirdness of the underground sensibility was something I brought to it. If you look at *Abraxas and the Earthman* and some of those short stories, they're genuinely weird. It's odd that a New York publisher would have published them, but it kind of shows you where they were at—where their model, everything they believed, had collapsed. And they were looking to these young people who could bring in bright, colorful artwork.

AK: Was Goodwin the editor of *Epic* magazine or the whole Epic line?

RV: Both. He was a great guy. I loved that guy. And the contracts were great for creators. I sold one-time publication rights to Marvel for those stories, so I own all that material. Plus, I got paid a decent rate, so it was win-win. It's like the whole industry was all of a sudden turning around in a big way. And the previous generation, it took them a while to get hip to it. I think Spiegelman figured it out first with *Arcade*, and then Crumb with *Weirdo*, but they were still working through the underground publishers. They were kind of behind the curve, and they were still stuck in black and white for the most part. It was hard for them to do color, where Marvel and *Heavy Metal* could use these new scanning and printing techniques. But guys like Sim and [Wendy and Richard] Pini who did *Elfquest*, they were so smart. They instantly saw the opportunity and laid the foundation for everything that's happened in the last thirty years.

AK: You came back to Vermont after you finished at the Kubert School?

RV: I spent a couple years down there, and that's where I met my wife. She worked at the art store, and we lived out on Lake Hopatcong for a little bit. But I had a son in Vermont and so I wanted to be close to him. I got the contract to do *Abraxas and the Earthman*, which was like sixty-four pages of color with plenty of time to do it, and it paid well, so it was like, *Hey, I don't have to be in New York anymore*. And of course, once we were back here, it was easy for me to visit Manhattan when I needed to. Her parents still lived in Jersey, so we'd shoot down, visit them, and I could go in and spend a day or two in Manhattan. And a lot of the business action was moving into the convention circuit. Comic book conventions were starting all over the country, and you'd go and there's the editor you need to talk to. You could have fun and talk comics and talk business all at the same time. I think that really helped make it a lot easier on me than playing the Manhattan game. A lot of guys like Miller and [Howard] Chaykin were in Manhattan, and it seemed like it . . . I don't want to say it restricted them, because they were both brilliant and they did incredible stuff. But I don't think it would have worked for me to be in Manhattan.

AK: So, your wife grew up in New Jersey. What was it like moving up here for her?

RV: She was really into it because she's Ukrainian, so the idea of having a little piece of land, having a garden, having flowers, a pond—that was her dream. When I signed the contract for *The One*, I was able to save enough for a down payment to buy the house, $48,000 for a house and six acres. Of course, we had to fix everything up. But we were really, really lucky. We got in, we got a great place, and it's all paid for now. Like I say, I'm blessed.

AK: You mentioned earlier that you bought comics and you bought records. What kind of music?

RV: It started out with the Beatles. Well, it actually probably started before then with listening to pop radio, just before the Beatles, but I can't say I was hot on it. But the Beatles—you heard those songs and you were just energized. Then right behind them, it was the Rolling Stones and all those guys. But it seemed like the Beatles had a new hit every couple of weeks, and the B side of the single was as good as the front side. It was just really amazing. I started playing a little music myself—my friends and I started a little band. My older brothers were into folk music. They would bring home the Kingston Trio and the Limeliters, and they brought home *The Freewheelin' Bob Dylan*. They didn't like it—they didn't like his voice. So, I brought it upstairs and I totally plugged into what he was doing with *Freewheelin'*. I got rid of the electric guitar and got an acoustic, and I started just singing and trying to learn songs for myself. I never got into performing or anything like that. There seemed to be an authenticity in his vision and in his voice and how he pulled all that together into a song that was as good, if not better, than the Beatles, and then the two of them seemed to be jumping off of each other. That got really exciting, and the Beatles got bigger and bigger and better and better. I was definitely into it. My younger brother, Michael, got the music bug, and he became a singer-songwriter and played in rock bands.

AK: One thing I'm curious about for artists who have worked for the major companies—what are some of your favorite characters you've drawn for Marvel and DC?

RV: I like all the characters. I like playing with every one of them. They've all got potential, and I find when I get the chance to play with them, I get a kick out of trying to add some sort of creative dimension to them that's built in but has never been explored before. So, I can't really say I have any favorites. I think one of my problems working at a place like DC is, I do bring this kind of iconoclastic underground sensibility, and I can't keep it out. You look at what Alan Moore can do—he can write a commercial comic, but my commercial comic is going to have vestiges of the underground in it, and I was constantly up against editors who were threatened by that, who were worried that their intellectual properties were being degraded by that.

AK: What was your first gig? Was *Aquaman* one of your first gigs where you got to do what you wanted with the character?

RV: No, *Swamp Thing* would have been my first one. Alan had ended his run, and the sense was, *Okay, everything's out of gas now, you gotta reboot it and get it going.* I was bringing in a lot of other small-time DC characters like Enemy Ace and the Demon, trying to give them a little angle that made sense to me, and of course playing them off Swamp Thing at the same time.

AK: What you've just highlighted is one of the things I love about these expansive character universes. There are all these nooks and crannies.

RV: Early on, there were more nooks and crannies. They've all been sort of pissed on now. But back in the day, no one had even thought of a lot of these characters—the Golden Gladiator, Roy Raymond, B'wana Beast—so I was able to just pick and choose and bring them in. My last run at *Swamp Thing* was a time-travel story, where Swamp Thing was falling backward in time, and each issue he'd go back to another era, and so I would find some Western characters, and I'd bring them all together and tie them into Swamp Thing's story, and then I'd go back to the King Arthur characters, the Shining Knight and the Demon, and then go back, back, back.

AK: Were you a fan of *The Flash* time-travel stories or the Earth-2 stories?

RV: The original ones, yes. It seemed like an incredible way to bring in all these Golden Age characters whom I'd never seen, but somehow I knew they existed. To see them alive on the page was really cool.

AK: You brought up something earlier that reflects on some of your work that I'm most familiar with. It's the idea that you've got these archetypes of a kind of character, and you like to take them apart. *Brat Pack* is an example; *The Maximortal* is another one. When I first read *Brat Pack*, I thought, *Oh my God, this Rick Veitch guy is scary!* There's a darkness in this work. So, I have two questions for you from that, and we'll do them separately. First, can you talk a bit more about deconstructing archetypes?

RV: Well, as we entered commercial comic book publishing in the eighties, there were still lots of vestiges of Dr. Wertham. So, these characters had characteristics that were obvious, but never explored. The basic one is sexual. These characters are all running around in skintight suits, and they've got kid sidekicks. The other one is violence. These are masked vigilantes, but they're presented kind of as happy characters. Our generation, not just me, felt that we had to push that. *Watchmen* is about that, *Dark Knight* is about that, and *Brat Pack* is about it—but *Brat Pack*, as an independent book, was free of any controlling influence at all other than what I wanted to do. I was angry at the time because of the way I'd been bounced out at DC over the Swamp Thing/Jesus episode. I had this underground sensibility, this punk sensibility, and I just poured it all out into the comic. Going back and looking at it now, one of the main themes of *Brat Pack*, outside of superheroes, is toxic parents, and I think the thing that gives that book its power is that I lived that, and I was expressing it organically, creatively, through my art form and through these characters that were essentially knock-offs of, or very similar to, existing commercial characters.

AK: Yeah, you could tell a Batman story without having it be Batman.

RV: And you could go in areas where they would never let you go.

AK: My second question was about the darkness component. Maybe you've gotten to that, with this issue of toxic parents.

RV: Well, *Brat Pack* came out after *Dark Knight* and *Watchmen*, so it wasn't like I invented that. I was definitely inspired by both those titles. A lot of people were. I think another thing that added to the darkness of it was that I was constrained to black and white. I was using airbrush and gray techniques, but it ends up becoming a very dark book, just the way it looks and feels, and a lot of the tricks I use with graphics have to do with darkness, so that might be a lot of it. But the punk sensibility is, *Let's just get in there, rip it up, piss everybody off*. And that was what it was about as well.

AK: Well, and then to jump from that back to *Two-Fisted Zombies*, I'm reading that like, *Where is this going to go?* There's a hopeful vein in it, and that made me glad. Was that just kind of where your head was at the time?

RV: Very much so—it was a pure expression.

AK: It was interesting to me, having read a lot of bleak underground comics, and *Skull* and *Insect Fear* and all those horror books, that there's something positive in it. I don't know if you see this, if you agree?

RV: I don't know if there's that much positive in it.

AK: I guess my thinking was, you have these two horrific rulers, right? But one's not as bad as the other . . .

RV: . . . but he gets killed and turned into a zombie, and everyone becomes a zombie. *Two-Fisted Zombies* ran into resistance from the underground community because it was superheroic. Somebody could probably make a case that it might have been the first dark superhero book, maybe after Spain [Rodriguez]'s Trashman. Trashman was a little ahead of it. But that darkness and that Kirbyesque look—I don't know. I don't think anybody else had done it yet.

AK: You were aware of the work of people like Spain? Did you ever meet those guys?

RV: Yeah, I was out there at the *Rolling Stone* party for their *History of Underground Comics* where Mark Estren got punched out by Ted Richards. I went to a party at S. Clay Wilson's where he had laughing gas in these big bags.

AK: Well, I guess that's the contrast in my head. The world S. Clay Wilson creates is completely bleak. There's not even really good or evil. But with *Two-Fisted Zombies*, some people, in their own screwed up way, are looking out for the welfare of others.

RV: You know, as we were putting the book together, one of the things my older brother said was, *Man, there's no sex in here*. So, he wrote a script

106 CONVERSATIONS WITH RICK VEITCH

that showed one of the characters in bed with his wife, and then the bad guy comes in and rapes her. Being in the underground, it's like it was expected.

AK: That's a question in itself—the morphology of the underground story. What are the pieces that make it what it is?

RV: Without those two scenes, *Two-Fisted Zombies* could be any independently published book.

AK: Your comic book reading was pretty consistent?

RV: Probably around *Two-Fisted Zombies*, I pared it down to only the really great shit. Whatever Kirby was doing, especially the Fourth World—that one brought everything he'd been doing to this incredible culmination. When that got canceled, it broke my heart. I was paying attention to what Kubert was doing because I liked his work, and the art of Russ Heath. I'm not sure if *Swamp Thing* and *The Shadow* had come out yet, but they were right on the horizon, and I zoomed in on them as soon as I saw them because of the quality and the fresh thinking that it showed that DC was able to do. But the Marvels were pretty terrible and the rest of the DCs were pretty terrible. They'd lost the thread with my generation. *Saturday Night Live* was coming on television, *National Lampoon*—this whole new type of humor. And it wasn't long until *Star Wars*. That came out the first year I was at the Kubert School. So, the sensibilities of popular culture were changing, and it took the old companies a few years to figure it out.

AK: My impression is that people like you were the exact market for the Kirby *New Gods* stuff.

RV: Yeah, we'd followed his Marvel trip all the way, and then he amped it up. He really he gave it everything he had.

AK: You brought up *Swamp Thing* and looking at [Bernie] Wrightson. How did guys like Wrightson affect your thinking?

RV: I knew that they weren't that much older than me. Bernie's just a couple years older than I am, but he's one of these prodigies. I'd seen his fan work in *Creepy* and a couple of other Creation Con things, so I knew he had the chops, and they immediately got him going on *Swamp Thing*. As soon as I saw it, it was like a message to me that the winds were changing at DC, that some editor understood what we were thinking out there in the real world.

AK: Were you a Jeff Jones fan?

RV: Oh yeah, the Studio guys were all great. And again, they were just a couple years ahead of me, so I could look at what they were doing and think, *Yeah, maybe I can do that.* They were definitely the inspiration for Bissette and Totleben and me. Sharing a house in New Jersey after we graduated, we saw ourselves like them and we tried to help each other. We kind of entered the commercial industry like a flying V, all holding together and giving each other jobs and helping each other pay the rent when needed. It was a really tight group. We're still really tight friends.

AK: Did Wrightson's work on *Swamp Thing* inform how you thought about the character?

RV: Swamp Thing was one of those characters that needed to be explored, which I think is the brilliance of what Alan and Steve and John did. They just broke it wide open. But [the Len Wein/Bernie Wrightson *Swamp Thing*] was beautifully constructed. Each issue walked you through another monster. And [Michael] Kaluta was great as well. I thought Kaluta's *Shadow* was much better explored. They really caught the Shadow. With Swamp Thing, even as beautiful and as great as it was, there was still this whole other dimension to go into—and fortunately we got to go there.

AK: To go back to Vermont—what does being from Vermont mean to you, if anything?

RV: Well, it's that community thing. I know that, when people ask me where I'm at, when I say Vermont, the first thing they go is, *Do you know Bernie [Sanders]?* And they'll be weeping because Bernie has been so inspiring. I really dig that. I wish he'd gone further. So, I like that part of the state. I like the fact that we've got a lot of programs to help low-income people in Vermont. I don't mind paying taxes to help people. I wish Vermont would get into the arts. A lot of people make a lot of noise about "art culture," but there's very little art in the schools, and very little support for any sort of art training. There are a lot of young, creative people in all the arts in Vermont, and it's a wasted resource. If they were trained and helped to pursue their careers in much the same vein I was, they would make Vermont better for everybody because they would make their money outside of Vermont and bring it in, and then they would hire people to fix their homes and to fix their cars and pay their property taxes. There's a lot of wasted creative energy in Vermont right now, I think.

AK: What you said about Vermont and community—there's this dichotomy between the state mottos of Vermont and New Hampshire: "Freedom and Unity" and "Live Free or Die."

RV: Yeah—the northern part of the state is different, though, from the southern part. And I think the southern part is more like the old Vermont, because there's no work here. People who can afford to live here have either got a trustafarian thing going on, or, like me, they've somehow figured out a way to get a job outside and to enjoy this beautiful place. But for a kid growing up here, there's nothing. Ten bucks an hour working at the ski area. That's

108 CONVERSATIONS WITH RICK VEITCH

it. I wish the people who run the state would have some sort of plan to train people and to give them some options. It's really kind of a shame.

AK: This opens up a time-travel question. As a kid, were you thinking *I want to be a cartoonist*?

RV: Yeah, I wanted to be a cartoonist. That was my thing. I knew it at the bottom of my guts: I wanted to be an artist, and comics were the thing. I could have been turned in another direction by someone who turned me on to fine art, but there was no one there.

AK: Can you talk more about purchasing comics and so on? Where did you pick up the undergrounds?

RV: For those, you'd have to go to Boston or somewhere and find a head shop. There was a head shop in Brattleboro, now that I think of it. Also, a lot of the young generation that was moving to Vermont, they'd just bring a stack of *Zap Comix* with them. They were lying around everywhere. Any of them that I got my hands on, I would try to save, because that's the kind of person I was. Once my brother Tom got into the undergrounds, we were able to get freebies, so he would send me a care package every once in a while, a big stack of whatever he had doubles on. When I was out there, undergrounds were everywhere, so I got to see everything.

AK: This is a loaded term, but would you view yourself as a collector?

RV: I've got my old comics, but I never even put them in bags. I've got all my old Marvels, just in a big plastic tub—I just read them and stick them back. I've never saved a comic in a plastic bag in my life. I've probably thrown away two fortunes' worth of books and comics and given away original art. So, I can't say that I'm a collector, but I'm a lover of it.

AK: I'm of that eighties generation that stuck all their comics in plastic bags. Were you ever a back-issue hunter?

RV: Once I started going to conventions, or when I was out in San Francisco, going to Gary Arlington's comic book store, that's how I fleshed out my Fourth World books and my *Swamp Things*—a quarter apiece, you could get this stuff. But in the early days, if you didn't buy it when it was on the stands, you didn't get it unless you could trade somebody or something.

AK: That's my other set of questions. I'm curious about trading comics between friends. Did that go on?

RV: Oh, yeah. In fact, I had these two friends who immigrated from England, and they had a stack of English comics—*Beano* and *Valiant* and all those—and I traded them a stack of American comics. So very early on, I got to read all that English stuff that also inspired the Brit guys that I ended up working with later. When we get together, we talk about those as much as we do about Superman and Batman.

AK: That's an interesting commonality. I hadn't thought about that. You had an anchor. With trading comics, were there relative values you were concerned with?

RV: No, it was just like *I'll give you these for those*. There was no money. There might have been places in the urban centers that did that. One time we were in Manhattan, though, and I found a copy of Stan Lee's little pamphlet *Secrets of the Comics*. I got it for a dime in a bookstore, so that was something.

AK: But it wasn't like someone had an *Archie* and you're like, *I want your Batman*.

RV: Nah.

AK: Did you ever read *Archie*?

RV: A little bit. It wasn't really my cup of tea, but again, I would be interested in anything that was a comic. I'd be interested not even in the comic itself, but the ads. Somehow the ads were totally cool. And the fact that there were the little dots—there's something about the whole damn thing, you know.

AK: Did you ever order anything out of the comics?

RV: I ordered all kinds of stuff from *Creepy*. They had this thing in the back called Captain Company and they never sent me anything, the fuckers.

AK: You were never a "6-Foot Monster" person?

RV: I probably coveted them, but I don't think I would send away. There was a definite belief in the household, coming from the parents, that you'd never get the stuff. And they were right.

AK: Can you talk a bit about *Treasure Chest*?

RV: It was cool. It was Catholic school, so you would pay a buck, and you would get a monthly copy of *Treasure Chest* for the whole year. There was really neat stuff in it. There would always be a couple religious things, but I recognized that some of the art was done by Joe Sinnott, who was inking Jack Kirby, and I was putting those two things together. I was beginning to see how styles work together and how one guy would look one way one time and another way another time. Just the fact we had this approved comic was neat, and it was very high-quality stuff. I found it a very interesting comic.

AK: Did you save *Treasure Chest*, too?

RV: I probably did, but I don't know if I have them anymore.

AK: I'm just thinking in terms of what's worth saving in a kid's mind.

RV: Well, I saved everything, and it wasn't just comics. I was just totally into any form of graphics. One of my friends and I would walk around the

110 CONVERSATIONS WITH RICK VEITCH

town, and if we saw one of those silkscreen posters for the Helldrivers at Rutland Fair, once the date went by, we'd go into the bar or barber shop, and ask, *Can we have the poster?* I saved all that shit, too. I loved anything that had a graphic sensibility. It was just totally attractive to me. And when the sixties posters came out, I was sending away for those. In the back of *Rolling Stone* and *Eye* magazine, you could buy these big posters of Dylan and stuff like that for a buck apiece. Or if you went to a head shop, they would have a big rack of posters. It was like catnip to me.

AK: Were films ever important to you?

RV: Yeah, films as well.

AK: Do you make a connection between visual storytelling in film and comics?

RV: Absolutely. *Two-Fisted Zombies* is me evolving a storytelling style as if I were a director. I remember seeing *A Clockwork Orange* and recognizing the camera setups as being very similar to Jack Kirby panels. I don't think anyone has ever made that connection between Kubrick and Kirby, but I saw it. With *2001* and *Jaws* and *Butch Cassidy and the Sundance Kid*, films got really interesting in the seventies. All of a sudden, a young director's aesthetic started to be established, and I think that would prove to be a real inspiration for young people who got into the creative arts.

AK: I never even made a connection in my head between movies and comics until I was reading one of the [Russ] Cochran EC reprints, and they had one of the artists reflecting on how that was where they spend their time.

RV: Yeah, and a couple of generations before me, like Kirby and Kubert and those guys, they totally went to the movies. Their big film was Orson Welles's *Citizen Kane*. That opened their minds in terms of how to approach a comic, that you could become much more Eisneresque. Eisner was a little ahead of the game on them—even ahead of *Citizen Kane*, I think. But that was a big stepping stone for that generation and the art form itself.

AK: Did you ever meet Jack Kirby?

RV: Yeah.

AK: What was that experience like?

RV: Well, I named my second son Kirby. That's how hardcore I was. We were at San Diego, and I had little Kirby in my arms with a little nametag. Jack was really old and really sick at the time, but he was shaking hands with people. There was a big line. I walked up and I just held little Kirby out to him, and I pointed to the nametag. And he looked at it and he went, *Yikes!* We shook hands, but I couldn't speak. I knew what was going to come out. My wife was right there and she talked—*Oh, my husband really loves your* *work*—but literally I was struck dumb in his presence. There were a couple of other times I saw him there where I didn't meet him one-on-one. There was one time early on, I was with Peter Laird and we were in one of the hotel lobbies, just chatting, and there was this commotion. We looked over and the sea of fans parted—and in walks Jack. Everyone was just in love with the guy—like, here's Jesus or something. And Pete and I just looked at each other and went, *It's Jack!* And we just sat there as he went in and took a seat, and people would come up to him, and he was gracious and would sign things. We just kept looking at each other, *It's Jack, it's Jack!* In my pantheon, he was right up there. Kubert was as well, but I got to know Joe on a personal level, so that kind of knocked him out of the pantheon because I knew him as a guy. But I was really, really fortunate to meet those guys.

AK: Kubert seemed to be just a profound influence on you guys, even before you went to the school.

RV: His work had this incredible integrity to it that we all responded to. If you saw a Joe Kubert comic, you'd buy it just because it was Kubert, and you'd study the panels because it was so beautiful. It got to the point where he was only doing covers, but I'd still buy it to study the cover. When he started the school, it was like all these threads that were part of my life suddenly came together into a coherent whole, and Joe was definitely the key point of that.

Here's why he was amazing beyond what he could do with his art. He had a deep belief in the worth of every human being, that everybody could pull themselves up, and that he would help anybody whom he saw that in. When he started his school he was looking for people who had a calling, and I had a calling. He recognized that in me, that first time we met. In fact, when I was struggling to get my grant and it wasn't coming through, I called him and told him I couldn't make it down to school, and he said, *I've been talking to Muriel about you. Why don't you come down, we'll figure something out.* So, I actually started the school with no funding the first couple of weeks, but then the grant came through and all of a sudden I was the rich kid. He was an extraordinary human being. Part of that belief was his heritage. He was Jewish and had come up through living in the Lower East Side, like a lot of those guys. And he just really believed that if anybody worked hard and was a straight shooter and honest, they would succeed and he would get behind them. That's what the school was all about. He didn't have to do that. He was the top cartoonist in the world, had plenty of money. But he decided he wanted to start a school and have twenty-five crazy young kids around and teach them how to do it.

AK: The way you described him, it sounds like that resonates with your world view, that idea of mutual support.

RV: Yep. He's an extraordinary human being. The luckiest thing that ever happened to me was meeting that guy.

AK: Can you talk more about some of the things you gained from him?

RV: One thing was, as focused as I was in my art, I also had a hard time focusing my creative energy. I might start drawing and be totally into it and having a great time, but my creative energy would be so powerful I'd jump up and run around the room or get involved with something else. I had a hard time focusing it. One of the great lessons he taught me without even trying was [what I could learn just] watching him work. He had an office off to the side of our big studio where we all were, and sometimes where I sat, I could see his drawing board, and he would be working on his commercial projects. He had this way of approaching his work and putting art on the board, this laser-beam focus. This is in the midst of an art school, where a lot of young people are coming up, and they need answers, and they need help, and they need this and that. It didn't matter. He was like a laser beam focusing on his work, and I started to imitate that. I said, *That's what I want.* So, as I would be doing my work, I'd feel that incredible energy, and I'd want to jump up. I'd go, *No, focus it, focus it, focus it,* and I would find I could draw five, six, seven, eight hours—all night. He saw me doing that and he was like, *You got it, Veitch, now get your shit together.* He kicked my butt in terms of learning to draw and peeling back all the self-taught stuff. He said, *Kirby's great, but you can't draw like Jack Kirby. You gotta learn the basics of anatomy first before you can exaggerate.* My first real classes in the foundations of art were through Joe.

AK: A longtime friend and colleague of yours, whom I won't name for the record, made a contrast between his approach to work and what he called your work ethic. Is that something that's been a lifelong part of how you've functioned? Or was that something you learned with Joe?

RV: I think Joe helped me bring it into focus. You can see from the material that I turned out as a kid, I was doing it. But I did have a problem with doing it for more than fifteen or twenty minutes. I don't know if it's ADD. I don't know what it was, but I'd be right in the middle of a pencil stroke and jump up, like I was unable to stop myself, and have to walk around the room or something. It's kind of weird. Just watching Joe, observing how he had trained himself, got me past that.

AK: Would you mind talking about this a little more? For me, it's almost like OCD, where there's this voice in my head: *Do something else, do something else.*

RV: I can't tell you if it was a voice or not. It was more like an intensity, that it would just reach this intense level. But it also might have been related to being able to take a drawing to a certain level and not knowing what to do next. That might've been a part of that. I did a lot of things that I never finished because I'd take it to a point and jump out of it. Joe got me past that. He recognized that I had that workhorse mentality, so he took a real interest in me through school and beyond.

AK: Since completing the Kubert School, you've been an employed cartoonist. What's that like with raising a family?

RV: It's feast or famine. It's the nature of the beast unless you want to do the Manhattan trip and get contracts and play that game. I could've done that, but at heart, I'm really about that creative expression I feel and getting that onto the page. So, I was always looking for a financial or contractual place where I could do what I wanted to do, free of a lot of outside influence, and make enough money to keep us going. We had incredibly great years. But then we had other years where I'd be lucky to scrape together $10,000. But it's okay, because it allows you to recharge your batteries. If you plug into this thing where you just do a monthly book your whole life, I think you burn out. I did not burn out probably until I was just finishing *Army@Love*. That was the point where I went, *I gotta take a break. I'm just exhausted.* I got back into it after a couple of years, but I just needed a break from doing it.

AK: What's the work you're proudest of, that you'd value higher than any of the others?

RV: It would be my dreamwork. This is how far out I took the idea of cartooning: once I got into independent publishing and I had a grub stake we'd made from some commercial comics, I started a comic called *Rare Bit Fiends*, which was a dream diary. It was my dreams in comic book form. Now, you're never going to make any money doing something like that, but I was able to put it out as a monthly comic for two and a half years. Things were tight, but I was able to do it, and in the process, I learned so much about myself and how our minds are structured, how the unconscious works, how it can provide a keel when you're navigating the oceans of life. That's what I got the most out of. And I think if anyone ever goes back and looks at my life, they'll look at that and go, *Wow, he's the first guy to do that. No one else ever did this really large chunk of personal dreamwork as a comic.* I think that is an achievement that's beyond just doing regular old superheroes.

AK: What are you up to now?

RV: I'm doing a couple kind of large projects. I've started a new company with my partner Steve Conley called Eureka Comics. We're focusing on using comics in schools as textbooks. Last year, we did a series of six graphic novels for McGraw-Hill that were essentially math workbooks mated with graphic novel fantasy characters. We're hoping to grow that business, because I'm very

From *Super Catchy* by Rick Veitch (Sun Comics, 2016). © Rick Veitch.

interested in using the art form in that way—and it pays a lot better than doing regular comics. I am doing a graphic novel—it's actually more like a graphic poem—with Ed Sanders, of the Fugs. He's working on a poem about the assassination of Robert F. Kennedy, and I'm illustrating that. We haven't got a publisher yet, but we're about halfway through the book. And I just did a new title called *Super Catchy* through CreateSpace, and I've launched a new imprint, which is called Sun Comics. I'm not sure where all that's going to go, but I'm looking for a new creative way to do the weird stuff I want without needing the overhead. So, print on demand, Amazon, CreateSpace—I've just been teaching myself that. My first title just came out. You can buy it on Amazon today.

AK: I'm intrigued by the idea of nonfiction, educational comics. What got you thinking about that?

RV: Bissette turned me on to a gig that Neil Gaiman, I think, had passed on to him, doing comics for a psychology program at the University of Quebec. It was funded by a grant from one of the biggest pharmaceutical companies, and it was like an $800,000 grant. So, I went up to the University of Quebec. They had this whole office full of people, and they needed fantasy comics to help kids understand social cues and social systems. It paid really well, but also it was really cool using these tools that I've got and actually helping people. I enjoyed that quite a bit. And I got thinking, *Well, maybe it's a way to make a better living.* I'm pushing sixty-five now, so I've got to think about retirement. I started looking around. I got my partner, and we came up with the idea of Eureka Comics. We got invited to a symposium at the World Bank of all places. We met all these highly placed people in education, internationally. We made our case for comics, and out of that we got the connection to McGraw-Hill and a pretty large set of contracts that we just finished fulfilling. They're talking about a whole bunch more, but we haven't signed it yet.

AK: And you guys are doing the creative work?

RV: Yeah, we do the whole creative part. I've been able to hire my son Kirby, who's just out of art school, as a colorist. And my son Ezra taught himself how to letter using Adobe Illustrator. They're kind of like my private studio, and I'm able to feed them freelance and get the work done under my auspices. It's kind of a best-of-both-worlds situation.

AK: Tell me a little bit more about this psychology project in Quebec—that's really intriguing.

RV: It still hasn't been released. Supposedly, they're just putting it together right now. It's called *Passport: A Guide to Life*, or something like that, and it uses dragons and fairies and unicorns, and there are a couple of human characters, and they'll interact with the fantasy characters and there will be some sort of social issue. One of them was about how sometimes it's embarrassing to invite someone into your house for the first time—there'll be a story about that. So, this is brought into the classroom, kids read the comic, and it gets them talking about their own feelings, but in this fantasy context. If you just ask a kid that question directly, he doesn't feel anything. But what they found is that through fantasy they can help kids with solutions and strategies for dealing with some of this stuff.

AK: And they're bilingual?

RV: I think they're going to be multilingual. They're in French and English right now, but they have told me there's going to be a Chinese version, which is one of the reasons they wanted the dragon character, because apparently the dragons have a certain symbolism in China. I have to say, too—with the McGraw-Hill work, they don't ask me to dumb down what I do, or to make my style more palatable. What I do is kind of edgy sometimes—even when I'm palatable, it's kind of edgy. But it seems like the educational structures now are more open to the graphic novel sensibility. They're seeing that their audiences, who are schoolkids, are really attracted to that kind of stuff, so they're more willing to mount the finances and everything needed for these kinds of programs.

AK: Well, I've kept you a while. Is there anything that you'd want to add?

RV: I don't know what to say, except I'm probably the luckiest guy you'll ever meet. My life could have gone in another, really bad direction if I hadn't gotten that grant and been able to pursue my lifelong dream. I fear I would have been one of those zombies walking around our towns with no goals and no money and no nothing. So, I thank my government for having a jobs training program when I needed it—*Ahem!*—and I hope that they will prove wise enough to do that for the current and following generations. I thank my lucky stars I got to do what I wanted to do.

Rick Veitch Interview: *1963*

DUY TANO / 2020

Transcript of an interview from *The Comics Cube* YouTube channel, November 18, 2020. The transcript has been lightly edited for clarity. Reprinted by permission of Duy Tano (*The Comics Cube*).

Comics Cube: Welcome back to *The Comics Cube*. I'm joined today by Mr. Rick Veitch, and today we're talking about *1963*. Hi, Mr. Veitch. How are you doing today?

Rick Veitch: Hey, I'm doing good. Thanks for getting ahold of me. Here in Vermont, in the USA, they've legalized cannabis. While we're talking, I'll be trimming my cannabis plants. It's harvest season this week, and we've got to get 'em all clipped and drying. So if you don't mind, I'll be clipping as we speak.

CC: That'll be fun. So, we're talking about *1963*. In case anyone is unfamiliar with *1963*, up here, where I'm pointing is a suggested video for the history of *1963* from *Strange Brain Parts*. [Tano indicates a link to "Whatever Happened to 1963?" from the *Strange Brain Parts* YouTube channel.] But it needs a little bit of fact checking because it basically said that Jim Valentino approached Steve Bissette, Steve Bissette approached Alan Moore, and then they approached you. That's not really true, is it? You were there first?

RV: You know, I'm not really sure. I know Jim approached Steve first, and whether Steve called me or called Alan, I don't really know.

CC: There's a comment in that video that basically said, Steve Bissette said you were there before Alan. And there's an interview with Alan that says you were there before Alan. Steve really puts you up front and center when he talks about *1963*. So how do you remember getting involved?

RV: I got a phone call from Steve. He and I had been working with Tundra. But Tundra was winding down; it was about to get sold to Kitchen Sink, and we could see the writing on the wall there, so we were looking for a new way to do our own comics outside of the large publishers, DC and Marvel, whom we'd been having a lot of problems with for the previous ten years. What's interesting about that time period is what was going on in the market. We were coming to the end of a really amazing decade of comics in America, the 1980s, when the distribution network had flowered. And the number of comic book stores had mushroomed all around the country, so that comics were selling better and better, and they'd freed themselves from the Comics Code, which had limited what could be in comics. It's kind of like a golden age of comics in America, the eighties. Just a lot of great stuff came out, and a lot of stuff that ended up shaping culture, like *Watchmen* and *From Hell*.

CC: And *Swamp Thing*.

RV: And *Swamp Thing*, especially. *Swamp Thing* was the one that really broke open DC Comics from their moribund, hidebound ways. But what was happening was that the market was exploding too fast. It was bubbling up. It had become a crazy collector's market where people were paying insane prices for comics that weren't worth anything. It was the beginning of people putting out endless Number Ones just for the collector markets. People were speculating on large boxes of comics before they were even printed. There was a weird speculator market going on to sell a lot of comics. A lot of comics never got to the stand, they just sat in boxes because these boxes were being bought and sold by shadowy dealers somewhere. A lot of it didn't make any sense at all. But at the same time, the Image guys had really kind of hit a home run out of the park by launching their imprint at the time they did. They were all refugees from Marvel. They were a lot of the top Marvel artists. And they decided to put their own company together, just at the right time. In the beginning, they used a lot of the rhetoric that my generation had used about creator rights. And it looked to us like, *Yeah, these guys, they're standing up for creators and stepping away from the big paychecks at Marvel and doing it themselves*. It looked like a really, really good thing for us. We didn't understand at the time how precarious the business was, but it was getting ready to explode in a very bad way, right while we were doing 1963. And that business landscape really helped shape and define what happened with 1963, and why the annual didn't happen, and why 1963 did not carry on. That was one of the big reasons.

CC: People see the Image founders as a bunch of rebels and mavericks, but you guys kind of paved the way for them.

RV: We were trying to. I mean, we were two different generations. Alan and Steve and I are at a certain age. And Todd [McFarlane] and Jim [Lee] and Jim [Valentino], those guys are ten, fifteen years younger. They're really ambitious people, but they're ambitious for themselves. Maybe not Valentino so much, because Valentino is our age. And I think he is more like on our side of the ledger on that one. But Alan, Steve, and I, and many other people in the eighties, stood up against the big publishers, not for personal gain but to bring the art form to its better potential. We all knew the stories of Siegel and Shuster, and Jack Kirby and all these guys who got ripped off by the companies and exploited. And so we all felt the need to change that. It wasn't just the creators—the retailers, the distributors, and the fans all kind of felt the same way. It was like, *We gotta fix this, this is a beautiful American—worldwide—art form, and it's being strangled by business practices.* So that's the difference. We were ambitious for ourselves to a point, but I think we were more ambitious for the art form itself. The Image guys were really about themselves, and that's the split right there.

CC: You and Alan and Steve had been working with each other for at least ten years at this point, because you were working together on *Swamp Thing*.

RV: That's when the three of us started working together. But Steve and I go back to the Kubert School in the mid seventies. We met at the Kubert School. We had this really tight creative relationship—worked on a lot of stuff together, lived together, or lived close to each other. A really great friendship. He is one of my best friends in life.

CC: And your relationship with Steve and Alan at this time was just aces, perfect, by 1992.

RV: Yeah, having worked on *Swamp Thing* together, I'd spent endless hours on the phone with Alan, talking about all kinds of great stuff, not just comics, but all this metaphysical stuff that he and I are into. I come at it through dreaming. He comes at it through magic. Trying to figure out what consciousness really is. Many, many pleasant hours talking to Alan on the phone and learning a lot about a lot of different stuff. I'm just in awe of his writing, because he would turn these scripts around in three days—a full *Swamp Thing* script, not a word out of place. It's just unbelievable what the guy did, and he was juggling *Watchmen* and who knows what else at the same time. He was just a fantastic artist and writer and production guy as well. And Steve is probably one of the most talented people I've ever met in my life. He can write, he can draw, he can do it all. I'm so very fortunate to have both those guys as my friends.

CC: Oh, Alan is in awe of you, too. I think at one point he said that if the American comics industry were ever on fire, somebody should save you so we can clone you and extricate the entire history of American comics.

RV: Well, you know, he's just being a wise guy.

CC: When you guys proposed *1963*, it was very different from the way Alan used to write scripts. Alan was a full-script guy, and he wanted to do

From *1963*, Book 1: *Mystery Incorporated* by Rick Veitch, Alan Moore, and Dave Gibbons (Image, 1993). © Rick Veitch and Alan Moore.

Marvel style. How did you guys feel about that? And how was that received by Valentino?

RV: I think Valentino loved it, because Valentino was a retro guy from day one. The whole concept was Alan's completely. Steve and I didn't have any input on the conceptualization of what 1963 was going to be. Our job was more to facilitate Alan's vision. And at first, I don't think we quite understood that it was meant to be deadpan. We thought it was like, *Oh, it's gonna be a little humorous. You know, we're gonna make this funny, satirical*, and he's like, *No, I want it completely deadpan. I want it with big dots. I want it on pulp paper. And the only humor is going to be in the ads.* He had this complete vision. He loved *Acme Novelty Library*. And he was seeing a package that was as packed with information and as perfectly designed, or attempted to be as perfectly designed, as *Acme Novelty Library*. I remember he said that in the beginning, so Steve and I took that and designed characters based on what Alan was telling us he wanted. And then it was our job to go out and figure out how to do the big-dots printing, the old style, Silver Age printing *and* to get it on pulp paper, because all this stuff was in the process of being lost. The American printing industry was moving toward these higher-end packages for comics, and there weren't any presses running anymore that were available to run this kind of stuff, much less create the big-dot films that they needed. But Jim Valentino put us in touch with the printers and Murphy Anderson. Murphy Anderson is a Silver Age artist who also ran a production company out of Connecticut. They still had the ability to make the big-dot color films, basically by cutting Rubylith with these teams of people. The printer was able to find a press that they were able to rehab, and they were able to find the right pulp paper, which had the right smell and the right feel, because 1963 is a tactile experience as well as a reading experience. It's meant to open up the gates of nostalgia to all us old, aging baby boomers who had our noses in comics when we were kids. And that was Steve and I, we were able to pull all that together.

CC: It is a tactile experience. It's not the same if you're just reading pictures of it on the internet. You worked on "Mystery Incorporated," which is a Fantastic Four takeoff; "USA," which is a Captain America takeoff; "Horus," which is a Thor takeoff but Egyptian; and "Tomorrow Syndicate," which is the last one, putting together the heroes and kind of making the Avengers. Do you have a favorite among those?

RV: No, I love them all. I think it's one of the most fun projects in terms of creativity that we ever worked on. I can remember getting the faxes in from Dave Gibbons on the inks when he first inked my stuff. I was just so knocked out—he totally caught it. And I remember getting the first printed samples in from the printer, the actual color on the pulp paper. It was just such a great, great feeling to know that we were really catching it. We really had it. And then Alan was coming in with the Bullpen Bulletin pages, and that was great, too, because after he'd finished writing it, he would call me up and read it to me in this breathless voice that I'd never heard before. But once I heard it, I knew that's exactly what Stan Lee was writing back in the day. And so that was really marvelous, too. That creative part of it was just great, especially in the first two or three months before the business part of it hit.

Steve and I, kind of stupidly, took on the production without payment. We just said, *We'll be the editors and the production people here, we'll make sure this thing happens.* But we didn't take any extra money for it, we just divided the profits up among the freelancers. Whoever worked on it got the exact same percentage. And Steve and I just sort of donated our time doing the production end of it. This was a huge mistake, because the production end of it was so complicated, and the learning curve was so steep, that Steve and I were in this unbelievable pressure cooker to get this thing produced and done and out on time. Timing was important, because as I mentioned before, the industry itself was just in the process of getting ready to explode. The way it worked is, you would solicit a book, and you would get a bunch of orders in. And if you didn't ship the book on time, those orders would have to be resolicited, and those orders could go down. And just as the bubble of this crazy money thing going on in comics exploded is when 1963 was released, so if our books had run late, our orders would have disappeared. So, we were desperate to get the books out on time. One thing I'm really proud of is that all six issues were released on time. I think it's the only Image comic that ever did that. And I kind of feel bad for the retailers who were probably stuck with boxes and boxes of books. But again, we didn't quite understand the ramifications of it, what was happening to the people on the other end of it. We were just trying to make a success of what we were doing.

CC: That's definitely true; I think everything was delayed. It has to be said, you guys are working on this in 1992, because it's got to come out in 1993. In 1992, among other things, was the death of Superman, and that really changed the market.

RV: Yeah, and at Marvel they were doing *Spider-Man* #1 and *X-Men* #1, selling like six and seven million copies. It was this huge speculator market. People were buying and selling these boxes of books, thinking they were going to be worth money, ignoring the fact that there were so many millions of them printed that they really *weren't* going to be worth money. In April 1993, when "Mystery Incorporated" was released, that's when the bubble burst. The whole thing came down. That was why we had to get the books out on time.

CC: Yeah, everyone has a copy of the death of Superman. People thought it was going to put their kids through college. But everyone has a copy, so nobody can sell it.

RV: A lot of us understood that, that it wasn't going to be worth anything. And I think if you read some of the background material in *1963* that Alan was writing, he makes fun of that—the collector thing. He's push-push-pushing at it, you know?

CC: You were talking about how this is a tactile experience, and how the production was tough. I actually just spoke to Bill Sienkiewicz about *Big Numbers*. Do you think Alan has a tendency to come up with these ideas, and then it ends up being more complicated than he thought it would be when he came up with it?

RV: I think he knows it's complicated. His whole life and career is to make comics a higher art form, and he does that not through promoting himself or collecting stuff. It's through his writing. He's got the most amazing mind. I think he's got what they call eidetic memory, where he actually sees things in his head. Like, he reads a comic book thirty years ago, and he can call it up in his memory to the point where he can, like, read it. It's astounding. And he's a voracious reader—he's read thousands of books and millions of comics. And he just absorbed it all in his head. And then he applies that to his storytelling. He asks a lot of his artists, and especially poor Bill [Sienkiewicz]. I have seen the scripts for *Big Numbers*. In fact, I've got a copy of *Big Numbers* #3, and it is so complicated. It's just unreal.

CC: Can you compare what it's like working with Alan in 1983 versus 1993, on *1963*?

RV: [*Laughs*] Well, in 1983 he was writing these incredibly dense scripts. I think the first script he ever sent me was for a story in *Epic*, and the first panel was six pages of typewritten description. The first panel!

CC: Single-spaced probably?

RV: Oh, yeah. He had this old Olympia Royal he was typing on in those days. And I've got the script for the *Double Image Eighty-Page Giant* annual here, the first eleven pages.

CC: So the first eleven pages of a script is what, two pages to Alan Moore?

RV: No, I mean eleven pages of comics. Maybe twenty-odd pages. But he starts out with this incredibly dense description of Mystery Incorporated dropping out of hyperspace into modern, Image New York. You know, it's like

124   CONVERSATIONS WITH RICK VEITCH

two pages for the first panel. But he also says to Jim [Veitch reads from the script], "On the other hand, since you're the artist, and have a better visual imagination than I do, please feel free to substitute something better if there's any scene that doesn't work for you visually." He essentially says that to every artist he works with: *I'm kind of going crazy here, but do whatever you want, as long as it works*. It's just the way he thinks. He sits down at the typewriter and, in a first draft, the whole thing comes out in superspeed, knocking this stuff out. It's really quite extraordinary.

CC: I've heard he doesn't do second drafts.

RV: Right. The rest of us heard that and just went, *Oh, my God*. [*Laughs*]

CC: Was it a different experience working with him doing 1963 Marvel-style?

RV: Yeah. He did write scripts, but he often phoned them in first because we were running so late. So, I get him on the phone, and I'd be roughing out the panels to his descriptions. Then he would finish typing it up and mail it in. And they were much simpler descriptions that we were getting, but then they would have all the dialogue in them as well. And I'd see if there's anything I had missed or that I had misunderstood on the phone. The whole schedule was so tight that he often had to phone in the stuff I didn't have. We didn't have computers in those days, so it was either faxes or mail to get documents back and forth.

CC: He still doesn't have a computer, does he?

RV: He's got a computer; he just isn't on the internet.

CC: So speaking of the marriage of old and new, new at the time being 1993: did you find it weird that you were having trouble creating a book with a production level that in 1963 would have been the default?

RV: Yeah, because we had to relearn a lot of stuff, and essentially we had to find a printing press that could print the thing. You can't get pulp, printed comics anymore. That's gone. The bigger learning curve, though, was working with Image. They were kind of in disarray. All those guys had made a huge pile of money, and they were going off and starting studios and buying homes and buying cars and talking to Hollywood. And you know, they call it the TOAD Syndrome: "take off and die." [*Laughs*] So they were kind of hard to deal with. Jim [Valentino] was great. I gotta say, Jim was the best thing that happened to us in this whole thing. He had an assistant coordinator, Randy, I can't remember his last name, and he was fantastic. But Steve and I weren't used to having to do our own marketing, solicitation, and production. So we were constantly being hit with, *Hey, we got to have this by tomorrow. We gotta have this by tomorrow, we gotta have this by the next day*. It was like every day, there would be something that Image needed from us. We were on this constant treadmill of learning how to do it, getting it done, and then getting it to them. And this put incredible pressure on Steve and me. We were like pulling all-nighters, all the time, and it was crazy. At the same time, Alan, uncharacteristically, was harder and harder to get ahold of. Usually, we could call him up and get hold of him. He's there, and we could solve problems if we had questions. But he wasn't around. He would disappear for a week, two weeks at a time. And then when we did get ahold of him, we'd have this laundry list of stuff we needed. So that created tension among us as well.

CC: Did you ever find out the reason he became so hard to get ahold of?

RV: I did. We didn't know it at the time. Later, he shared with me that he had been going through a kind of personal crisis that he couldn't share with us at the time. I don't know if I can really discuss it. I would say that I read an interview with him not long ago, where he talked about that time when he was first getting into magic—he was exploring magic, using psychedelics, and he had a mini nervous breakdown. I think that's the way he described it. I think he was in turmoil. But he wasn't able to tell us that, so we just didn't know what was going on.

CC: With the Image guys, they had a lot of success, starting studios and everything. Do you think it was too much, too soon for those guys?

RV: Yeah, I think it was. And I think they missed an incredible opportunity to shape comics in a really healthy way moving forward. Then instead, they became a corrosive force on the art form. But they were younger. They didn't understand.

CC: Was it also a factor that you guys were coming from DC, and those guys had come from Marvel? Was that a factor at all, or not?

RV: I don't think so.

CC: I just want to point out that 1963 has an insanely talented lineup, because aside from you and Alan and Steve, you had John Totleben, Dave Gibbons, Don Simpson, Chester Brown, and John Workman, and then Murphy Anderson on production. That is an *incredibly* deep lineup.

RV: [*Laughs*] Well, they were all our friends, and we wanted to take care of them all. We saw that we were going to make some money, and we wanted to bring our friends in, too, because we knew that if they had capital, they would do the kind of comics they really wanted to do, and that would be good for our art form.

CC: That's such a deep lineup that if one of you were running late, I feel like the others could have just jumped right in and helped out.

RV: That's kind of what happened at the end. Dave Gibbons just saved the day with "Tomorrow Syndicate," because it was running so late, and by then

126 CONVERSATIONS WITH RICK VEITCH

Steve had left the project. And he inked it and lettered it in record time. And we just got it in under the wire. Thank you Dave Gibbons, wherever you are.

CC: That's interesting, because you're the credited artist here.

RV: I'm the penciller, and I'm also the colorist, using the name Merry Marvin Kilroy. But Dave lettered that, and he did it in record time, while his wife was sick. Just unbelievable.

CC: Can you talk about the 1992 San Diego Comicon and what happened there?

RV: Yeah, it was like something right out of a movie. We were down on the floor, and Don Simpson came down and said, *Hey, you've got to come up here—the Image guys want to talk to you!* So we followed him up to the biggest hall; it holds like five thousand people, and it's full of Image fans. And the Image guys are holding court up there. Todd McFarlane's got the mic, and he's doing his thing on stage. The pitch was that they wanted to announce [1963] on stage, that moment, but that we had to agree to Jim Lee taking over the annual, which would've been the ultimate ending of *1963*. We were kind of stuck, because we couldn't get ahold of Alan from San Diego. We had to make the decision ourselves. I think I was more open to it than Steve was, and ultimately Jim Valentino came down, and we talked it all out. Jim Lee said he really wanted to do this, and that he would. I'm not sure if he could have stopped the project. I don't know if it had to have his vote to even happen. That's a good question for Valentino, but we agreed to it. They announced it and they brought us up on stage. Todd and Rob [Liefeld] and these guys were throwing hats and stuff down to the crowd; the crowd surged [toward] the stage. The security guards grabbed us and pulled us away from the crowd and out the back door as the whole place went crazy.

CC: It went crazy because it was announced that Jim Lee would be drawing the annual?

RV: No, it went crazy because Alan Moore was going to be working with Image. But also because of the craziness of the whole Image thing. People were just rabid for it, so as they were throwing this merch out to the fans, the fans rushed the stage, and we had to be pulled out by security. It was like being a rock star.

CC: That's insane. Was there an artist in place for the annual before Jim Lee kind of put you on the spot?

RV: No, I'm not sure what we were thinking along those lines yet. I would think it would have been Valentino, but I do not remember how we were planning that.

CC: Yeah, Jim Valentino drew the Johnny Beyond feature. I would have assumed that he would've been the one to draw the modern one. He actually did a follow-up to *1963* in *Shadowhawk*, which no one ever talks about.

RV: It's one of these little-seen things. He was as much a part of it as we were. He was just fantastic.

CC: It seems weird to me that the Image founders would try to compete with each other—Jim Lee kind of "taking" the project from Valentino. Did they come off to you as friends, or just people who ended up being in the same company together and starting something up together?

RV: Yeah, I can't say they were very friendly to us. Especially Todd and Jim and Rob—they were very up front about how they wanted to be the belle of the ball. They want to be number one, they want to be stars. With Steve and Alan and me, I don't think that was our goal.

CC: Before *1963* was even released and Jim Lee was announced as drawing an Alan Moore comic, Todd hired Alan to write an issue of *Spawn*. Did that cause waves within the whole thing?

RV: It did with Steve. I wasn't bothered by it. I thought, if Alan can get an offer to do an issue of *Spawn* and make half a million bucks, God bless him! And I knew him well enough to know that he wouldn't let us down. He would finish the project with us as described; he wouldn't just let it dangle. Steve had been working with Alan for a number of years on *From Hell* in *Taboo*, so I think there was some tension there—you know, Steve trying to edit and organize Alan to get scripts to Eddie [Campbell] to finish *From Hell*, so that could be in *Taboo*. That was a tension thing. Steve was bringing some of that baggage to it. He was pretty unhappy with it, and I think in a later interview he saw it as abandonment of us, but I don't see that at all. He had an opportunity to bang out a script and make a bunch of money. I would have done it!

CC: What led to the annual not being completed? I mean, I know Jim Lee said he was going to take a break for a year, but that seems like a weird thing considering he committed to doing the annual.

RV: I know a lot of people are looking to blame someone for it, but it's a bigger situation. Part of it is the nature of the business, which was falling apart at the time. They'd gone from selling six million copies of *Spider-Man* to selling fifty thousand in the course of six months. The whole industry was coming down, so it didn't make a lot of sense to throw a lot of effort into putting out comics until the air had cleared and we figured out where the business really was. The biggest problem, I think, was the partnership of Rick and Steve and Alan. I think if we had been able to hold our partnership together

128   CONVERSATIONS WITH RICK VEITCH

as friends, then we would have been able to come up with a solution, and we would have had an annual of some sort—and I bet you we also would have had more '63 comics following it. But we couldn't hold it together, the three of us, so if there's blame, it's Rick, Alan, and Steve.

CC: I wanted to ask about that, because it's well documented that Steve and Alan had a falling out. What was your stance at the time, and how is your relationship with them now? Because you ended up working with Alan at Awesome and ABC after that.

RV: It's sort of like knowing and loving a couple that divorce. They're all pissed at each other, but you love them both. I'm the monkey in the middle of these two guys. What happened was, Steve and I were under unbelievable pressure to get these books out on time, and we were doing it, but like I say, every day was just an incredible struggle, and Steve cracked first. I was just finishing putting the production for book 5 together, "Horus." Out of the blue, Steve sent us a fax basically resigning from the project. I'd been talking to him every day. I had no idea this was coming at me, and Alan didn't, either. I remember we got on the phone afterward, and we just couldn't understand what he was doing. We tried to get ahold of him; he wouldn't pick up the phone. I probably should've tried harder. I should've driven over to his house and tried to talk sense to him, but I was exhausted and I was kind of mad at him because he had dumped the last book in my lap. We had been taking turns running the production, and he was supposed to be production guy on the sixth book. And by walking away, that meant there was only one person left to do it, so that was a pretty crazy month, I'll tell you.

CC: That was a crazy sixth book, too, because it's not just the production. You ended up using a bunch of other characters in the multiverse Alternity spread.

RV: Importantly, the coloring starts to change, too. It goes from the big dots to all of a sudden this airbrush coloring, and that's what he was planning for the annual, where the big-dot characters land in Image New York. So you get a taste of where that was going.

CC: Do you think—I'm going to try and word this as nicely as I can—do you think Jim Lee would have been the right person to draw it?

RV: Yeah, he's fantastic. But the script I have here is dated December 1993. So the last issue of '63 shipped in September. Jim Lee didn't see the script until December.

CC: Wow.

RV: By then he'd probably lost interest. This is another thing that I think is our fault: Steve and I thought Jim Valentino was dealing with Jim Lee. And

Jim Valentino thought Steve and I were dealing with Jim Lee, so Jim Lee didn't hear from us all during this.

CC: So ever since he took the assignment at the 1992 Comicon, he didn't know anything about it?

RV: Other than that the comics were coming out, but we weren't in touch with him, calling him up and telling him how things are going and making sure he was on board, because we thought Valentino was doing it. Valentino thought we were doing it.

CC: Oh, wow—that's fascinating.

RV: By the time the script came out, he had decided to take a sabbatical from doing comics. But again, I think if Steve and Alan and Rick had their shit together, we would have gotten that annual done somehow and finished the project off, because that's the type of people we were. But it was such a miserable thing that happened to our personal relationship that it just died right there.

CC: And you and Steve kept on trying to get it reprinted, right?

RV: Yeah, that was the thing: at least we could reprint the six issues. And we also tried various schemes to do the annual as well, but by then Steve had done an interview with *The Comics Journal* where he kind of went after Alan and said a lot of things that Alan didn't like, and Alan broke off his relationship with Steve. So that essentially kills it right there. I tried to bring the two of them together—you know how it is, we know people that love each other but are mad—but it didn't work, and *1963* became a casualty of that.

CC: Is it one-sided, or do both of them not want to work it out?

RV: I think Steve would like to work it out, but Alan just shut him down. I would try to talk Alan into speaking to Steve. He didn't talk negatively about Steve, he would just sort of gently say, "No, no, I don't want to work with him anymore," and he'd go on to other things.

CC: You guys ended up splitting the characters from *1963*. Steve Bissette got N-Man, Fury, the Hypernaut, Commander Solo and Her Screaming Sky-dogs. Did you and Alan split the rest, or did you get the rest of it?

RV: Alan and I own it, but I don't think anything will ever be done with it, because he's quit comics. I think it's pretty much over with. That was the last nail in the coffin in terms of our three-way friendship and partnership, because any time when you have to break something apart like that, contractually, with lawyers, it just sucks. It's just terrible. So that was the last bad taste in the mouth of *1963*, right there.

CC: And that happened around 1998, right?

RV: I can't remember what year it was.

CC: I heard you tried taking this to Dynamite.

RV: Yeah, they talked to me about buying it. Their offer was abysmally low. Dynamite wanted to do a collection, and at first Alan said, "Okay, as long as my name isn't in it." But then he made it clear that if we went ahead, he would never speak to me again, so I knew then that I didn't want *that*. And I knew that he didn't want to have it out there. As a partner he had the right to say no, just like as a partner I would have the right to say no.

CC: Is it tough being friends with Alan Moore?

RV: No, it's been a very fruitful relationship. I consider myself really lucky to have met the guy. He's an extraordinary person, an extraordinary mind, and what he's done to comics—I mean, they used to have a saying in DC Comics that certain characters like Superman and Batman were the lightning in the bottle, and that whenever you created a character you wanted to catch the lightning in the bottle. Well, Alan is the lightning in the bottle. He can take any character and rehab it and bring depth and wisdom to it that no one else can. I look back at his time at DC and I just wonder why they never gave him Superman. Because we'd be living in a different world if Alan had taken Superman on and done a full run on it.

CC: I was just talking to his daughter Leah, and she was saying that as much money as *Watchmen* has made DC, they probably would have made more money if they just gave him back *Watchmen* and kept him on the staff.

RV: Yeah. If I had been Paul Levitz, I would have established a personal relationship with Alan Moore. I would have called him up, and whatever he needed, and whatever he wanted, I would have done it and kept him. I mean, could you imagine DC with Alan and Dave Gibbons doing *Superman*, and Frank [Miller] doing *Batman*? But they missed it. They were greedy, and they killed the goose that laid the golden egg, and they paid for it. I was privy to a lot of the shit that they did to Alan, and it's awful. It's no wonder he's angry and he's walked away from comics.

CC: You got some of that too, though, with your last *Swamp Thing* issue.

RV: Oh, yeah. But not like him, because like I say, he was the lightning in the bottle, he was the prize, and they just didn't handle him right. You know, if they had been enlightened businessmen, we'd be living in a different world right now.

CC: And that's true also for Image, and for DC the second time—WildStorm and all that. Speaking of lightning in a bottle—I know this has nothing to do with 1963, but how did it feel when Alan Moore ended *Swamp Thing* and said that the perfect person to follow him on *Swamp Thing* on writing duties was you?

RV: Well, you know—on the phone to me, he and I would make jokes that I was committing career suicide. It's like following the Beatles onstage. The guy is just so good. But I felt I wanted to do it because I love the characters and I loved working with Karen Berger, who was just a fantastic editor. So, I took it on. It was a mistake, because it ultimately blew up in my face, but I still got to do a lot of good comics.

CC: It's a legendary run that followed a legendary run. Going back to 1963, I just want to talk about the creative side of it a bit. You put it in the 1960s-type storytelling, but you guys were using modern science. It gives us this cognitive dissonance in terms of the way we're experiencing it. How did you guys approach that type of marriage of old and new?

RV: Well, that's Alan. One of his areas of study is hyperphysics, and that's one of the great things I would learn from him on the phone. He would read these scientific journals on how quantum [physics] works and how multiple dimensions work and all that kind of stuff, and he'd explain it to me so I could understand it. That's what he was bringing in to 1963, figuring that Crystal Man, being this Reed Richards, big-brain kind of guy, would know this stuff, even in 1963.

CC: Oh, so that was the concept behind it. And you explored a lot of these themes as you moved forward into Awesome and into America's Best Comics.

RV: Here's another part of the 1963 tragedy: if we'd held it together, we wouldn't have been working for Awesome, and there wouldn't have been ABC. Alan would have been exploring all this retro stuff he had in him through 1963, and we all would have benefited from it. We'd probably still be doing them today.

CC: It would have been a line on its own. So, it's stuff like that what you did with Greyshirt, Tom Strong, et cetera, that would have shown up in 1963?

RV: Sure, and Supreme. Because Alan really is a Superman writer. He wants to do Superman, and he would have brought him into 1963 somehow.

CC: Yeah, that's insane that they never gave him Superman, now that you mention it. With 1963, you went insane on these ads, and you teased 1963½. Was this a real thing that was going to happen eventually, or . . . ?

RV: No, what it was, was Paul Mavrides, an underground cartoonist who worked for *Zap*, had a project called 1963 in the works that we didn't know about until we were a couple issues in, and he sent word to us, going, "Hey, I'm doing 1963, too!" I think it was Mark Bode who was kind of a middleman between us and helped us work it out where we said, *If you just change your title to "1963½," we'll give you promotional space inside our books*. And he thought that was a great thing. So part of the story of 1963½ is in "Tomorrow Syndicate."

CC: Oh, I did not know that! That's cool.

RV: Paul never finished 1963½, so I don't know whatever happened to that. But he was a nice guy to let us have the title.

CC: These are based on old Silver Age Marvel comics. Do you have a favorite Marvel comic?

RV: I grew up on Marvels; I caught it right at the beginning. I think my first Marvel comic was *Fantastic Four* #3, and I just bought every Marvel after that. Jack Kirby is the guy for me. In fact, I named my number two son Kirby in honor of Jack. It was such a great thing growing up, that you'd go down to the store every two weeks and there's a new Jack Kirby Marvel comic, just full of the most amazing graphics and story ideas, and all that Marvel stuff in the background. It was really great—but no single favorite.

CC: *Fantastic Four* #3, I think that was also Alan's first Marvel comic. Do you have anything else to say about 1963 as we wrap up?

RV: I'd just like to apologize to all the fans out there that we blew it. And I don't think Jim Lee is the culprit here; I think it was a much larger mess than just Jim. I take blame for us three partners, who should've held it together, but we didn't. I apologize to the fans; I would have liked nothing better than to have continued this work, but it just didn't happen.

CC: That's supergracious of you, to take the blame for three people.

RV: Well, I kicked myself because there were times when I could have talked sense to Steve. You know, we go back so far, and we were so tight, but I was just exhausted, and I was mad because the thing was dumped in my lap, so I didn't do what I should have done.

CC: Do you and Steve still talk? Do you still have plans on working together?

RV: We're still friends. We don't work together, but on a day-to-day basis, we're still good friends. We've got this amazing history together. Put us in the same room and creative sparks fly, still.

CC: Is there anything you're working on that you'd like to plug right now?

RV: Well, if people want to see my new stuff they can just go on Amazon. I've been releasing a new *Maximortal* work called *Boy Maximortal*. I've been releasing new issues of *Rare Bit Fiends*, my dream comic. And I've been doing this series called Panel Vision, which are comic books that are one panel per page, and I think I've released four of those now. I'm doing all that through Amazon. If you look me up there, you'll find it.

CC: And my last question is, how do you think things would have been different if you had done 1963 in the last ten years, instead of in 1993?

RV: Boy, that's a good question. We wouldn't have made as much money, that's for sure. Sales have just dwindled. The whole market is down to nothing now. It was perfectly timed for its day, to do it thirty years after 1963, in 1993. It was also Alan making a point about how Image comics were getting lamer and lamer. He was going to show how the rich past of comics stood up against modern Image comics. When he writes the dialogue for the Image characters—he's this incredible literary mimic, and he writes just like Rob Liefeld and Todd McFarlane. It's kind of hilarious when you read it.

CC: Is that in the script? The ten pages of script?

RV: Yeah.

CC: Is that anything you'd ever be willing to share? I'm guessing no.

RV: I would have to scan it and put it on the internet. It might already be out there, because I'm not the only one with it. This copy came from Homage Studios. It came from Jim Lee to me.

CC: Oh, really!

RV: Yeah, so it must be out there. But if not, I could probably scan it and get it out there.

CC: It would be funny if I could just show a graphic of a line of dialogue as you're saying it . . .

RV: Maybe I can read something. Here's Bedrock: "Are these dweebs for real?"

CC: [*Laughs*]

RV: There's also a set of interviews we did for *Comics Feature* or one of those comics mags, where we did interviews in character. There's Roarin' Rick and Affable Al, and Sturdy Steve and Merry Marvin Kilroy. That's on the internet somewhere, and that's really worth a read if you can dig it up.

CC: I'll go look for that. My real last question: we talked about how the comics market has dwindled, and how that burst in 1992 and 1993. What exactly do you think is causing the lower sales now, and how do you think we could fix it?

RV: I don't think it can be fixed. There are a lot of different issues. One of them is that print is changing over to digital, and comics are right there. There are still people that love the printed comic, but there are very few magazines that are printed anymore; they all go digital. Comics have to make that transition. If you listen to what Jim Lee's talking about in his interviews as publisher, that's where DC is moving. They're pulling out of the direct sales market. The direct sales market is now thirty, forty years old, and it's dwindled down to nothing. Where we used to have fourteen distributors, we now have one, Diamond. Since they have had a monopoly, the quality of comics has gone down, the sales have gone down. It's just a dying form, and I don't think there is a way to resuscitate that. So, look to the future as digital, and there might be a way to sell digital products, and if you also wanted the print one, you could press a button and get it in the mail or something, but I don't think there are going to be comics stores anymore.

CC: How much do you think quality has to do with it? Because a lot of fans my age—I'm thirty-eight—so a lot of fans my age are like, *Oh, it's because comics suck now*, and *Back in my day* . . .

RV: [*Laughs*] Yeah, but the reason they suck is because of the business side. In 1998, when the second collapse happened in comics, they created a system where there were only five publishers who got a decent deal with Diamond, and all the rest of us were cut out. They cut out the grassroots power of American comics, which had really been what had empowered the eighties, where all these people were just coming out of the cracks making comics all over the place and they could get them distributed! Now, once 1998 happened, all that ended, and the small, little-guy publishers were starved, and they couldn't get their books out. So that's what's wrong: this powerful, creative upswell was halted by the business guys for their own profits. So maybe when we get to digital, that groundswell will come back up, all that creativity. There are a lot of people out there doing great comics that are never seen, never on shelves.

CC: Do you think crowdfunding could be the answer to that?

RV: It seems to be. I haven't done it myself, but a lot of people are working that way, and even some of the publishers who have great deals with Diamond are over there crowdfunding on Kickstarter, so it tells you that their system just ain't working anymore.

Rick Veitch Interview: Panel Vision and Greyshirt

DUY TANO / 2021

Transcript of an episode from *The Comics Cube* YouTube channel, March 2, 2021. This transcript has been lightly edited for clarity. Reprinted by permission of Duy Tano (*The Comics Cube*).

Comics Cube: Welcome back to *The Comics Cube*, everyone. Rick Veitch is back, and first we're going to talk about Panel Vision. For the people viewing this who don't know what Panel Vision is, would you mind telling us what your elevator pitch is for it?

Rick Veitch: Well, I'm not really good at elevator pitches, but essentially, it's creating comics that utilize one panel per page. So, it's still comic books, but it's a different way of creating comics and hopefully, for the reader, of experiencing comics. I had been working with the Amazon Prime Kindle program, which is a print-on-demand program. And I realized that with the pricing of the books, you could put together a 108-page book for the same price that you can put together a 40-page book. It sounds crazy, but that's how they price it per unit. So it allowed me to expand the possibility of what the book could be. I'd been inspired years ago by a book I'd seen in Italy, by [Alejandro] Jodorowsky and Moebius, called *The Eyes of the Cat*. I don't have a copy of it, but I'm sure a lot of viewers will know it. It wasn't a commercial project; it was done as a gift to the friends of the publisher, Les Humanoïdes. And it instantly became this collector's item because they only printed like two thousand of them. I got to see it in 1981 or something in Italy, and I was like, *I want to work like that someday*. And Panel Vision has allowed me to do it.

CC: That's awesome. When I read the descriptions for Panel Vision, it said, "Rick Veitch is using the medium and pushing it to new boundaries." Then I saw that you were doing it one panel per page, and I thought, *One panel per page and pushing the boundaries of the medium? How's that gonna work?* Because you basically removed the concept of a layout. But then I got

136   CONVERSATIONS WITH RICK VEITCH

it on my Kindle. Did you optimize it for the Kindle? Because I feel like it's a different reading experience.

RV: That's exactly the point. It's a different reading experience. It's comics, it's pure comics, but it's different from what we were used to. And by taking away the page layout, it asks the reader to linger on each panel and spend a little more time, and so as the artist, as the creator, I'm trying to work things into the panel. Subtle things, clues, anything I can get in there to give the thing a little more depth and a little more width—and I think it works.

CC: There have been five Panel Vision books so far: *Super Catchy*, *Otzi*, *Redemption*, *The Spotted Stone*, and your latest one is *Tombstone Hand*. You're known for your love of dreams. Those all kind of follow dream logic. Am I correct in that assessment?

RV: Not really—I mean, there is some dream logic in there, especially in *Redemption* and *Super Catchy*. But I think *Otzi* and *Spotted Stone* and *Tombstone Hand* all work as stories. They're like little singular parables. The idea is that you give someone just a book. That's all you get. There are no ads, there are no other stories. There's nothing else. It's an experience unto itself. And I like that feeling that I can give somebody that.

CC: I've always wanted to ask this: who influenced you to do that inking style that you have, with very thick, expressive lines?

RV: Probably Joe Kubert. I studied at the Kubert School—I was part of that first-year class with [Stephen R.] Bissette and [John] Totleben, and [Tom] Yeates, and those guys. Joe had an extreme influence on me breaking out of how I was working at the time, which was essentially thinking like Jack Kirby, and making me look at real illustrators and understand the methods and materials of brush and pen. I have to say there are three [artists]—Totleben, Bissette, and Yeates—I learned a lot from working with them one-on-one, because all three of them are masters of the pen-and-ink skill.

CC: I really appreciate the way that you can cartoon, as well. The way that you can go from realistic to cartoony is very versatile. The thing that I noticed about *Tombstone Hand* when I was reading it, compared to the other Panel Vision books, is that at first it gives the impression of being a more straightforward story than the other ones. And then it goes off into a more insightful discussion about life and what comes after. Are these questions that you continually ask yourself and you always want to explore?

RV: Oh, yeah, yeah—the great mystery of life. I mean, that's why we're here. I think with *Tombstone Hand*, when I began the book, all I really had was the idea of a standoff in a grave, where one guy's in the grave—he's wounded—and there's another guy outside the grave with a rifle. I wanted

From *Tombstone Hand* by Rick Veitch (Sun Comics, 2021). © Rick Veitch.

138 CONVERSATIONS WITH RICK VEITCH

to explore that kind of standoff. How would the guy in the grave get out? And the story itself kind of evolved organically. Another aspect of working in Panel Vision is that for most of them, I work on one panel a day.

CC: Oh, really?

RV: Yeah, and I don't really know what's going to happen next. But I'll finish the panel, and then the rest of the day and into the first part of the next day, I'm thinking about the possibilities: *Well, what if I went this way with it? And what if I did this, and what if I did this?* But it allows the thing to grow organically, almost like a plant. And as the creator, I'm in a sort of trance, I think is the word for it. Where I'm in that story, and I'm feeling my way through all possibilities to get to the best thing that it can be.

CC: So you didn't script this out? When you do something like *Redemption*, where it's the comic and then just a word underneath—that's all stream of consciousness, would you say?

RV: Well, it's a daily panel. Each day, I did a panel. And with *Redemption*, I knew I wanted to do a story where a guy fell asleep and had a dream. And then in the dream, he fell asleep and had a dream. And then within that dream, he fell asleep, so it was a dream within a dream within a dream. Everything else is just sort of psychedelia.

CC: I've noticed another common theme among the five Panel Vision books: it's kind of a theme about isolation. You like to explore people who are kind of on their own. Is this a conscious thing?

RV: It's not a conscious thing, but it's probably how I live. We live up on a mountaintop, and we're kind of isolated. I'm not in an urban area very often. I'm a country person, so isolation is kind of how I live.

CC: And that shows in your work. In *Tombstone Hand*, how did you come up with the idea of the character who gets shot and basically has one foot in the grave and one foot not in the grave throughout the whole story?

RV: Well, it was like I grew him. When you open the book, and it's four panels of a shadow moving across the barren landscape, that's how I entered into it. As I was drawing those panels, I was thinking, *Who is this guy? What's he doing? Why is he going here?* Day by day, I would build the story. I knew I was going to get to the grave. But how I got there, I didn't know, and what happened afterward I didn't know.

CC: As the writer and the artist of all these books, do you even still pencil, or do you just go straight to ink?

RV: Well, working with a Cintiq is how I work now, digitally mostly. Except when I'm doing commissions—then I work with pen and ink. But with a Cintiq, you can go right from layouts to inks, because you can correct any mistake immediately. So, why not? It saves like a third of the time. It's a really good system.

CC: You've been in the industry for over forty years at this point. How have these tools influenced the way that your style has changed, your working process has changed? You've always kind of been an early adopter.

RV: Well, maybe that, but I've also always been an artist that uses photos for reference. My studio used to be filled with tens of thousands of reference books, because if I needed a tank, I wanted it to look like a real tank. And if I needed a horse—I'm not a good horse drawer, so I would have a book of horses that I can sort of swipe and stuff. Now, working digitally, I don't need the books, because I've got another screen right next to me with Google. And virtually anything I need, I can find and get the visual details of it correct. It also works really well with setting up how the body is going to pose or something like that. You can find all kinds of cool action poses just by calling "soccer match" up on Google. I'll find these guys jumping around and doing all this crazy stuff. You can turn those poses into an action scene, and it has a lifelike feel to it that I couldn't get on my own.

CC: I've never thought of actually transposing one image in one context into another context altogether. That's very interesting. So, I bought all five of the Panel Vision books on my Kindle. I was gonna buy them on paper, and then I realized the shipping would murder me. But I don't regret buying it on the Kindle, because I feel like there is something to the fact that every time I turned the page, the next image would automatically occupy the same space. I felt like it was moving, like it was both a comic and maybe a piece of animation.

RV: Yeah, I can see what you mean. Panel by panel by panel, it moves. That's a good thought. I mean, it does fit in with the digital environment, although it's kind of a quick read. But my hope is that people go back and reread the books, because like I say, there are little clues and little subtle things that are put there in the background, and how the characters act and so on that make it worthwhile, I believe, for people who go back and reread them.

CC: I agree, they reward rereading. Why do you think it is difficult for some artists to transition to the digital format?

RV: A lot of a lot of the problem is age, I think. I'm a baby boomer and I'm pushing seventy years old. And my generation has a hard time learning software and keeping up with software and dealing with the daily frustrations of doing your art on a computer. I've been able to adapt to it because I started early, but a lot of my friends still don't, and God bless them, because they're brilliant pen and ink people. You know, they *should* be working analog. But for me as a production artist, I enjoy the feel of it. Running the stylus over the

140   CONVERSATIONS WITH RICK VEITCH

glass. Boy, it feels great. And there's a lot less impact on the wrist, which is an issue if you get old and you've drawn six thousand pages. How you're using your wrist and your fingers becomes really important.

CC: Especially since now you don't have to go over it in pencil and then in ink.

RV: And then erase, and erasing is the hardest one—that'll just ruin your wrist.

CC: All the pressure, yeah. You headed the Comicon website, it must have been twenty years ago now.

RV: Started in 1998.

CC: So, twenty-three years ago. You've always kind of been at the forefront of these developments. Is that just your mindset, or . . . ?

RV: I don't know. I mean, as a personal creator, I'm always looking for creative space to really explore this medium of comics, which I just love. And I think when we started Comicon, and I did it with my partner, Steve Conley, we were looking for a new way to get out there, because Diamond and DC Comics had just destroyed distribution for independent books. We had lost the marketplace, you know, they were squeezing everybody out. So, we were looking for the next venue to get it out there, and the internet just happened to happen at that point.

CC: That's more true than ever now—I think the biggest publisher of comics right now is Webtoon. How's it feel, being one of the early innovators of moving comics to digital?

RV: I don't think about that. I know that it was a lot of work, running Comicon. The best part of it was that we ran a news site called the *Splash*. And you can't find this on the internet. It's all gone now. But this is going to tie into our discussion about ABC. It was all at the same time—we were doing ABC comics, I was running the *Splash*, which is sort of like the Drudge Report of comics. And we were sort of beating up Paul Levitz at DC Comics as we were working for them. So it was kind of an odd relationship.

CC: I went to that website every day, back when you actually had to go to websites, instead of waiting for them to pop up on your newsfeeds to see if they have an update.

RV: You should have seen the little tools I had to [use to] actually make that. It was this thing where I'd have to put in the headline and then put in the copy. And then the next day, I'd have to move it all down and put in the next story and then move them down and put in the next story, day by day.

CC: And now they have templates for that.

RV: It was essentially a blog before there was a term for "blogging."

CC: You mentioned ABC. In 1999, ABC launched: America's Best Comics. It came out of the "ruins" of Awesome Entertainment, where you were also working with Alan Moore. You were working with Alan Moore on the flashback sequences for *Supreme*, and then you were with ABC, working with Alan Moore on Greyshirt, which is a tribute to Will Eisner's *The Spirit*. So, between 1963, *Supreme*, and Greyshirt, you guys homaged Silver Age Marvel, the [Mort] Weisinger–era Superman, as well as the Golden Age Superman, and Will Eisner's *The Spirit*. What is it about retro pieces that attracts you?

RV: Well, we lived it. We bought that stuff on the newsstand when it first came out. When Alan and I get on the phone, we just wallow in it. He's got this memory. He can call up any page he's read from the time he was a little kid and describe the details to you. I'm not quite as good at that, but I absorbed all this material. And we would just get talking for hours sometimes about Curt Swan's Superman, and what Eisner did, and then of course the Marvel stuff. I think Alan with 1963, more than anybody, defined the modern retro comic. When he told Steve Bissette and me what we were going to be doing, we initially thought that it was going to be like a joke, and that we should draw sarcastically, even, but he was like, *No, no, I want it completely straight*. I think the term he used was, *There was a time when comics were in a state of grace, and that's what we want to do*. And so the humor in 1963 is in the ads. The books themselves try to duplicate the exact spirit of that time, not only in how they read and look, but the paper stock and how they're colored; 1963 is kind of like a tactile experience.

So out of that, when Alan went to work for Awesome and he knew he was going to take over *Supreme*, he knew he wanted to do some retro stuff. He originally approached Curt Swan to do that material, but Curt had health problems and wasn't able to do it, so he tapped me, and I was delighted to do it. The important element to the Awesome stuff, which carried over to the ABC material, was Todd Klein, the letterer, because we were working Supreme in all these different timeframes. We were doing EC comics, we were doing early Superman comics, we're doing midcentury Superman comics. Everything that Alan wanted to do meant that Todd was instrumental in the design and implementation of authentic lettering, hand lettering. It just looked perfect. And when Awesome collapsed and Alan was in the wind all of a sudden, he wanted to keep that team together, because he liked what we were able to do. It was Homage Studios that got to him first. He and Homage started to put together that deal. I wasn't really part of the deal itself. I was just the early artist that was attached to it.

CC: Could you tell that he was going to bring you along?

RV: Well, he just called me one day. We worked on *Swamp Thing* together, going way, way, way back, so it wasn't odd to get a phone call out of the blue, saying he's got this new project, and he sees me as a part of it. And it's a blast to work with him.

CC: Personally, I was surprised that you were not part of the *Tom Strong* team. Because *Tom Strong* to me felt like a direct lift from *Supreme*, basically a lateral move. I was surprised that you were not on it.

RV: Well, I don't know—I think *Tom Strong* looks fantastic. My stuff doesn't stand up to what those guys were doing. But I can do that retro stuff, and I can make it look right, and I can evoke it. We couldn't quite get the color and the pulp paper that we had with *1963*. But I think we carried it forward quite a bit. We kind of defined "retro," up to that point.

CC: Why do you think some retro comics don't work? *1963* wasn't the only one. There was a whole line of comics: *Big Bang*, some other stuff that was coming out. And I just feel like they fell flat, I guess.

RV: I don't know, comparing anything to what Alan Moore's doing falls flat. I'm the guy who followed him on *Swamp Thing*, right? So I know this— the guy's so good.

CC: A tall order, but you did it, though.

RV: Yeah, I did it, but I'm just saying. *Big Bang* might seem like it falls flat, but if Alan Moore wasn't there, you know, working that side of the street, *Big Bang* would just be seen as fantastic. The guy is so good. He makes everybody else seem like midgets around him. He's a fantastic literary mimic, that's one of the things that people don't realize about him. He reads endlessly. And he has this mind that can absorb all this stuff and then bring it up and mimic other writers, which we certainly saw in *The League of Extraordinary Gentlemen*. But all the retro stuff, and even the *1963* stuff when he had to mimic the new Image characters—he wrote dumb all of a sudden. He really got it.

CC: Would you say that working with Alan brought out the best in you?

RV: Oh, always. Always. It's a real treat and honor to work with him. He , is the greatest writer of comics, probably ever. And he certainly defined the whole era, beginning with Marvelman. Yeah, he is the big bang of it. Although as artists, we're absolutely important to it as well. I think the tragedy of it— and this brings us to ABC—is the business always worked around him in a negative way and kind of hog-tied him with the ABC deal, in a really bad way. And here we are today: he's given up comics.

CC: Before I dive deep into ABC, you told me the last time that in play back in the eighties was the possibility of Alan and Dave Gibbons on *Superman*, and Frank Miller on *Batman*?

RV: I don't know if it was a possibility. It was just a thought I had.

CC: Ah, okay. If that was true, I don't understand why that didn't happen—because that was a no-brainer!

RV: Well, I think it's DC not seeing the potential. I mean, they certainly must have seen what Dave and Alan did on that Superman, Batman, Wonder Woman thing, "For the Man Who Has Everything." They nailed it. They absolutely nailed it. But they had something else in their head and they didn't see the potential.

CC: The thing about ABC to me was—and I tell everybody who worked on ABC this—when ABC dropped, I was down to collecting like two comics. I was already sixteen, and I was gonna give up comics because, you know, other interests, meaning girls. But then ABC dropped, and I just couldn't believe that one guy was conceptualizing and writing all of this. I just thought that was fascinating. Also, I had recently discovered Will Eisner. I had already known of your work before. You were the only artist there whose work I'd actually known before ABC, so when I saw that you were doing a Spirit pastiche, I was really very interested. I saw that first sketch that you did with Greyshirt reading a newspaper. What is it about Will Eisner that's so special?

RV: Well—where do you begin. I had the great good fortune to meet Will when I was at the Kubert School. He came twice and spoke, and then afterward we got to hang out downstairs. He was the first person that ever said the words "graphic novel" to me. He was telling us flat out, *All this superhero stuff is great entertainment, but it only takes the art form to a certain level. What you kids need to do is to up the game a notch. And we need a term to describe comics that are above superheroes.* That's where the term "graphic novel" came from. I don't know if he originated it, but he was definitely pushing it. He also laid out this other side to my life, which a lot of people don't even know, which is that comics are an incredible informational art form that can be used to teach and to advertise and to get information across. He said to us that the American military had done a study in the fifties about the best medium to get information across, and it was comics. That's where his work with the Pentagon began: he started putting out a magazine called *PS: The Preventive Maintenance Monthly*, working with the Pentagon. So, I've taken this to heart in my life. I work with educators and universities, doing comics. It's better financially—it pays a lot more than even working for DC or Marvel. It pays commercial art rates, which are probably three times what comic book rates are, especially in terms of what you have to do to get a page done. Comic book rates are pretty measly. This has supported me behind the scenes to do things like *The Spotted Stone*, the stuff I really love. I can take on one of these high-end projects, work hard for two or three months, and then I can take the rest of the year off and do the kind of comics I want to do.

CC: This is a common theme throughout the interviews that I do, that comics don't pay too well. So if you're doing comics, you have to really love comics, and the commercial art pays way more.

RV: Yeah, but with commercial art you're pleasing the client, whereas with comics you pretty much run wild. The stuff we did with DC and Vertigo, there was very little structure to it. A few things: they want to make sure Superman looks right and Batman looks right. But they were looking for us to be wildly creative and explore ourselves, so it worked really well in that sense. And I have to say, DC Comics had a terrific royalty plan, so all that material I did in the eighties for DC, I'm still receiving royalties for, which I can't say for any other publisher.

CC: That's pretty cool. So, Will Eisner told you that there's more to comics than superheroes. How did you feel about that as somebody who obviously loves superheroes?

RV: Well, I'm originally an underground comics guy. I came out of the San Francisco scene. My first comic was for Last Gasp in San Francisco. Yes, I worked in mainstream comics, but I didn't belong there. I was too crazy and too ready to blow things up. But I found Eisner really inspiring in the sense that he saw what we did as an authentic art form that had just emerged in the twentieth century and that we were just taking the first baby steps into what could develop out of that. Certainly we've seen, in the last thirty years, fantastic approaches to doing comics, and in comics that is so much more valuable than the latest Spider-Man or Batman.

CC: With Will Eisner, there's so much experimentation in *The Spirit*. How does it compare, riffing on somebody like Kirby in 1963 versus riffing on Eisner in Greyshirt?

RV: Well, I don't know what the difference is. Both of them just did fantastic work. You can't say that Jack Kirby wasn't imaginative! He certainly was. Eisner was working with a studio, so a lot of his stuff was done not by him but by other people, and I think he made his reputation on a handful of stories. There are a lot of Spirit stories that aren't that good, especially during the war. I think he had other guys doing the work. But there are maybe twenty, twenty-five stories that are perfect, absolutely every single word in the right place, perfectly paced. You read that story and you come out the other end and you're like—*Yeah! That's it!* It sticks with you forever. That's what we wanted to do.

CC: Do you have a particular one in mind when you're thinking about the perfect Spirit story?

RV: There's the one that's ten minutes in this guy's life ["Ten Minutes"]. He's playing the pinball machine and he ends up in the subway. He kills somebody, the shopkeeper's on the floor, he's dying and he's going, *Oh, you bum.* It's this incredible slice of life, and then it builds to this crescendo where he gets killed on the subway.

CC: Yeah, I read that when I was in high school and it was like, *Wow, 1940s comics, I didn't know!* Can you talk about what went into the design of Greyshirt?

RV: Well, Alan envisioned cities in the world of ABC, and so he asked me to design the technology for Indigo City. I came up with the idea of gas-powered cars and the idea that there was this meteor that had landed and created the bay in Indigo City, little things like that to round it out. I knew he wanted him in a suit with a hat, but we didn't want him to look like the Spirit, so I spent some time trying to figure out—like, rather than the domino mask we'll give him the bandanna on his lower face, which you can do all kinds of cool, shadowy things with, wrinkles and things to make it interesting. Then I brought out his eyes—he's got these really angry eyes and angry brow. The thing that finally pulled it together was his hat, which is not a big, wide-brimmed Spirit hat. It's like a little trilby with a curve to it, and it cocks on his head sideways. When we had that, it was like, *Yeah, that's him.*

CC: And the cane . . .

RV: We hardly ever use the cane as a weapon, but it was just something that he would carry around, and he had these little daggers in his shoes that would allow him to jab into a building and climb up the side of it if he needed, little things like that. But essentially, he was just a guy out there fighting crime.

CC: I thought the first Greyshirt story was incredible, with the amnesia, because it's one of those things where I didn't see the ending coming. But the second story that you did, "How Things Work Out"—that one's a classic. How did you guys do that?

RV: Well, that was Alan. He envisioned the whole thing. What's great about him, and I've been on the phone with him when it's happened, is he'll call up and go, *I don't have an idea about anything,* and we'll start talking about this and talking about that, and all of a sudden he'll go, *I got it,* and he'll download a complete story with dialogue out of his head. It's weird how he does it. I think that's how "How Things Work Out" happened. He just saw it—*Oh yeah, a building, four panels, four time frames*—and then he sewed the stories through it.

CC: Was it easy or difficult to execute?

RV: The beauty of Alan Moore's scripts is he thinks everything out visually. He makes a little comic in his own notebook before he types it. That's one of his secrets, he sort of lies around and gets stoned and draws the thing out in his little scribbly stuff, so he figures out the visual problems usually. In the script he'll spend the time to describe it all to you, with the caveat, *If it doesn't work, Rick, you figure it out, whatever works for you*, but a lot of times it's all there.

CC: You've worked with him for a long time, since *Swamp Thing*. How often did it actually happen that what he wrote didn't work?

RV: I can't think of—oh, only once. We did a story with Swamp Thing called "My Blue Heaven." Swamp Thing lands on this planet in outer space and populates it, there's Constantine and Abby, and he built to this point that Swamp Thing becomes enraged and rips the Abby creature apart—and I just couldn't do it. He wanted me to make it look like Swamp Thing was ripping Abby into pieces, and I just couldn't do it. I ended up having him just knock her head off, which wasn't quite as bad.

CC: That would be kind of traumatic to draw.

RV: Yeah, I mean, we all loved Abby. But when Alan writes your script, it's a complete script, with everything thought out.

CC: The only exception to that was 1963, right? With Greyshirt you were back to full script. Did you have a favorite Greyshirt episode among the first twelve that you did?

RV: Boy, I like them all. "How Things Work Out" has got to be the best one. I think that got nominated for an Eisner along the way. We also did one that was one of those alphabet stories that Eisner would do—A is for this and B is for that—and it was an homage to Will, who had just passed away. I thought that worked out really well, too.

CC: Yeah, that was for *Tomorrow Stories Special* #1. For #12 you did a crossover with Cobweb. You were the first one to do a crossover, I think, with the ABC characters. Before that, we readers didn't even know they were all taking place in the same world.

RV: Ah, that's interesting.

CC: We had no idea, because Cobweb and Greyshirt both lived in Indigo City, but they didn't look like the same thing. Cobweb was all over the place. Did you have a favorite character from "Greyshirt," aside from Greyshirt?

RV: Well, remember, too, it wasn't just the *Tomorrow Stories* Greyshirt, but we also did a graphic novel of Greyshirt.

CC: *Indigo Sunset.*

RV: Which I wrote. It's all me, except I got to work with Russ Heath, Dave Gibbons, John Severin . . .

CC: David Lloyd, Frank Cho . . .

RV: That was pretty awesome, to be able to work with Russ Heath and John Severin—I mean, oh man, my God.

CC: Getting to *Greyshirt: Indigo Sunset*, I was actually surprised when I saw it because I had read that *Tomorrow Stories* didn't particularly sell very well. Would you say that?

RV: That'd be a question for Scott Dunbier. I don't really know the numbers on it.

CC: Do you think readers have a hard time with anthologies?

RV: Could be, could be. I know Alan loved it, because it allowed him to play with these toys in a sandbox. It was a great read because you get three stories in the book. But they still haven't collected all that stuff, either. I don't know if that's ever going to happen.

CC: Oh yeah, I have them.

RV: But it's not all of them, is it?

CC: It doesn't have the specials, which is unfortunate. And it doesn't have your "A to Z" story.

RV: We also did "America's Best Heroes," which I penciled and Andrew Pepoy inked, and then I used the Photoshop big-dot coloring style so that you really had that look of an old comic. I thought that worked out really well, that was fun.

CC: I love that one! Getting to *Indigo Sunset*, what went into your proposal? Why did you want to continue to explore Greyshirt?

RV: Just because we were in the middle of it and the potential was there to do it. I don't know if Scott [Dunbier] came up with the idea of a spin-off or if it was me.

CC: I'm fascinated by the way that you produced it, because all of your covers have nothing to do with the main story. You basically have this back matter at the end, which is the newspaper, and the newspaper's front page would be about what would happen on the cover. What led to that conceit?

RV: Probably because I didn't know what was going to be in the stories yet when I did the covers. You have to do the covers a couple of months early, and so I was looking for a great cover design more than a cover that had something to do with the main story. Then I had these images—*Well, we could make a story out of this*—and so it made sense to fit it in the back end. I think it was also a nice surprise for the readers who actually waded through all that material back there to find out, *Oh yeah, it's the cover.*

CC: And it was not just Eisner; in the first issue itself you see some Dan DeCarlo in there. Where did the conceit to do a tribute to so many different comic book artists come from? And how do you as an artist manage to make them look so cohesive? There's a sequence in the first one where you go from them looking like a Dan DeCarlo picture and then the next page is more realistic. How do you manage that kind of transition?

RV: It's in my genes. I've absorbed so many comics at this point, I just have to look at something and go, *Yeah, this is how to do it*, and I'll be able to ape it enough to get it across. It just fit in with everything we were doing with ABC and that we had been doing with Awesome, which was just to explore all these avenues of comics that were being ignored. I think one of the most important things to understand about ABC is that comics were in crisis right at that time. There was collapse of distribution, and the comics that were coming out, like the Image comics, were really bad—they'd given up even trying to have stories. It was just all these guys standing around, chests puffed out—stupid stuff. Alan saw ABC as a remedy to that. He thought, *We can build the comics industry back again if there are great comics*, and he took it upon himself to solve that problem. That's part of what ABC was all about.

CC: What a novel idea!

RV: Yeah, and the workload was unbelievable. It was like four titles, and I think it was one every two weeks he had to have a script for. He was working with all kinds of artists all over the world, and one of the ways he works with artists is by phone. He calls you up and talks to you, gets a feel for you, and of course he's already familiar with your work. So he was a really, really overworked guy doing ABC comics. The tragedy of it all is that Homage sold the contract to DC Comics, which was Alan's blood enemy at that point, and it put Alan in a horrendous situation that no good came of.

CC: He said he didn't want to screw over all the artists who'd already signed on.

RV: That was it. We were, I think, three books in; I was working on the third issue at that point. He brought all these people together and he felt a responsibility not to pull a rug out from under them, and he didn't feel that there was any alternative, although my counsel at the time was, we should just pull this back and we'll try Dark Horse or one of these other guys or Image or somebody. But Jim [Lee] and Scott flew out to England on the day the news broke, and they gave him the news of what they were doing and sort of painted a picture of it that made it agreeable to him to move forward. All the promises that were made ended up being baloney once DC had their hooks in him again, though, and it was a very miserable period for him, not only in the comics but [Warner Bros.] was making all these films from his work, so DC was under pressure from Warner to control this guy—and of course you can't control Alan, he's something else completely. But it all ended badly, and Alan's out of comics.

CC: Alan has a reputation on the internet among fans, and I think the reason he has that reputation is that he's not on the internet to defend himself.

RV: Well, I think also he's outraged at how he's been treated, and when he gives an interview it comes out. He's pissed off that they did this to him, and he knows his worth. He's a bankable star who transformed comics, and for that he got tied up in the spider web of business stuff that he didn't want anything to do with. He just wanted to do great comics and to help build the art form into a beautiful thing, and the businessmen just screwed him over.

CC: Even the story of staying with DC because he didn't want to screw over the artist; I think that kind of thing says a lot about him that gets overlooked by a lot of people who want to judge him for being cranky or grumpy or whatever it is.

RV: He's an honest blue-collar bloke, and he has great respect for everybody and everybody's work. He knows how hard it is to draw comics, because he tried to do it himself and he never quite made it to that higher level to do it professionally. His love of the form is real. It's the business end of it that's just been a mess.

CC: Of all the ABC books, I think his love of the form, of experimentation with layouts and everything, was most obvious in both *Promethea* and in Greyshirt.

RV: It's *Swamp Thing*, too. He would take every page and try to figure out a new way of laying out a comic. You'd get the script and it would be all these new, fresh ideas. So, this is something that's [always] been part of him.

CC: Even in something like *V for Vendetta* or *Watchmen* or *From Hell*, even when he's sticking to a grid, it's still an innovative way to use the grid.

RV: Absolutely, absolutely. In fact, here's a story for you. In 1981, I was in Italy at a comics festival and I met Dave Gibbons, first time. We were both young men. He gave me a handful of 2000 *AD* comics to read, and I looked through them all and there was one story in there that knocked me out. It was told backward in time.

CC: Is it "The Reversible Man"?

RV: I can't think if that was the title or not. I didn't remember who wrote and drew it, but I remembered that story. It was like a Will Eisner–level story, and I said, *Someday I'm going to swipe that; I'm going to keep it in the back of my head.* So, you fast-forward to the mid-, late eighties. I'm on the phone with

150   CONVERSATIONS WITH RICK VEITCH

Alan, he calls up, *I don't have any ideas, we need an idea for a story*, and I said, *Wait, I read this story one time that was told completely backward*. And Alan said, *Oh, you liked that?* And it was him! Before Alan Moore was famous, he had knocked my socks off with this story out of the blue.

CC: That's awesome! So, getting back to *Indigo Sunset*, I don't imagine that the first twelve episodes of Greyshirt were all meant to tie in together, were they?

RV: No, they were meant to be urban slice-of-life stories that Greyshirt, like the Spirit, is just peripherally part of, and so we meet all these people living in Indigo City and going through some sort of comic book story, and Greyshirt might show up at the end or in the middle. *Indigo Sunset* was meant to flesh out Greyshirt, to give him an origin, the reason why he's crime fighting.

CC: And you ended up fleshing out the whole world.

RV: Well, I had those twelve stories to begin with, and so I tied them together in any way I could and developed characters that were in one story and tied them in with characters in other stories, so it's like a spider web.

CC: How much of that puzzle did you figure out before you wrote the book?

RV: There was an outline that I typed out, but one of the great things about comics is that trance I mentioned earlier. You're in the middle of making a comic book and you're in a weird creative trance that's really neat. You've always got it in the back of your head: you're driving down the road and— *What if Greyshirt met Cobweb and did this, what if they were lovers*. That all of a sudden opens this whole story or gives you some sort of plot twist that you can add to an existing story. It's really fun. I gotta say, I feel like I'm blessed to have been able to do this my whole life.

CC: I was really blown away because I got this in the trade paperback—great cover by the way, anytime you do the whole blinds-as-shadows thing it's always great. Each issue starts off with a one-page black-and-white sequence, and for the first three issues I think it's just Greyshirt helping out a random passerby or whatever, and then later on you realize that they are actually people in the main story. Do you feel satisfaction in pulling off that kind of magic trick?

RV: I hope that readers stick around long enough to take it in, because some readers just blow right through it. It's too subtle for them. But I always love to get three issues in and have the reader go, *A-ha, that's what he's doing!*

CC: Is there any point in Greyshirt where you stopped actively trying to channel Will Eisner?

RV: It's always got Will in there, and Will's one of the foundation stones of comics storytelling and graphic novels. But as you can see, I was spreading out—it's a gangster comic. There hasn't been a gangster comic in a long time.

So I went back and found this DVD with hundreds of old gangster comics on it, and I was able to read them all and feed that into it as well.

CC: Yeah, I see people like Matt Baker in your work, especially in the second issue. Another thing that I thought was fascinating was, despite the fact that it is a "realistic" gangster comic that just happens to have sci-fi and ghosts in it, there's a sequence here that I thought was fascinating [*holds up a page from* Greyshirt: Indigo Sunset *with a character occupying the gutter between panels*].

RV: Ah right, he's like outside of the story. He's haunting the story, and at one point he sticks his hand in and pushes a book and freaks out the character.

CC: How do you come up with that kind of thing?

RV: Cannabis. We should mention that people who would like this book can go to my website rickveitch.com. I have it for sale because they sent me a box of these, so anyone who needs one, just go to my website.

CC: You have these backup features in *Indigo Sunset* that you mentioned. You got David Lloyd, Dave Gibbons, Frank Cho, Russ Heath, John Severin. For the one with Russ Heath, you were poking a lot of fun at Roy Lichtenstein.

RV: Lichtenstein is such an important person in the art world, and the fact that a lot of his stuff came from Russ is undeniable.

CC: Did that always bug you?

RV: Originally it did, but I've come more and more to appreciate what Lichtenstein did. He is the first person to take a comic book panel and put it on a wall, and so he forces you to look at the panel. When you look at the panel without consciously thinking about it, you know that there's a story leading up to it and there's a story going out the other end to an ending, so it carries this ghost story with it, and it makes it kind of marvelous. You could actually apply that thinking to any painting after you've seen Lichtenstein. You look at the *Mona Lisa*—what's the story? How did she get there, and what happened to Mona Lisa afterward? It adds a whole new dimension to painting in my mind.

CC: I have that with [Edward Hopper's] *Nighthawks*.

RV: Having studied with Joe Kubert, I got to hear some stories because Lichtenstein actually reached out to the war comics artists back in the early sixties. This is a fantastic story. He was beginning to be famous and they were putting on a big gallery show, and he invited the DC Comics war artists to come, and that was Joe Kubert, Russ Heath, Irv Novick, Mort Drucker maybe. They get to the show, and Roy Lichtenstein and Irv Novick look at each other and go—*You!* They knew each other—they'd been in the army together in a sign painting unit back in Japan at the end of the war. So Roy Lichtenstein was swiping his old sergeant.

152 CONVERSATIONS WITH RICK VEITCH

CC: So he knew he was swiping them.

RV: Yeah, he knew. He tried to apologize. He did a talk to the National Cartoonists Society trying to explain what he was doing, and he said, *I'm not trying to steal from you guys, but this thing took off, I have to follow it through now.* You know, it's making millions of dollars. And they understood because they were all commercial artists and they were hoping that they could make that step up with what they were doing to the gallery scene, but none of them were able to do it. But Lichtenstein—there's something very positive about what he did for comics.

CC: That's a perspective changer for me, because I've always just kind of seen him as a guy who swiped and made money from other people's work.

RV: No, I think he had a lot going on up here and he just fell into that one. He's part of this pop art thing, and you've got Andy Warhol doing a Tide box or a Brillo pad box, and it's just empty—there's nothing to it. With a comic book panel, there's something to it. He's bringing you an emotion, he's bringing you the synthesis between words and pictures and also just that weird campiness of old romance comics and war comics. So, I think he did a good thing.

CC: I have a really random question here: how come Dave Gibbons did not draw? He wrote and you drew.

RV: I think it was because we were in a bar somewhere, and I just said, *Write me a story*, and we came up with this idea as we were hanging out in the bar.

CC: And how did it feel working with John Severin?

RV: Oh man, the guy's the greatest. I've been looking at his stuff since the EC Comics days. An extraordinary period artist. When I was at the Kubert School, Joe was publishing a magazine called *Sojourn*, and Severin was doing this Western. We got to see the original art and work with it as we were doing the production on the book. It was just extraordinary, absolutely extraordinary.

CC: The third issue of *Indigo Sunset* is told in song. Do you have a background in songwriting at all, or was that a first for you?

RV: No, but I like old-time music, and what jumped out at me was, my lead characters were Frankie and Johnny, and so I could just rework the old "Frankie and Johnny were lovers" into "Frankie and Johnny were partners," and I stretched it out from there.

CC: You also had all of the back matter that I thought was very rewarding. The comic strips in the back—you were just having a ball there.

RV: They had to be done quickly because there wasn't a big budget for the back material. I can't remember what I was paid, but for the whole thing it wasn't a big payment, so I would have to knock those out really quickly, and that became part of the joke, you know, *What is this?* And the fact that we could bring in Weeping Gorilla was a nice touch, too, I thought.

CC: Yeah, the Weeping Gorilla one was the first time I was like, *Wait, maybe they are all in the same universe.* I actually had an argument with my brother asking if the Chuckling Duck and Weeping Gorilla were having a conversation.

RV: I don't think we meant to [do that], but if you want to read it that way . . .

CC: There's this one here where he says, "you just can't get a good cup of java in this town anymore," and Chuckling Duck is like, "Substance free is the only way to be!"

RV: There you go, a completely random connection—that's comics, right?

CC: Moving on to the *Tomorrow Stories Specials*, you have a story in each one. This is basically where ABC ends. The first one is the Eisner tribute. He had just passed away. How meaningful was that for you guys to work on?

RV: He was like the king of comics—although Jack Kirby was, too—but he was such an inspiration to all of us, and it came as a shock because he was so active right into his eighties that when he died it was just like, *Wait, what happened, he can't be gone*, because he was like the grandfather of all of us. Brilliant, brilliant man.

CC: He was still working on *The Plot* [*The Secret Story of the Protocols of the Elders of Zion*], I think, or he had just finished *The Plot* when he passed, and with no degeneration in his art quality. It was amazing. That last panel in that Eisner tribute that you did, which is him drawing under the wildwood, I thought that was very touching.

RV: Thank you.

CC: And then you managed to close out ABC basically, because aside from the *A to Z* books, those were the last things that Alan did for ABC. You closed it off with America's Best Heroes.

RV: That was a blast. We were kind of thinking Wally Wood when he wrote the script, and I did Wally Wood as best I could, but then we brought in Andrew Pepoy, who just nailed it with the inks, and by then I'd figured out how to Photoshop big-dot color so it looked really authentic, and we were able to make it look really great. I was really happy with that one.

CC: It's also a tactile experience. I felt like I'd just picked up a back issue.

RV: There's like a double cover, too: there's the regular cover on the front, you open it up and then there's the America's Best cover right underneath it.

CC: How did it feel being one of only I think three artists to draw all or most of the characters in ABC?

RV: I don't know, I don't really think like that. It just happened. People call and say, *Will you do this*, and you jump into it. There's no real plan to it all, I'm afraid.

CC: That last one was really fun. You had Tom Strong doing this riddle thing, and it's like a callback to those old Justice League comics. Very fun. And then finally you did *A to Z*.

RV: That was with Steve Moore. Another writer who I think suffered from being so close to Alan.

CC: Having the same last name!

RV: He's passed away, too, which is sad. He's another guy who's able to structure a story perfectly, just like a song can be perfectly structured. He had that ability to make a story like that, and the last one I got to work on was like that, I thought.

CC: How did the *Splash* work its way into the dynamics of ABC?

RV: I was running Comicon.com. It was the very beginning of the web era. We were just trying to figure out how to keep people coming to the site day by day, and so it made sense for us to start a little news site. And it began with me finding news items on the internet that were about comics and stuff like that. One of the stories I was following was the Marvel bankruptcy, which was in the *New York Times* and the *Wall Street Journal*, so I could write a little news story and keep comic fans up to date about it. Out of the blue, I received a package from somebody who worked for Marvel and had received a severance deal. They were being sued by the Marvel investors to get that money back. I had the proof, the documents, and I had this headline, "Marvel Sues Freelancers," and so the *Splash* blew up on the internet. It was like the perfect clickbait before there was a word for clickbait.

The story developed and we built this following, and all of a sudden I got approached by a lot of people embedded in the industry who were pissed off at what DC and Diamond had done by basically monopolizing the direct sales market. They were really mad that this beautiful thing we had all worked to build had been taken by these greed heads. So all of a sudden I had people feeding me information about what was going on inside Marvel, DC, Diamond, Dark Horse, and the rest of them, and the *Splash* became kind of like the Drudge Report, where a couple of times a week I'd have this bombshell story about what [Paul] Levitz was doing or what was going on at Marvel and stuff like that—and they were frantic. They didn't understand how I was able to find out what was going on inside. And to this day I could never reveal the names of the people who spoke to me, because I promised them I never would. I had insiders telling me exactly what was going on at Marvel and DC, so this created this insane dynamic especially with Paul Levitz, because we were ahead of him all the time in terms of the deals he was doing with Diamond; he was pulping magazines. It was an absolutely crazy dynamic.

CC: For ABC, did that put you in an awkward situation?

RV: It was totally awkward, but at the same time no one called me on it. It wasn't like they called up and said, *You're not working for us anymore.* Maybe it was because I was working for ABC, which was supposed to be off to the side of DC Comics. It just kind of went on, and to this day they don't know how I did it.

CC: How do you feel about it now in 2021, with DC breaking away from Diamond? You're talking about the Marvel bankruptcy—I'm kind of seeing similar signs for DC.

RV: It's the end result of some really bad decisions that were made to make short-term profits back in the day. The people who run the business in comics are not thinking about the art form. They're thinking about the next two quarters and how they're going to make money and explain why they're making money or not to the people above them, and beyond that it's out of their hands, really. My goal has always been to promote the art form, to explore the art form, to feed the art form, and maybe the collapse or the semicollapse that we're watching now is actually a good thing, because maybe new ways to get comics from creators to readers will develop.

CC: I think you've absolutely succeeded. I think you're one of the great innovators of comics.

RV: Well, thank you. I'm a lifer, I'll tell you that. I've been doing it since I was a little kid.

CC: There is a rumor going around—and I don't buy into it at all—that DC might be selling its properties. If you had a chance to get Greyshirt back, could you happily do more Greyshirt?

RV: I would. I mean, I would do more Greyshirt for DC if they wanted to, and I think they should do a collected Greyshirt—that's great material to be a great book. Alan will never be part of it, but I'm sure he wouldn't mind if I ran with it.

CC: Yeah, clearly you can do Greyshirt on your own.

RV: The whole comics industry is under threat right now, so it's probably best for everybody to wait and see where everything lands, because it's all shaking apart. We're all watching Diamond, going, *Wow, are they gonna be able to survive with no DC Comics?* And if they can't survive, what happens? Does Marvel not survive, then? The companies that now control DC and Marvel are AT&T and Disney, and comic book publishing is this little infinitesimal nothing to them. It's a bad time for comics right now, a very bad time. I saw a thing on the internet the other day that of this month's Marvel comics, 37 percent of them were Spider-Man, and this month's DC comics, 33 percent of them were Batman.

CC: And I bet the other 33 percent is Superman.

RV: They've forgotten the art form, and people like Alan and Dave and I, all these guys who love comics, we love it as an art form, and we look to Will Eisner, who was an inspiration, who went around telling us, *This is a real thing, you've got to grow it and nurture it and explore it*. It's theoretically possible to do something interesting at Marvel or DC. In reality, it doesn't happen. They're doing the house stuff over and over and over again. They're trying to sell to a market that's shrinking day by day. I think it'll be a while before it all sorts out, and it makes me happy that I've got my own thing going with Panel Vision and *The Maximortal*.

CC: Are there plans for more Panel Vision books?

RV: Oh yeah, I'm not going to stop until they take the pencil from my cold, dead hand.

CC: So far there're five Panel Vision books out. You can get them on Amazon, and you can also get *Greyshirt: Indigo Sunset* from rickveitch.com. Just to close us out, speaking of comics as an art form, are you following any comics artists right now?

RV: Not really. I would love to if I were more in touch with it. I see beautiful art on the internet. But the nearest comic book store is a hundred miles away from where I live, because any of them that were closer have closed, so I don't get to go in and browse anymore, and I'm not the kind of person who wants to do a pull list and get the same crap month after month. I'm looking for interesting stuff. And there are no conventions. That's where I used to pick up the Fantagraphics stuff. I'm pretty much out of touch with everything except what I'm doing.

CC: What's the last comic book that you read that blew you away?

RV: Boy, I can't remember. It's been a while.

CC: Okay, thank you so much, Mr. Veitch. This was great—I really appreciate you coming back on the show.

Here Comes the Sun: The Twenty-First-Century Rick Veitch Universe

STEPHEN R. BISSETTE / 2023

© 2023 Stephen R. Bissette, April 2023, Mountains of Madness, Vermont. Published by permission.

For the past decade or more, Rick Veitch has nurtured at least two new creative and commercial paths. At a time when most cartoonists his age (if they've lived long enough, that is) have retired, Veitch has collaborated on a procession of nonfiction educational graphic novels with creative and business partner Steve Conley. The income from these projects essentially frees up Veitch to pursue his most personal projects, returning to self-publishing-via-print-on-demand under his Sun Comics imprint, a moniker Veitch applied to his first-ever serialized comic book creations during his grade-school-to-high-school years.

This interview was conducted with Rick Veitch via email between March 22 and April 8, 2023, and the final manuscript was proofed by Rick to ensure accuracy.

FOUNDATIONS AND EARTHQUAKES

Stephen R. Bissette: Rick, if you were to summarize for someone unfamiliar with your bodies of work your comics career as chapters, as "story arcs" from the 1960s to present—Sun Comics to Sun Comics, if you will—what would those arcs, those chapters, be?

Rick Veitch:

Original Sun Comics: my homemade comics starting in fourth grade and continuing into high school.

158   CONVERSATIONS WITH RICK VEITCH

Undergrounds: *Crazymouse, Two-Fisted Zombies*, and continuing right through to the present day.

Kubert School: A dozen or so *Sgt. Rock* backup stories.

Creative Burnouts: Collaborations with S. R. Bissette on undergrounds, *Epic Illustrated*, and *1941: The Illustrated Story*.

Epic Comics and *Epic Illustrated*: a dozen or so short stories and three graphic novels, *Abraxas, Heartburst*, and *The One*.

Swamp Thing.

Turtles/Tundra: *Brat Pack, The Maximortal*, and *TMNT*.

Image: *1963*.

King Hell: *Rare Bit Fiends*.

Mainstream: *The Question, Daredevil, Supreme*, and *Teknophage*.

ABC: Greyshirt.

Vertigo: *Can't Get No* and *Army@Love*.

Eureka Comics: educational and informational comics for McGraw-Hill, PBS, *Wired*, the University of Quebec, the University of Vermont, and the International Monetary Fund.

Modern Sun Comics.

These bleed in and out of each other, of course. Have I forgotten anything?

SRB: I think you've covered it! You've returned to Sun Comics as your imprint of choice for self-publishing. Your childhood Sun Comics were something special, and you've given us glimpses of some of the covers in your recent print-on-demand volumes. Given the recent University Press of Mississippi book collection of one young cartoonist's created-during-childhood comics (*Into the Jungle! A Boy's Comic Strip History of World War II* by Jimmy Kugler, 2023), will we ever see a POD collected edition of the original Sun Comics that have survived the past six-plus decades?

RV: Probably not while I'm alive. I'm glad I did that stuff and I guess it has some sort of small historical value as juvenilia, but it's really awful and I have a hard time looking at it, much less inflicting it on other people. The early Sun Comics are to be included in my archive wherever that ends up, so maybe someone in the future might be so inspired. There are also wads of underground spew I did in high school that are cringeworthy and should never see the light of day.

SRB: At what point in your mainstream comics career were you when you first met Steve Conley, and where and how did you two meet?

RV: We first met at an early Spirits [of Independence] show, Austin, Texas, I think. I didn't have computer skills yet, but I had already collaborated on a computer comic with Jack Weiner for *Taboo* and was looking for other examples of this new emerging form. And there was Steve fresh out of high school and doing fully realized computer comics! This is before there was special software available, so everything had to be designed from scratch.

SRB: Comicon.com emerged from you and Steve Conley getting together, and the meeting of the minds that followed. What skill sets did each of you bring to the table, and why launch something like Comicon online, and the even more labor-intensive (initially) news site associated with it?

RV: Comicon.com came out of the collapse of the distribution system in 1998. We could see the writing on the wall for independent and self-published comics with the Diamond monopoly slowly strangling us. We both shared that idealism that powered Spirits [of Independence], and we both saw the emerging World Wide Web as a new way to do comics free of the corporate greed heads. Steve had the computer skills; in fact, he was a professional website developer at that time. I wanted a way to duplicate what I did at comic book conventions: interact with fans, sell art and books. He had just been to a web seminar where various themes for websites were discussed, and one of them was "convention." So in a single phone call we came up with the basic concept of an online comic book convention and the name Comicon.com.

I was just getting set up on my first Mac. I remember Steve teaching me how to cut and paste! But I knew a lot of creators and was able to call my famous friends and pitch them on this idea of getting a "table" at our "con." The thing kind of worked right from the start. We charged a small fee for the tables, which were basic web pages, and we sold banner ads. This brought in enough coin to pay for our server costs. Steve and I rode herd on it, but it didn't generate enough income to pay us.

The news part of the site found us. To build viewership, we were posting interesting things we found on the internet to a basic link page we called the *Splash*. This was before the word "blogging" had been coined, but that's essentially what we were doing. Then a person who had been laid off by Marvel got sued for their severance pay. They couldn't interest the [*Comics*] *Journal* or the [*Comics*] *Buyer's Guide* in the story, so they sent it to us. We ran it on the *Splash* with the headline "Marvel Sues Freelancers," and all hell broke loose. Views spiked, and I started getting emails from people within the industry offering to be sources for info on what was really going on behind the scenes. It turns out a lot of folks were really pissed to discover that their direct sales market had been co-opted by Diamond and the big publishers. So, the *Splash* kind of became the Drudge Report of comics, which was a lot of fun!

SRB: I'd like to get a snapshot of the importance of the *Splash* to your interests in the marketplace and industry as they existed at that time, Rick. What were some of the other stories you covered on the *Splash* that particularly mattered to you? Can you tag a year to some of those events?

RV: All this happened in the first few years of the new millennium. Easily the most important story we covered was the Marvel bankruptcy and takeover by one of Marvel's licensees, Toy Biz, run by Ike Perlmutter and Avi Arad. Those two guys understood the value of the Marvel characters and built a Hollywood powerhouse out of the financial ruins that still rules the box office today.

But my interests were just in understanding what was going on behind the scenes in the business and tweaking those in power. Just as we saw the potential in the internet, so did the big guys, and we covered Diamond's first baby steps in that direction. They were partnering with Next Planet Over, which was the earliest internet start-up doing comics. But they were doing it behind DC's back and we had sources feeding us the particulars, so that caused an uproar. We were never able to discern exactly what DC's financial stake in Diamond was when [Steve] Geppi's real estate holdings collapsed, though.

SRB: Recalling your decision to step away from the *Splash* and Comicon.com management, what were the factors involved—and who did you (and/or Steve) pass the torch to, so to speak?

RV: There were multiple factors. First, we brought on another news site, Newsarama, which did a great job of covering all aspects of the comics biz, although without the wise-ass attitude of the *Splash*. Second, the big companies quickly became adept at plugging the leaks and working in secrecy, so there were fewer and fewer juicy scoops. Third was my health. I'd been diagnosed with rheumatoid arthritis, and that made everything more difficult for me.

SRB: Since that's nobody's business but your own, let's get into a different series of past problems. Is it fair to say that Comicon.com and the *Splash* emerged out of the direct sales market implosion of the mid-1990s and ensuing Diamond Distributors monopoly?

RV: Yes. But part of the equation was Spirits of Independence. And another part was an idealistic belief that the new internet technology could free us from gatekeepers like Diamond.

SRB: What was the Spirits of Independence tour? How many of those did you participate in?

RV: Spirits was a dedicated series of conventions focused on the growing self-publishing phenomenon in comics. It was the brainchild of Dave Sim. I don't have a record of how many I did, but I know it was a lot of them. It seemed I was on a plane at least one weekend a month in those days, either to a regular show or a Spirits stop.

SRB: Do you recall when the Spirits tour took place—can you provide a reference point, if memory serves, between the Spirits tour and the last of the Diamond and Capital [City] distributor trade shows (in which an individual self-publisher like King Hell could pay for table space and directly communicate with retailers over a weekend)?

RV: Spirits was a freewheeling direct-to-consumer experience, in contrast to the highly regulated pecking order of the trade shows. The first one was in Austin in 1995 and the last in Montreal in 1997. By the time Montreal happened, we were all still feeding Capital and the small distributors with books but not being paid. I spent that weekend trying to get Dave Sim to see what I was seeing, which was that we needed to build a new pipeline of self-distribution or we were going to get buried. Dave wasn't buying it. He saw distributors as unimportant "service people" and predicted that new distribution outlets would quickly spring up in the wake of the ongoing meltdown. He was in a weird state, partly from exhaustion and partly because someone had given him a huge bag of pot. Dave of the analytical steel-trap mind had been replaced by magical-thinking stoner Dave, and I couldn't get any sense out of him. When I left Montreal, I was convinced we were screwed and it was time to reinvent what I was doing.

SRB: How were the Spirits tours different from other comic book conventions of that era, and different from the distributor trade shows?

RV: They were grassroots affairs, organized by self-publishers in partnership with local retailers. There was no overwhelming presence of Marvel and DC like at the distributor shows. Spirits was clearly building momentum, as a lot of creators came out of the woodwork with personal visions of doing comics outside the norm. And it was clearly growing an appreciative audience ready and willing to try the new stuff. But lack of distribution proved to be the choke point.

SRB: We all felt that choke hold. How, and for how long, did you sustain your self-publishing venture as long as you did after the demise of Capital Distribution and the other, smaller distributors?

RV: When Capital went down, all those sales went with it, and it became clear I couldn't sustain a monthly book. But graphic novel sales were beginning to really blossom, and I had a lot of material in inventory. So I got serious about desktop publishing, acquiring the hardware and learning the software to put together paperback collections of my *Epic Illustrated* work (all of which I retained rights to): *Abraxas and the Earthman*, *Shiny Beasts*, and

162   CONVERSATIONS WITH RICK VEITCH

Heartburst. I was also able to keep my Heroica material in print: *Brat Pack* and *The Maximortal*. And to continue collecting my *Rare Bit Fiends* dream comics: *Pocket Universe* and *Crypto Zoo*. I was working with printers in China, importing pallets of books, putting out a couple titles a year, and offering the backlist through Diamond.

SRB: In hindsight—in terms of how you saw that crucial period and axis point, personally, professionally, and in the broader terms of North American comics and graphic novel history—what would you want people to know about the 1990s' independent and self-publishing movement? Any popular misconceptions or distortions of that history, as you lived it, that you'd want to offer a corrective for, looking back almost three decades later?

RV: My evaluation is that the collapse of the distribution system into a monopoly with shady connections to the major superhero publishers (sometimes referred to as the Diamond Age of Comics) was a catastrophe for the art form in North America on the same scale as [Dr. Fredric] Wertham and the Code. While it turned out to be good business for a few greed heads in the early years, that soon began to unravel. The grassroots creative energy that wanted to break loose, as demonstrated by Spirits, was strangled in the cradle. Readers looking for something other than Batman, whom [the] Spirits [of Independence creators] were aiming to entertain, went away. Twenty-five years later, the direct sales market is a husk. The art form of comics was once again sold down the river, this time to serve as a launchpad for corporate intellectual properties.

SRB: What were the specific fiscal events that led to your terminating the 1990s King Hell self-publishing imprint and venture? How had the implosion of the direct sales marketplace—from which the King Hell self-publishing venture blossomed—impacted your ability to continue self-publishing?

RV: The Diamond monopoly was boiling the frogs of indie comics. First, they put us in the back of the catalog with tiny graphics ("Geppi's Ghetto," as it was called), changing the discount structure so indie books cost retailers more than books from their five "exclusive" publishers. Finally they limited relisting, which cut off the last lifeline for the small nonexclusive publishers. This had a constricting effect on the breadth and depth of the comics art form in the US, turning the once-vibrant direct sales market into a channel for the corporate superhero slush that haunts us to this day.

SRB: Given the chronology, it would also appear (correct me if I'm wrong) that your active creative participation in *Supreme* for publisher Rob Liefeld, and your work with the ABC line for Jim Lee, kept you busy around or during this same period. How did your participation in those projects begin?

RV: I was mixing self-publishing, sales of original art through Comicon.com, and work-for-hire freelance to pay the bills. The *Supreme* gig began with a phone call from Eric Stephenson, who was editing the title. The story I got was that Alan originally wanted Curt Swan for the retro sequences but that Curt was in ill health, so it fell to me. The ABC line grew out of that when Liefeld's publishing venture collapsed. Jim Lee offered Alan a home at WildStorm, and Alan wanted to keep working with the creative team of *Supreme*: Chris Sprouse, myself, and Todd Klein. I got the call from [editor] Scott Dunbier.

SRB: The *Supreme* arc you were part of, working again with Alan, also seemed to be part of the "retro" work you'd been doing with your part of the 1963 miniseries, which Image published. Was it satisfying to extend and take that revisionist take on the Golden Age and Silver Age comics (the latter of which were part of your youth, as a reader) to another level? Did it also resonate with your earlier Sun Comics of your own youthful creative labors?

RV: Alan's plan for 1963 was to create a DC side to it with knock-offs of their Silver Age characters. His retro explorations had multiple inspirations, I think; partly his attempt to pull mainstream superheroes back from the grim and gritty tone *Watchmen* had helped launch, partly because he felt a kind of surreal connection between the world Mort Weisinger shaped and his own delving into magic and the imagination, and partly pure wallowing in nostalgia. The fact that he was such an extraordinary literary mimic made it all work, I think. As for me, I really enjoy working in the styles of artists from my youth. I'm not into magic per se but share a deep interest in the nature of consciousness with Alan and spent many hours on the phone discussing the connections he was making. I'm not sure if readers were ever able to understand it in those terms, though.

SRB: What happened with *Supreme*? Did Alan, you, and your creative partners get to complete that project before the collapse of Liefeld's publishing mini-empire?

RV: The first story arc was finished, the second story arc got cut off with a couple issues to go, and a third story arc was planned that never got going. It involved Supreme traveling into a piece of Supremium (his version of Kryptonite) and meeting up with all the Superman knock-offs.

SRB: You mentioned how your part of the ABC line with Jim Lee emerged from the rubble (if you will) of *Supreme*. However, your part of the ABC line tapped a very different vein of past American comics history, specifically Will Eisner's *The Spirit* and its aesthetic, kinetics, and vocabulary. What was that like for you, especially given how our mentor Joe Kubert had provided (however briefly) a direct connection with Eisner, via Will's visit to the Kubert School?

164   CONVERSATIONS WITH RICK VEITCH

RV: I was delighted to provide the visuals as Alan explored every nook and cranny in the comic book universe. We were still at it ten years ago, before he quit comics, developing a series that was like *The League of Extraordinary Gentlemen* of superheroes, with a knock-off of every character ever published in a single story! What I liked best was how Alan could write an eight-pager that worked so flawlessly it left an indelible imprint on the mind like the very best *Spirit* tales. My own personal connection to Eisner and *The Spirit* is strong but no stronger than my connection to all the other stuff that rang my chimes as a kid. When I got to write Greyshirt on my own, I gave him a distinct crime comics feel rather than the Eisneresque pastiche of Alan's stories.

SRB: Did you ever get to talk to Eisner about Greyshirt?

RV: I didn't.

SRB: How did it play out with the ABC line? You ended up at DC Comics again, as did Alan, to see it all through.

RV: Like pretty much every project I worked on with Alan, on the creative side it was a peak life experience and on the business side pretty much a plane crash. Although with ABC, the plane came down on a home for widows and orphans before skidding into an electric substation and causing a nuclear plant to melt down. We were about three issues into the ABC launch at WildStorm when we woke up to learn Jim Lee had sold his business to DC! He somehow convinced Alan to stay on board by promising autonomy from any DC interference, but that was to prove to be a promise that couldn't be kept. Paul Levitz took a hands-on position and began demanding changes to the material almost immediately, causing Alan no small amount of grief. Then the Hollywood guys got into the act with *V for Vendetta* and *Watchmen* being filmed and marketed. Alan was clear that he wanted nothing to do with the films, giving any money earned to his collaborators and having his name left off them, but it wasn't enough for the corporate/movie/comics axis, who seemed intent on using him to market their wares. They happily proceeded to put Alan through hell. The end result, today, being that Jim Lee has replaced Paul Levitz as publisher of a hollowed-out DC Comics and Alan Moore, our greatest living writer of comics and the one person who could have made sense of their line, has fled the field.

For my part, I was the last holdout from the original ABC stable to sign on to the DC version. I had sworn never to work there again because of the *Swamp Thing* #88 debacle but was told they would "reconsider" their decision if I came on board. I was also getting calls from Dan Raspler and Karen Berger with offers of work. Diamond was making it harder and harder to self-publish. But the key thing was health insurance. I was pushing fifty, with a family, and in those pre-Obamacare days it was impossible to get health insurance unless you were part of a group plan, which were all run by the corporations. So I swallowed my pride and went back to work for DC.

SRB: I'm curious how your work with Alan on the so-called retro stories—*1963*, *Supreme*, and Greyshirt—might have played a role in your own conception of your Heroica universe. Conceptually, it could be argued that starting with *The One* and continuing through *Brat Pack* and *The Maximortal*, you had already been dealing quite directly with familiar "retro" comic book archetypes and mythos, including the very Cold War superheroes our generation had grown up with, and that *Army@Love* (as its title implies, riffing on DC's venerable *Our Army at War* series) also fit this through-line.

RV: The retro stuff with Alan was all about tone; catching that sweet spot that Neil Gaiman called the "state of grace" of early comics. The Heroica is a completely different animal. Yes, it is fed by the original archetypes of comics, but it is more akin to underground comix than the Silver Age. I'm after the dark, hairy underbelly of the art form and trying to give form to the transcendent idea behind superheroes.

SRB: Were there any specific narrative springboards or imagery from any of the 1990s trinity of the Moore/Veitch "retro" body of work—again, *1963*, *Supreme*, and Greyshirt—or from that real-world freelance experience (rather than the content of the stories, the industry upheavals and changes you'd observed) that subsequently materialized in the later Heroica work?

RV: Not from the retro work but definitely from the business skullduggery.

SRB: Let's come back to that a little later, Rick.

OLD DOG, NEW TRICKS

SRB: May we focus for a bit on the personal and professional development of your digital art skills? You mentioned earlier Steve Conley's role in your cultivating those skills, and you cited a collaborative story you did with your neighbor Jack Weiner. You were simultaneously a "late bloomer" and an "early adopter" of home computing to create comic art; can you recall, what was your first-ever introduction to digital art—as a viewer, or reader?

RV: It was probably *Shatter*, a digitally drawn comic by Mike Saenz published by First Comics in the mid-eighties [fourteen issues, 1985–1988]. The art was very low resolution with lots of jagged pixels visible, but it was an interesting experiment.[1] It was obvious that computer art wasn't ready for prime time but that it was going to develop and evolve, so I was keeping an eye on it.

SRB: Had you experimented with digital art prior to working with Jack Weiner to create and complete the story "A Touch of Vinyl" (published in *Taboo* #3)—which as I remember Jack created the published artwork for using an Amiga—or was that your first hands-on collaboration to create digitally crafted comics artwork?

RV: I had not done anything digitally before working with Jack on "A Touch of Vinyl." In fact, I didn't have a computer or know the first thing about them at the time, which was maybe 1989? He had an Amiga 2000, and his brother worked down at MassArt [the Massachusetts College of Art and Design] with access to scanners and laser printers. What I liked about the output he was getting was that it was higher resolution than *Shatter* with the ability to make softer-edged lines and tones. It seemed a good vehicle to do "fumetti," or photo comics, which was something I'd always wanted to try.

SRB: Tell us what you can about Jack, please. He's a forgotten participant in this aspect of your own personal and professional creative development, deserving of some overdue attention.

RV: Jack Weiner had graduated from MassArt and was an accomplished print maker. He and his wife, Mary, decided to move to Vermont, build a cabin, and homestead. As it happened, I bought the house next door, and we met and became friends based on shared interests in art and cannabis. The most interesting thing about Jack, of course, is that he claimed to be an alien abductee. There are books written about the abduction, *The Allagash Incident* is one of them, and he appeared on television a number of times to tell his story.

He wasn't into comics like we were, but under my influence began to see the potential in them. And he was an early adapter of computer skills. While there wasn't any dedicated software in 1989 to make comics, the Amiga was designed to handle digital images, and Jack just figured out how to import photos, make the panels, and put in word balloons, captions, and dialogue. I wrote the script to "A Touch of Vinyl" and we did photo shoots together, scanning the photos and importing them into the art. It was a blast, and the nutty story of a guy in love with his blow-up doll still cracks us up when we read it.

Jack continues to make digital comics, having contributed a number of pieces to my dream comic, *Rare Bit Fiends*.

SRB: To the best of your knowledge, what was Steve Conley doing with digital art and comic art prior to the two of you meeting? What aspect of his work led to your wanting to cultivate your own skill set as a budding digital artist and cartoonist, and enlisting Steve's aid to do so?

From *Heartburst* by Rick Veitch (Marvel/Epic, 1984). © Rick Veitch.

RV: Steve told me his high school had an early Mac that no one knew how to run, so he took it upon himself to get it going and from there began to explore how to make comics on it. There were no tablets or styluses yet, so he taught himself to draw with the mouse! When the World Wide Web started to come online, he was at the cutting edge, teaching himself how to write code and create websites.

My own involvement began, not with making art on a computer, but in wanting to master desktop publishing. I had kept all the original painted art to my *Epic* work, along with the copyrights, and wanted to collect it in new editions. The scanning technology of the early eighties had been pretty hit or miss, mostly miss, so I was eager to get the color to look like it did on the originals rather than dim and tinted like it did in *Epic*. This meant getting a computer, learning the basics, then learning graphics programs, then acquiring a good scanner and the skills to adjust the color. There were no training programs where I lived, so I had to teach myself everything over a period of years but ultimately was able

168 CONVERSATIONS WITH RICK VEITCH

to assemble complete books with the art looking exactly as I wanted and work directly with printers. It was an important step for me.

Creating new art digitally came later with the advent of more powerful desktop computers, dedicated comic book software, and input devices like tablets, styluses, and ultimately the Cintiq displays.

SRB: What was the first King Hell reprint collection you digitally prepared for publication, and how labor intensive was that first venture? How many reprint collections did you complete and publish under the King Hell imprint?

RV: I think the first one I did was *Brat Pack* in 2003. It was a pretty grueling exercise in frustration because I was teaching myself each step in the process as I worked. I had access to the original art, so I scanned that and stripped in the lettering from an overlay in Photoshop. Then I had to learn Adobe InDesign to do the page layout and output. When you put the whole learning curve together, it's not unlike learning a musical instrument. You spend a lot of time making mistakes until things start to jell and you're making music!

The first batch, *The One*, *The Maximortal*, *Rabid Eye*, and *Pocket Universe*, were all done old style with me hiring production people to do everything. Both editions of *Brat Pack*, *Crypto Zoo*, *Shiny Beasts*, *Abraxas and the Earthman*, and *Heartburst* were produced by me on the desktop.

SRB: What was the first freelance professional (not self-published) artwork and/or comics work you created and delivered digitally?

RV: That was a short story I did for a European edition of *Wired* magazine. I had this new software program from Japan, Manga Studio EX, that I needed to learn, so I bit the bullet and pushed my way through.

SRB: Did you continue collaborating with others—as you had with Jack and then Steve Conley—via digital and desktop tools?

RV: The whole workflow is digital these days. For some of the Eureka projects, we've had a virtual bullpen working on files simultaneously.

SRB: At what point did you find yourself transitioning into working primarily with digital drawing tools? Are you still doing any "by-hand-only" work, or has digital creation as well as production become your primary drawing toolset?

RV: I still work with pen and ink for commissions, but for comics production I've found that digital saves at least 30 percent on time. It also works to help my stuff improve in the areas I'm weak in. The thing that sealed the deal for me was the Cintiq display that you draw on directly with a stylus. They have a great natural feel, they are easy on the wrist because you don't have to bear down like with a pen, and I've been able to set mine up so my back doesn't ache like it used to after hours at the drawing board. And of course with my elderly vision it's a godsend to be able to zoom in on something and get the details right.

SRB: For years, easily a decade or more, your working with an airbrush on your black-and-white and color comics stories and graphic novels lent them a style that transcended your earlier pen-and-brush-and-ink work. Has working digitally taken you to a new level, in terms of the published work?

RV: My newer stuff looks cleaner and more focused, I think. But it still lacks that wild line spontaneity artists like you and Joe Kubert made look so easy. I was always a reference artist, my studio crammed with books so I could draw things to look correct, but I was limited to what I had on hand. Now I've got Google Image Search for near infinite reference material on any subject.

SRB: I recall you telling me at one point how working digitally, you could finally "ink" in a way you'd never been able to before, realizing a level of facility and precision you couldn't achieve with a real-world brush. Of the tools you've mentioned, which digital program or tool provided that breakthrough?

RV: The Cintiq pen display working with Clip Studio Paint (the latest version of Manga Studio) is just an extraordinary pairing. The big time-saver is that I can go from layouts directly to finished inks, saving having to do the whole penciling stage. Corrections are so easy that working directly in the digital equivalent of ink makes sense. And we haven't even discussed lettering! Clip Studio has a robust lettering engine included, saving the step of hand lettering, of course, but also of having to bring the file into Adobe Illustrator. Clip Studio does *everything* we do in one program.

SRB: Given this new digital realm, what are the differences, for you, between working in black-and-white or color now?

RV: Color is easier in digital than the old methods. In the old days, doing color with an airbrush required hours of tedious stencil cutting. Digitally I can now accomplish the same thing in seconds. I've also started exploring working with digital oils, something I never attempted using tubes of paint and canvas.

SRB: From your very first comic book cover (*Two-Fisted Zombies*), your cover art has been exceptional, always reveling in a vivid, often iconic power and clarity; the individual comic book covers for your serialized series like *The One* riffed on familiar commercial iconography with startling impact. Has this aspect of your work been furthered by your working digitally these days? Have digital tools made it easier to seize, capitalize on, and extrapolate from personal, or culturally resonant, images?

RV: From what I can see of the current crop of covers, a lot of people are co-opting historical and cultural iconography to the point that it has become sort of trite. So I'm trying to pull new stuff out of the back of my brain pan. At the same time, I've got all the great paintings ever done available on my desktop so I can look to what makes the great stuff great. Color is something I didn't get a lot of training on, but now it is easy to pull an amazing color palette out of an existing painting and use it to color my own piece.

The art of designing covers for maximum impact is something I absorbed being around Joe Kubert. But in this day and age, the cover no longer sells the book on a newsstand. Ninety percent of them just show superheroes standing around with their fists clenched and their chests out. I'm always going to be shooting for something more.

READIN' WRITIN' 'RITHMATIC

SRB: When and how did you and Steve Conley begin creatively collaborating, outside of Comicon.com and the journalism site? What was your first collaborative comic project?

RV: Our first big Eureka Comics project for McGraw-Hill Education was six math workbooks in full graphic novel style. But we didn't collaborate on the art; he did three volumes and I did three. I think the first time we worked on the art together was on the Nepal book for the International Monetary Fund. He did finishes over my layouts.

SRB: What year did you and Steve form Eureka?

RV: Two thousand thirteen.

SRB: Okay, let's dig into the educational graphic novels, as this is a virtually unknown realm for most of your readers, fans, and most fellow professionals. What led to you getting involved in the first place, and what was your first gig in the educational comics and graphic novel niche?

RV: The big breakthrough gig came through you, Steve. It was for the University of Quebec at Montreal, and since there were deadlines involved, you passed on it and gave it to me (thanks!).[2] It was a series of short comics stories that were designed to help children deal with emotional and family issues using fantasy characters. The project was funded by GlaxoSmithKline, the giant pharmaceutical producer, to the tune of $900,000. So I got a taste of working for real commercial art rates rather than the measly rates comic book companies had been paying us. And I enjoyed the challenge of working with teams of educators and shaping the comics to fit the needs of the client.

All inspired by Will Eisner's visit to our class in the Kubert School, where he explained his own work in educational and informational comics.

SRB: In what year was that first project with the University of Quebec started, when was it completed, when was it published? What form did it take—as in, what was that first graphic novel titled, how many pages was it, what was it, exactly, and where and how was it distributed once published?

RV: I think it was around 2012 or so. I have no idea how, or even if, it saw publication. One of the weird things about doing educational comics is, once the job is completed, that's it. They don't send copies or even share the fate of the project!

SRB: Did you write and draw it, and what was the process on that first venture, for you?

RV: I designed the characters and did the art based on their scripts and specifications.

SRB: I remember that Will Eisner visit in 1977 to the Kubert School—before the publication of *A Contract with God*, about which Will was very secretive, but candid about what it meant to him—and his conversation with Joe about the educational comics (the term "graphic novel" hadn't been codified as yet) industries. For the benefit of those who weren't there, what are your recollections of Will and Joe's conversation?

RV: I remember Will got there late, so we had a short session. Will introduced us to the term "graphic novel," which he was pushing as a way to create legitimacy in the eyes of book publishers. He described his work with educational comics and the military. One factoid he gave us, which I've never been able to find anywhere else, was that the military had done a study on various media to determine which one worked best to convey information into memory, and it was comics.

SRB: I recall some time after Will's visit, Joe took over producing Will's military educational periodical, *PS: The Preventive Maintenance Monthly*—I think that was after our time, though, or did you work with Joe on that at any point?

RV: That was a couple years after we left, I think.

SRB: We saw, while still students at the Kubert School, the material manifestation of the link between Eisner and Kubert and educational comics, via the projects Joe brought in to the "work study" after-hours projects. You worked on some of those, Rick, and given the context of your work in educational graphic novels since the University of Quebec debut project, I'd like to tap your memories of the educational projects Joe had you and I and our classmates working on occasionally. Do you remember any of the specific projects Joe was shepherding through production and completion back in the late 1970s?

172 CONVERSATIONS WITH RICK VEITCH

RV: Two creative ones I remember were *Sparky the Firedog* and *Magazineland*. Joe had you and I do rough layouts for the whole of *Sparky*, then help with backgrounds. I'm not sure if we did layouts for *Magazineland* (which was a promotional comic for the Sparta Printing Company, which printed all comic books).[3] I did the machinery and architecture, both pencils and outlining in ink, then Joe slapped in the blacks. I think you and I worked together doing the color guides for both those, too. Amazing hands-on learning process while making a few bucks!

There was also a big paste-up job all the students worked on that was an educational reading system for schools. We took existing panels from old DC stories and relettered the dialogue into upper and lower case. Then we touched them up and did the camera-ready mechanicals.[4] Years later my nephew told me those books were in his school and helped him get over a hatred of reading!

SRB: Did you have any freelance experiences with educational comics and/or PSA-type gigs between the Kubert School years and your initial venture with the University of Quebec?

RV: Yes. I did a bunch of stuff for PBS. One was to accompany study materials for their *Nature* series "The Secret Life of the Brain." They also published a few issues of *Nature Comics*, which I contributed to. And I did a story for *Wired* magazine.

SRB: That initial work for PBS—were those illustrations for text essays or comic stories?

RV: Comics.

SRB: Were you writing and drawing for PBS, *Nature Comics*, and *Wired*, or working from scripts? What was your process—and, given the educational content, did these jobs require editorial review and changes to what you'd initially delivered (more stringent than, say, mainstream commercial comic book jobs)?

RV: Some I wrote, some I drew from scripts. Mark Evanier wrote a couple of the *Nature Comics* stories. Yes, there was a heavier editorial eye on these projects than we were used to at DC. But not obnoxiously so.

SRB: You say on the University of Quebec job, you "enjoyed the challenge of working with teams of educators and shaping the comics to fit the needs of the client." On that first major effort, what changes did you make in your workflow; what was the process for working with a team of educators? I imagine with the higher page rates, given the educational agenda, you would be making considerable adjustments to your previous "standard operating procedures" as an artist, as an essential creative contributor to a much larger team effort than you were used to—and a team unaccustomed to the comics medium, at that.

RV: The only major change was to not have free reign with my imagination like I do writing and drawing fantasy comics. These were for educational purposes, so everyone on the team was working to get the information correct and easy to digest. There are also social considerations and the need not to offend people. These social considerations have gotten more and more stringent over the years as the cultural wars have bled into the education system. Since using comics in the classroom is a relatively new development, there was a sense of exploration, too; like "what works in this medium?"

SRB: I'd like to get a handle on this previously "secret" body of work— what was the step-by-step, job-by-job chronology that led from that initial University of Quebec venture to you and Steve Conley formalizing what you now have to offer under your Eureka studio umbrella?

RV: After the University of Quebec gig, I could see the potential to develop a business that specialized in comics for educational and informational clients. But I knew something like that required more than I could provide on my own. I had worked on Comicon.com for over ten years with Steve until we sold it in 2012. I knew he had the skills such an undertaking required and asked him if he was interested. We formed Eureka and started going around doing the dog-and-pony show to potential clients. We generated a lot of interest at first, but no real jobs. The breakthrough came when we took part in a symposium in Washington, DC, with educators and publishers on all levels. There we made the connection to McGraw-Hill. While everyone at MH liked our pitch that comics would be a good way to educate kids, we couldn't get them to pull the trigger on a paying project, as it seemed there were factions within the company that resisted the idea of comics in the classroom. So Steve came up with a strategy, asking MH to challenge us with a subject of their choosing that we would turn into a demonstration project on our own dime. They agreed and asked for a short story on the Scopes Monkey Trial. We did it up, and they liked what they saw enough to ask us down to their HQ in Columbus [Ohio], where we did more presentations. It was on that trip we got the go-ahead on the six math workbooks.

SRB: Given the changing educational landscapes over the years that you, and you and Steve Conley, have been creating graphic novels for this new market, what has been the smoothest experience you've had on a project, and why do you think it worked out as it did?

RV: Considering the demands of educational comics to precisely convey information while not offending anyone, almost all our projects have gone reasonably smoothly. Part of the reason is Steve Conley's ability to navigate the corporate and institutional needs so adroitly. If it was just me, we would have run into problems quickly. See next answer for the one crazy job . . .

SRB: Similar question, inverted: what has been the *roughest*, most labor-and-revision-intensive project of those you've done to date? What was it that required additional attention, work, and revisions, and why do you think that happened as it did?

RV: The problem job was the math workbooks, a series of six forty-page graphic novels demonstrating math principles. We were just turning in the last one after six months of intensive work when our publisher, McGraw-Hill Education, got caught in a culture war storm. One of their textbooks in Texas was found to describe African slaves as "workers," and this blew up in the media.[5] McGraw-Hill responded by doing a company-wide reevaluation of all materials in the pipeline for social consciousness issues. One of our graphic novels had fantasy characters in a dungeon using math to figure a way out, and it was decided that showing any sort of jail scenario would be hurtful to kids who had relatives in prison! So we had to rejig about fifteen pages from scratch, changing the dungeon to a maze. They paid us handsomely to do the revisions, but it was a heartbreaker.

SRB: Over the years you and Steve have worked together on these projects, you've described to me an informal "studio" setup, similar in many ways to how Will Eisner used to work, going back to his Spirit days (when creators like Jules Feiffer, Wally Wood, Lou Fine, and others worked with and under Will to forge the *Spirit* weeklies), except in how workflow no longer requires everything to be "in house," in a brick-and-mortar studio, but using the internet to move stages of labor back and forth. Could you describe for us how you and Steve have worked together, and who else have you brought in to work with the two of you?

RV: We've got a free-form arrangement that changes with the needs of each job. Sometimes I'll take point and sometimes Steve will. Sometimes that will depend on which of the concept drawings the client chooses and sometimes on which of us has time in their schedule or needs the freelance income at the moment. In terms of the art and writing, we have interchangeable skills with differing styles, and that can be fun to explore. But Steve almost always rides herd on the digital side of any project and takes care of a lot of the back and forth with the clients. I keep the books and make sure everyone is paid on time.

We've used my sons, Ezra and Kirby, on some of the jobs. We are able to collaborate on the internet, all using the same programs (Photoshop and Clip Studio) with the working files shared on Dropbox. It's a great system.

SRB: Do you have a larger stable of fellow artists and writers you work with?

RV: We haven't expanded the artist stable beyond ourselves, Ez, and Kirby, but we can see a time coming when we will be digging into our Rolodexes for talent.

SRB: Out of the work you and Steve have completed, are there any "standout" projects or passages you're particularly pleased with, proud of?

RV: I'm equally proud of them all.

SRB: Based on what you've described—without inappropriately asking for business specifics—in a given recent year, what portion of your time or year have you dedicated to the educational graphic novel labors? What does that leave open for you to pursue your own personal, self-published projects?

RV: If I can set up my schedule so a quarter is for Eureka projects and the rest for my own Sun Comics stuff, that's ideal.

SRB: Do you see this field of endeavor growing in the near future, Rick? What, in your mind, does the educational graphic novel and graphic textbook landscape look like down the road?

RV: I believe the potential is huge, not just for Eureka but for any savvy, talented cartoonists who can navigate corporate waters. Every organization that has a story it wants to tell can benefit from presenting it in the comics medium. And we are only at the beginning of getting modern comics into the educational sphere and tested for their effectiveness as learning tools. If Will Eisner's factoid about the military's testing of comics proves true, then it's going to be revolutionary for education and for cartoonists.

SRB: How can people see and read this body of work; is there any way to purchase any of it? This whole world of educational graphic novels is completely invisible to most of the community that will be reading this book.

RV: I wish there were a storehouse of this stuff I could point people to, Steve. Best I can offer are the samples we posted at the eurekacomics.com site.[6]

NEW BEGINNINGS

SRB: Before we get into your current print-on-demand phase of self-publishing, let's not presume readers have any idea of what used to go into the production process of making a comic book, of publishing a graphic novel. Your first comic book, cocreated with your brother Tom Veitch and published by Ron Turner's Last Gasp, was *Two-Fisted Zombies*. What was the delivery and production process for such a venture back in the early 1970s? What was the physical process; what did it entail?

176   CONVERSATIONS WITH RICK VEITCH

RV: That was a loosey-goosey underground publisher, so everything was unstructured and laid back. I drew the comic, leaving the word balloons empty, then sent it to Tom, who scripted and lettered it. He delivered the finished art to Last Gasp, who shot the films and sent it to the printer. No deadlines; we made our own timetable. The publisher would wait until they had four finished books in hand and gang print for cost savings.

SRB: Once you were freelancing for the mainstream comic book publishers, what did that process involve—completion of steps, delivery of your completed work (as an artist and, later, as a writer), the production process from leaving your studio door to published comic book or graphic novel—and how did that differ in four-color comic books from the fully painted comics stories and serialized work you did for *Heavy Metal*, *Epic Illustrated*, graphic novels starting from *1941: The Illustrated Story*, et cetera?

RV: Workflow on a monthly book for, say, DC went like this: writer sends script to editor, editor sends edited script to penciller, penciller sends pencils to letterer, letterer sends lettered pages to inker, inker sends inked pages back to editor, who sends out copies to the colorist and gives the [color guides] to DC production, who prepare it for the printer. I've played pretty much all of those roles in my day. The fully painted art was delivered to Marvel/*Epic*/*Heavy Metal*, who had it scanned. In those early days they used big drum scanners that did a dozen pieces at a time. There was no correction for color after scanning, so a lot of it was pretty dreadful.

SRB: And every one of those steps you detail between your studio and the respective editors/publisher involved some form of transport—the post office, UPS, Federal Express, or your taking the work into New York City from Vermont yourself to hand-deliver—with the same often required to go from editor to letterer, et cetera. You've detailed some of your digital evolution and process, but prior to that, you began self-publishing, working with Preney Print and Litho in Canada, then with overseas printers. When did you begin doing your own self-publisher book design work, and what was the physical process, pre–digital era, for you? What were the physical steps involved?

RV: Predigital, I would do all the creative chores, then send the physical interior original art on to Preney, who shot the films, produced a blue line proof, then printed the book. The cover art scanning and production was done by Murphy Anderson's studio, who were running early desktop publishing tech.

SRB: And, for the record, Murphy's operation was based in New Jersey, so the workflow involved Vermont-to-New-Jersey-to-Canada and back. We worked intensely with Murphy and his son on the production work for *1963*, with Murphy's expertise playing a crucial role in establishing and maintaining the illusion of comic books having been published in the year 1963, though we were doing all the work in 1992 and 1993.

RV: I'll let you explain how that color process worked.

SRB: As a result of that foundational work with Murphy Anderson and Murphy Junior, I remember you telling me about subsequently cooking up your own digital approach to re-creating the look and "feel" of Golden Age and Silver Age comic book four-color technologies and cosmetics. Did you apply your own techniques to published work, and if so, what were those? Would you care to share some of that process and technique with us here?

RV: I've always loved the pulp and big-dot color in old comics. So once I got used to working with Photoshop, I figured out how to scan in old comics and then "sample" the big-dot color and "paint" it under new line work. It's a bit tedious, but the effect is really good. I first used the technique commercially for the America's Best Heroes story in *Tomorrow Stories Special* #1.

SRB: What was your first exposure to the earliest print-on-demand technology? I recall a bookshop in Manchester, Vermont, being the first place and time I was conscious of print-on-demand books, with a finite catalog of titles they could print on the spot for customers.

RV: When I was doing the *Splash*, one of my beats was the emerging technology for digital publishing. This involved reporting on the birth and development of digital comics, the tablets that were being envisioned, digital ink, and print-on-demand. We were all looking to the future not knowing which formats and technologies would win out. I did a panel with Scott McCloud around 2003 and asked him to comment on the future of print-on-demand comics, and he yelled, "*THIS IS THE PROBLEM! DEAD TREES!*"

SRB: What limitations of the early print-on-demand (POD) books steered you clear of that potential alternative to offset printing and traditional distribution? What elements of POD seemed promising, or prompted you to keep it in mind as a possible future vehicle?

RV: I myself wasn't considering POD in the early days. I was waiting for a digital platform to arrive that would be a good fit for what I did. But I was reporting on POD as part of the *Splash*. The examples I did see of POD seemed shoddy. The printing was okay, but the bindings came apart when you opened them.

SRB: What was the point at which you decided to finally engage with print-on-demand as a vehicle to return to self-publishing?

RV: Over a pastrami melt and French fries at the Windsor Diner [in Windsor, Vermont], you showed me some monster movie magazines that your friends were doing via CreateSpace, which was part of Amazon. The printing was good and the bindings were rugged. These POD books were ready for prime time. The quality inspired me to look into it more deeply, and what I found was intriguing. CreateSpace/Amazon offered a complete ecosystem that included not only the printing but distribution, point of sale, fulfillment, and regular royalty payments. Here was a way to connect directly to my readers and bypass the gatekeepers who had stifled self-published comics in the late-stage direct sales market.

SRB: Your first POD original had a curious format: nonnarrative, modest-sized "landscape" books, with a single panel per page, as freeform as your "Li'l Tiny Comics" and your poetry comics and graphic novels. Why did you decide to begin with these "Panel Vision" projects?

RV: I'd had the Panel Vision idea of telling a story with one panel per page in the back of my head for a long time but could never figure out a way to make it work with a publisher in the traditional direct sales market. POD freed me from having to even consider the needs and requirements of publishers, distributors, or retailers. I could just approach a project as a stand-alone piece of art, not something that had to climb the greasy pole in the marketplace. This was the liberating "Ahaa!" moment that sold me on POD.

SRB: As a comics historian, I could cite one-panel-per-page book-format comic creations (pre–graphic novel, or proto–graphic novel, if you will) going back to the very beginning of the twentieth century, including the works of Frans Masereel, Lynd Ward, and others, but would I be wrong to recall Alejandro Jodorowsky and Jean "Moebius" Giraud's *Les yeux du chat/Eyes of the Cat* chapbook as a singular work you turned me on to, that really caught our attention? Would that accurately and fairly be a gestalt leading directly to *Can't Get No* and your first POD graphic novels, *Super Catchy*, *The Spotted Stone*, et cetera?

RV: We also had a couple of Jules Feiffer's books when I was a kid: *Hostileman* and *Tantrum*. But, yes, I got to see and read a copy of *Eyes of the Cat* when I went to Lucca [Italy], in 1981. I was really taken by it; not just the story and art, which were gobsmackingly brilliant, but the one-panel-per-page format, the bright yellow paper it was printed on, and the fact that it wasn't a commercial project but a limited printing gift that Les Humanoïdes sent out to everyone who joined their fan club. More than any other influence, that book stuck in my mind and led to me exploring Panel Vision.

SRB: *Super Catchy* (2016) was such a remarkable first effort for the new Sun Comics launch. The compact, horizontal format, forty-eight pages, full color, reading like a stream-of-consciousness concoction—how did this come together, organically?

RV: It began with a handful of illustrations I did as practice while first learning to use the Cintiq and the art programs. I was basing the illustrations on 1950s magazine advertisements, changing the happy consumers to super-heroes on a lark. When I decided to give POD a try, and to work in Panel Vision mode, I picked them up and built it out from there. Only when the art was done and being colored did I add the Super Catchy angle and write the captions.

SRB: Superheroes, superheroines, and their iconography dominate *Super Catchy*. Is this an extension of, or apart from, your previous and ongoing genre efforts, and the Heroica Universe?

RV: *Super Catchy* and all the Panel Vision books are more closely related to my *Epic* period. In those early days, I would spend two or three months working on a single short story that I wrote, drew, and lettered. Each one was different and allowed me to explore a new fantasy trope. I felt I was able to push boundaries in my work in those days, helped by an audience that was more open to stories coming out of left field! There's not a single Panel Vision book that could be successfully pitched to a publisher in this day and age. They kind of require the POD ecosystem.

SRB: How difficult was it for you to master the production the original CreateSpace platform utilized, the template it required?

RV: I'm an aging baby boomer, so learning software is always difficult. In the first couple POD jobs, I made all the mistakes and almost gave up in frustration more than once. But thankfully I hung with it and now can make it do what I need. The payoff for all the hassle has been a hundredfold.

SRB: What were the color lessons learned from doing—and once it was in print holding in your hands and being able to study the results of—*Super Catchy*?

RV: It seemed to me that certain methods of color application translated better to the POD printing process. I think the heavier painted approach ended up a little muddy, while the use of tints and gradients, in Photoshop, had a lighter look, which I liked. The other lesson was cost. To do a forty-four-page book in the Kindle color was expensive, so I had to price it at $12.95, which is a little steep for forty-four pages. The black-and-white per unit costs are much friendlier and allow for bigger, fatter page counts for a reasonable consumer price. Kindle has since added a higher-quality color printing option, which I haven't tried yet.

SRB: You were on board with POD at Amazon early enough to briefly experience CreateSpace, then struggled through the momentous shift in production necessitated by Amazon dissolving the CreateSpace platform and supplanting it with Kindle for POD as well as digital books. Which of your POD books were completed via CreateSpace, and what were the benefits of CreateSpace, per your experience? What was lost, what was gained, with the switch to Kindle?

RV: *Super Catchy*, *The Spotted Stone*, *Otzi*, *Rare Bit Fiends* #22 and #23, and *Boy Maximortal* #1 were CreateSpace. All the rest Kindle Direct.

CreateSpace worked with Adobe InDesign, which I was familiar with. But InDesign wasn't essential to the simple, stripped-down aspect of doing a black-and-white comic. I can do what I do in a more basic page layout program like Pages; it was just another pain in the ass to get up to speed with yet another software program.

So not much lost for me, although designing rich books like *Cryptic Cinema* [2017, a genre film book by Bissette] will be more difficult, but not impossible, after the change. The upside is that Kindle Direct and Pages work super slick together. The directions on the "How-To" page are simple and spot on. And they are adding new features and updates to the Kindle system since they made the change. The CreateSpace platform had been left dormant for quite a few years before they pulled the plug.

SRB: At what point did you utilize the Kindle platform to publish digital editions of Sun Comics as well as POD physical books?

RV: In 2021 I started putting out digital editions of all the Sun Comics books.

SRB: What have the returns been, short-term, on POD physical editions, and Kindle digital editions, for Sun Comics?

RV: Digital represents just 30 percent of all orders so far in 2023. My total sales of paperback/hardcover/digital in 2022 were 31 percent higher than 2021.

SRB: Let's step through all the Panel Vision books you've done to date. *The Spotted Stone* (2017) was a completely different creation, still dreamlike and mercurial but more satisfying as a narrative read, in many ways extrapolating upon, and distilling down, elements of *Can't Get No*. What was the initial impetus, and what was your approach to seeing through *The Spotted Stone*?

RV: It was another project that I had begun a few years before but dropped because I couldn't interest any publisher in it. If you look closely at the art, you can tell the first ten panels were done in traditional pen and ink, and the rest of the book digitally. The POD option made it possible for me to pick it up again and bring the story to fruition.

SRB: As I remember, *The Spotted Stone* garnered much more immediate and positive feedback, and received some favorable attention, which is quite an achievement for a POD project. That said, as with all POD ventures, we haven't the kind of metaphoric yardsticks we depended upon during the 1990s direct market experiences, where initial orders and (hopefully) reorders allowed us to really track progress, success, or failure based on preorders and print runs. How did *The Spotted Stone* go over, and at this early stage in the game, how were you measuring any kind of POD "success"?

From *Otzi* by Rick Veitch (Sun Comics, 2018). © Rick Veitch.

RV: *The Spotted Stone* seems to have hit a sweet spot for a lot of readers. It was a very simple and quick read that resonated with people coming to grips with how modern technology kind of dehumanizes us. I think that simplicity is why it got nominated for an Eisner. You've been an Eisner judge, so you know what a chore it is to plow through mountains of thick graphic novels over a few days. *The Spotted Stone* kind of stood out because it was so simple, basic, and easy to absorb. More than one person told me they had an emotional reaction to the sequence where the girl is on the new planet and then lives a long, full life in just a handful of panels. I think we all feel that about our lives sometimes; that they are going by too fast.

For me, it proved that the Panel Vision concept could work and was worthy of further exploration. This opened up a new creative dimension in my comics-making career, which I am grateful for. Each Panel Vision book has been its own thing, a singular art experience unmarred by ads or editorial hoohaa.

Saleswise, it is always difficult to get modern readers to try anything new. But *The Spotted Stone* has been the best seller of all the Panel Vision books and continues to do decent backlist numbers. When I release a new *Maximortal* or *Rare Bit Fiends*, Amazon offers customers some of my other titles, and you can see by the orders that this results in new readers.

SRB: Though similarly dreamlike and fluid in its all-visual narrative, *Otzi* was another monumental change of pace, unusual in the Panel Vision series in that your springboard was a real-world archaeological artifact—a once-living person, in fact, frozen, semimummified, from the Copper Age. Ötzi, a.k.a. "the Iceman," has been referred to as "a natural mummy," discovered back in the fall of 1991 in the Ötztal Alps (hence the nickname he has been given) in the region of Tisenjoch, on the border between Austria and Italy.[7] He lived sometime between 3350 and 3105 BC, and his age [at time of death] has been estimated in the mid-forties, perhaps a ripe old age in Chalcolithic Europe in his day. Where did you first read about ol' Ötzi, and how much research did you do before starting work on the Panel Vision project? What kind of visual reference did you compile and keep at hand?

RV: *Otzi* the book evolved out of me again trying to teach myself new technology and software (this seems to be the curse of the computer age). I'd gotten an iPad with an iPencil, which was proving to be another neat way to draw digitally, with the added attraction of being mobile. There was a great little art program for it called ProCreate, and I was playing around with that and getting a good ink line. I drew the first panel as a simple landscape. Then on a whim, added a little figure climbing the hill in the foreground. I needed to dress and equip him and ended up looking at photos of the real Ötzi for inspiration. Before I knew it, there was a story and Otzi was the star!

SRB: Oh, man, that is very cool. Your meditation on Otzi is presented, as in *The Spotted Stone*, as a shared experiential narrative: we are with Otzi during his last breaths and accidental death, in your words: "his final journey . . . waylaid by wormholes, parallel universes, internet start-ups and the very fringes of chaos" (quoting your Amazon descriptive text). Did you preconceive aspects of Otzi's journey after drawing that first image, or did it emerge as you drew each panel and page?

RV: *Otzi* was done one panel a day with very little preconceived ideas. I was working on an educational comics job during the day, and in the evening after dinner, I'd sip a glass of wine and smoke a little cannabis and let my imagination run free on the iPad. All I had at the beginning was a vague idea of a guy jumping from rock to rock in a weird river of floating rocks. So I started him on his journey to find this river of rocks, and the story emerged from there. The daily panel format is fun, since you kind of carry the previous panel around with you for a full day, in that creative trance state, trying out any number of different options for the next step. The evolution of the chaotic rocks into something more structured came out of that. And having Otzi captured and reborn in a parallel universe followed.

SRB: Otzi joins a procession of your heroes undergoing radical transformation, much like John Isaac in *Abraxas and the Earthman* and all your Heroica protagonists. Otzi doesn't pursue his fate: it happens to him, he is swept up in it, without the reference points you and your reader could bring to interpreting his experience. Were you consciously approaching *Otzi* as a distillation of this core component of your work, or did that sort of "present itself" in the process of realizing the project?

RV: Pretty much all superheroes follow the radical transformation line, so it's kind of in my storytelling DNA. But as I mention above, *Otzi* was a journey of discovery for me and continued to surprise me all along the way. This way of working is one of the side benefits of the POD ecosystem. As an artist mining his imagination, I don't have to shape a single thought or idea to the needs of editors, publishers, distributors, or retailers. That's a really nice creative space to inhabit.

SRB: Leapfrogging from a Copper Age protagonist adrift to a modern-age protagonist exploring primal aquifers, did you give yourself the same license on *Redemption* (2019)? It almost reads like a fusion of *The Spotted Stone* and *Otzi*.

RV: Yes, I was growing a story, a panel a day, organically, like a plant. All I had going into it was the idea of a character falling asleep inside a dream and waking up in another dream.

SRB: Room to dream, room to grow! The longer page count—eighty-four pages—was that predetermined, or as in *Otzi*, is this the length it organically took on, as if of its own volition?

RV: I don't set any predetermined page counts for the Panel Vision books. They are what they want to be. This might be a good place to mention that the POD per-unit pricing is conducive to this kind of creative impulse. Kindle charges the same unit price per black-and-white book whether it's 40 pages or 108. This is in contrast to regular printing costs that go up by the page. So, costwise, POD makes the panel-per-page format feasible.

SRB: Your "dialogue" with your readers becomes more overt with this Panel Vision project, more schematic, if you will. Why break from Panel

Vision's template with *Redemption*, introducing single-word captions beneath each panel/page and a half-dozen sporting word balloons?

RV: Why not? The only hard and fast rule of Panel Vision is that it's a panel per page. Anything else goes. The wide-open possibilities of Panel Vision are what attract me to it. I grew up with the undergrounds and early *Heavy Metal*, and I loved the fact you never knew what was coming as comix creators stretched the form in all directions like Silly Putty. The comics art form, in my opinion, has grown too stilted and calcified by the needs of the commercial interests. It needs a stick of dynamite shoved up its ass!

SRB: *Redemption* functions (for me) as an extension of your ongoing *Rare Bit Fiends*, a dreamlike metaphor for what you're dealing with, day to day: as in *Can't Get No* and *The Spotted Stone*, your protagonist in *Redemption* is torn between remaining anchored, fettered, to "normal" existence, or cutting loose to embrace the allure, the promise, of what he's glimpsed beyond this earthly plane of existence. It sounds banal as I describe it (sorry about that), but your expression of the struggle is lucid, pure, and strongly felt, and that last line is a gem!

RV: I got lost in the middle of that story and asked you to have a look at it for creative input.

SRB: I had notions, but honestly, wasn't sure *what* to suggest—

RV: You kind of shied away, but the process of asking opened a door in my brain, and the rest of the story presented itself. Like a lot of my stuff, it points to a part of ourselves that the world of scientific rationalism denies; that thing that Jack Kirby so perfectly realized in "The Source."[8] As I sail into my seventh decade on Earth, I'm here to say the Source is real and we can experience it if we pull ourselves away from all the mad crap fighting for our attention. Not a bad message, I think.

SRB: It's more than a little daunting to be asked, "What do you think I should do here?" when what you're doing in the Panel Vision projects so completely comes from you, your inner self.

RV: More than once you've pointed out something in a story I'd been working on that really helped me see it in a new way.

SRB: I'll do better next time! *Redemption* is very Jungian—no surprise, given your Carl Jung studies and readings and *Rare Bit Fiends*. You mentioned to me you're deep-diving back into Jung's texts just now. Where has that been taking you? How has it changed your perspectives (on the world, our world, your world, your dreaming, your comics work)?

RV: I had begun dipping into Jung in my early twenties when I first really got into dreamwork. His model of the psyche and approach to using the unconscious as a tool helped me develop as a human being and find my way in the world. But for decades I saw it mostly as a self-help program; that if I paid attention to my dreams, they would help me get my shit together. Which is what happened; until later in life, after churning through decades of dream-work and dream art, I began having amazing meditative experiences accompanied by bizarre coincidences. Trying to make sense of it, I went back to Jung and started digging deeper, and it was all there; psychological processes he had documented in his patients and researched in history that mirrored my own. I just couldn't understand what he was talking about when I was younger because I hadn't had the experience.

SRB: Back to Panel Vision—though at this point, you took a break from the format, and we'll circle back around to your relaunch of *Rare Bit Fiends* as POD and launch of *Boy Maximortal* via POD—after taking a breather, you completed a fifth Panel Vision opus, *Tombstone Hand* (2021). It's a major shift into a new genre, a new set of images and iconography, tapping the Western genre; what was its genesis?

RV: Going in, I had the opening image of a shadow moving over a field of rocks. And a vague plot device of a standoff, where a wounded guy is telling the guy who shot him what he's seeing as he dies. So shaping it as a Western set in a graveyard made the most sense. I stuck to my one-panel-a-day regimen, which gave me a lot of time to consider my next move in the story. I challenged myself to avoid the obvious and try to bring something really unexpected to each plot point. I think *Tombstone Hand* is the best of the Panel Vision books. The story works like a one-act play; a traditional beginning, middle, and end tale with a spooky mystical vibe, solid characters, and a number of sweet O. Henry twists. It's a great little read that fits the Panel Vision format nicely.

SRB: You're right, though I'd argue it's more Ambrose Bierce than O. Henry—a little bit of Sergio Leone (as Cheyenne says in *Once Upon a Time in the West*, "people like that have something inside, something to do with death"). Coming on the heels of *Redemption* being a meditation on life, was this a mirror image or inversion, a conscious decision to meditate on death?

RV: It grew into a meditation on death because I had to make the reader believe the guy who'd been shot was dying and seeing into the afterlife. But it's fair to say at my advanced age, probably everything I do has a whiff of impending demise. The Leone influence is deep and wide, of course, but I hope in *Tombstone Hand* I got deeper than the surface posturing people usually take away from Leone movies. The best of them have really great things going on structure-wise that transcend Clint shooting the bad guys.

186 CONVERSATIONS WITH RICK VEITCH

SRB: One of the first "in-progress" comic stories I ever saw your original art pages for was a Western you had been drawing back in the 1970s, pages you showed me when we first met at the Kubert School. Does *Tombstone Hand* echo that in any way?

RV: No. That was an immature work, an example of the "surface posturing" I mention above.

SRB: You've worked in just about every genre in comics *except* Westerns. What's your read on Westerns as a genre? Is *Tombstone Hand* your distillation of what it means to you?

RV: I think whenever you put your mind to a project, it distills what you've absorbed, what you feel, who you are. But I can't say I have any sage-like opinion on the Western genre. There have been masterpieces of the genre in film, and there have been droves of dreck. I can't say many Western comics have really rung my chimes, either. [Franco-Belgian *bandes dessinées* writer Jean-Michel Charlier and artist Jean "Moebius" Giraud's] *Blueberry* is one for the ages. I enjoyed a few issues of *Jonah Hex* back in the day. But I'm kind of out of touch with modern comics, so I don't know if anyone recently has been exploring Westerns with any panache.

"THE SLEEPER HAS AWAKENED"

SRB: The comics genre you essentially invented was your dream comics, which you returned to after two decades with the first of the POD *Rare Bit Fiends*, #22, which you published via POD in December 2016, right between your pioneer Panel Vision titles *Super Catchy* (August 21, 2016) and *The Spotted Stone* (January 20, 2017). How long had you been working on the contents of #22, and why pick up the numbering from your original off-set-press-published direct sales market run instead of starting anew with a new number 1, perhaps a new title?

RV: I didn't invent the genre of dream comics. In the early days of the comic strip there were about a dozen knock-offs of [Winsor] McCay's *Dreams of the Rarebit Fiend*. Fellini did dream comics in the late fifties.

SRB: Well, yes, and Jack Kirby and Joe Simon launched *The Strange World of Your Dreams* in 1952, which Kirby returned to with the even shorter-lived *Spirit World* in 1971, and there was a syndicated comic strip in the late 1940s scripted by Dr. Albert Edward Wiggam called *Let's Explore Your Mind* that sometimes got into dream interpretation, but you took those fetal forms to a whole new level, Rick.

From *Roarin' Rick's Rare Bit Fiends* #24 (Sun Comics, 2020). © Rick Veitch.

RV: My contribution to the genre is to focus on it in a big way, producing a large amount of dream art and providing a more complete context for understanding what dreams are, how they work, and why they do what they do. That and providing a place for other dream artists to publish their stuff. Restarting a title at #1 is a trick to goose sales in the direct sales market. But with POD, I'm free of those concerns. I'm proud of publishing twenty-odd issues of my dream comic and want people to know it has a long heritage.

SRB: What was it like diving back into those heady pages? What was your fresh approach strategy?

RV: The POD option arrived at an opportune time, as I was really compelled to get back into *Rare Bit Fiends* by what was going on in my dreams. An autonomous dream character had started showing up, one who spoke to me directly by name and was intent on showing me various works of art. Dreams had also made a point of teaching me simple meditation tricks, which, when I applied them to my real-world meditations, opened my eyes to a new reality. All this sent me back to Jung, looking for some sort of equivalence in his writing, and sure enough, there was Mercurius, an alchemical figure who operates as a middleman between the waking ego and the deep self in dreams. This evolved into "The Art of Mercurius," in which I tried to document the art pieces Mercurius was intent on showing me, many of which seemed to involve philosophical concepts or models of particle physics. This stage of late-life dreaming was and is really exciting and fulfilling. I'm glad I've got *Rare Bit Fiends* to share it and help me come to grips with it.

SRB: You've continued with the series (the most recently published, at the time we're talking, being #25 in May 2022). How has it been doing for you, in terms of reader response, in terms of sales?

RV: Readers want the Heroica stuff more than *Rare Bit Fiends*, but I've got a dedicated audience of about seven hundred readers per issue. And the back issues continue to sell. *RBF* #22, released in 2016, sold a hundred copies last year. Part of the POD financial ecosystem is that I now have control of my backlist. With each new release, because of the way Amazon presents things to customers, the older titles find new readers. I think it's called "Long Tail" marketing. And I'm collecting the chapters into hardcover collections, which is nice.

SRB: The hardcover editions are magnificent. We're amid a tsunami of autobiographical and memoir graphic novels, many of which have been mainstream best sellers that have even spilled over into other media adaptations (e.g., *American Splendor* the movie, *Persepolis* the animated feature film, *Fun Home* the stage musical), but *Rare Bit Fiends* is the most unique memoir of all.

How do you see your dream comics work fitting into the twenty-first-century cultural and pop cultural landscape?

RV: I don't see *RBF* as a pop culture artifact. It's deeper than that, a unique art statement providing a fifty-year record of the dreams of a modern human being that culminate in a real transformation late in life. For anyone who is searching for meaning in their interior lives, it provides a model and, more importantly, a reason to keep going. Decades of dreamworking churn through all the bullshit we have accumulated and open a door to something really beautiful and indelible. There is a treasure at the end of the quest!

SRB: Well, I did say "cultural," as I agree with you completely about the scope and importance of what you've accomplished with *Rare Bit*. What contemporaries of yours on this path have done similar work—in comics and/or in other media—that you'd want to bring to the attention of others?

RV: Aleksandar Zograf has been doing dream comics for at least as long as I have. Others that come to mind are Bob Kathman, David Reisman, Robert Crumb. Then, of course, [Akira] Kurosawa made the magnificent dream film *Dreams* [夢/ *Yume*, 1990]. Paul McCartney has written a number of songs based on dreams including "Let It Be" and "Yesterday." Keith Richards got "Satisfaction" from a dream. Somebody really needs to write the history of dream art going back to biblical times!

SRB: And how has the return to deep-reading the works of Carl Jung (which you mentioned earlier) fueled your current dreams, and your perspective on the whole of the *Rare Bit* life project?

RV: It reinforced my belief that I was on the right track. I was having visionary experiences that didn't make sense to rational scientific sensibilities, but Jung had spent many years documenting similar experiences and explaining them in the context of his model of the psyche. "The Art of Mercurius" gives the whole *Rare Bit* project a completeness, one that begins with the chaotic dreams of youth and ends with a rich dialogue with the deep parts of the Self. That's not to say there isn't more; dreamwork continues on a daily and nightly basis. But the life arc of my dreams is there for anyone who cares to dip into it.

SRB: Will you be putting all the collected *Rare Bit* runs into hardcover form via POD?

RV: Yes. I've got two titles, *Azoth* and *Pocket Universe*, in hardcover already. As my inventory of *Rabid Eye* and *Crypto Zoo* paperbacks sells out, I'll move them to hardcover, too.

SRB: What has it been like after a little over two decades to return to your original concept for *Maximortal* and expand and extend the series with the ongoing new work? Had you long planned or had in mind the new series, *Boy Maximortal* (2017–present)?

RV: Yes, the Heroica was a long-range, multivolume plan. And it was always percolating in the back of my mind over the decades. It feels really good to be working on it again with the hope of finishing the whole cycle before I croak.

SRB: Given the long break between the last published Heroica *Super Special* (two issues, 1996) and the first installment of the serialized *Boy Maximortal*, were there major components you'd rethought, reconceived, from your original plans?

RV: Not in any significant way. I knew what the bones of the story were back in 1991. But that left lots of room to flesh things out, to explore certain themes and see connections that were invisible to me in the beginning.

SRB: Before you were done with the 1990s run, your "meta" approach turned further in and over on itself. At the end of Heroica *Super Special* #1 and in #2, you showed us Doctor Blasphemy reading the first and second book of the Heroica. How did this "loop" between the comics you've created and that we're reading—the very comics the fictional characters (or at least one of them) are demonstrably cognizant of—inform your approach to *Boy Maximortal*?

RV: In the very beginning, the Maximortal is presented as a higher-dimensional being, so linear time becomes plastic around him, folding in and out of itself. In the *Super Specials* he's revealing to Blasphemy that he's pure information, and every toy, every comic book, every film and bubble gum card with his kisser on it, is him. I'm also creating an alternative structure to the Heroica so that if I finish it and it is published in a giant omnibus format, the *Super Specials* could act like introductory chapters to each novel.

SRB: *Boy Maximortal* #1 was published in October 2017, between the Panel Vision *Spotted Stone* and *Otzi*, between *Rare Bit* #22 and #23. How were you staggering your workloads, so to speak? You were juggling your freelance projects, prominent among those the Eureka jobs with Steve Conley, and with the launch of *Boy Maximortal*, three POD ventures.

RV: I don't work as hard as I did when I was writing and drawing a monthly series. I usually spend four or five hours a day working now instead of the ten or more when I was doing *Swamp Thing*. I still have deadlines with some of the Eureka jobs, but they pay well enough that I'm left with plenty of time for my personal creative works like Panel Vision, *Rare Bit Fiends*, and *Boy Maximortal*. I'm in a much more comfortable creative space these days than when I was hustling the mainstream comics biz.

Notes

1. *Shatter* premiered in direct sale market comics shops via a one-shot special and as a backup series in Mike Grell's *John Sable: Freelance* #25–30. The artwork was created using the then-available original Macintosh Plus in MacPaint; later issues in the series were completed using FullPaint by Ann Arbor Softworks. The series was scripted by co-creator Peter B. Gillis. Mike Saenz left the project with #3 (Saenz subsequently created the first software system designed to make comic art, ComicWorks, for the software company Macromind). *Shatter* #4–8 were illustrated by artists Steve Erwin and Bob Dienethal using traditional drawing tools; the pages were then scanned and manipulated to simulate digital art. Charlie Athanas took over art creation for #9–14, drawing directly on his Macintosh Plus with a mouse, reworking his manually-drawn-with-pencil roughs by redrawing them into digital form. The collected *Shatter* was published in trade paperback format by Ballantine Books (1988) and, later, by AiT/Planet Lar (2006).

2. This was a contact sent my way by mutual friend Neil Gaiman, a query and opportunity presented during my time teaching at the Center for Cartoon Studies in White River Junction, Vermont (2005–2020), when taking on *any* intensive and/or long-term freelance work was impossible for me, given our weekly faculty workload at CCS. "But I know who might be interested," I said, redirecting the parties involved to Rick Veitch . . . and the rest, as you see, is history.

3. *Magazineland USA* was published to commemorate World Color Press Day (June 18, 1977); it was produced by the Joe Kubert School of Cartoon and Graphic Art, with pencils and finishes by Joe Kubert and Rick Veitch. I recall Rick doing a lot of pencil work on this one. At the time, World Color Press printed almost all the four-color comic books, and had done so for decades. By the late 1980s, World Color had lost its near monopoly, closing their doors by 1990.

4. I recently stumbled across a copy of one of the publications, *Super AA* #4, in my files. If memory serves, this magazine-size comic book was originally packaged as part of a boxed set, containing numerous issues letter-coded ("A," "AA," and so on) to indicate their respective study levels. The inside front cover describes the series as "a Motivational Reading Kit by Kathleen Thompson," published in 1978 by Warner Educational Services; the cover sports the Warner Bros. corporate logo and that of SRA (Science Research Associates, Inc., a subsidiary of IBM). To see Rick's online peek at the 1977 *SRA Super A* and *Super B* projects, go to https://eurekacomics.com/#/portfolio/portfolio/sra-super-a-and-super-b/.

5. The controversy referenced previously existing, in-use textbooks, *not* Eureka's educational graphic novels. Erupting late September–early October 2015, the initially offending caption was in McGraw-Hill's ninth-grade textbook *World Geography*, accompanying a

chapter 5 illustration entitled "Patterns of Immigration." Houston freshman Coby Burren brought it to the attention of his mother, Roni Dean-Burren; her social media post on the topic went viral, and more examples of language and history deliberately laundered by Texas's Board of Education were shared. See Tom Dart, "Textbook Passage Referring to Slaves as 'Workers' Prompts Outcry," *The Guardian*, October 5, 2015, https://www.theguardian.com/education/2015/oct/05/mcgraw-hill-textbook-slaves-workers-texas. Dart writes: "In 2010, Christian conservatives on the Texas board of education approved a curriculum that they saw as redressing liberal biases by promoting such topics as religion's role in the founding of America, Reaganism, the undermining of American sovereignty by the United Nations and why the McCarthyism of the 1950s was not so bad after all. It was suggested that the slave trade be termed the 'Atlantic triangular trade.'"

6. See https://eurekacomics.com/ and be sure to click on the "open" tab at the right edge of the pictured virtual book cover to enter the site. The list of published projects includes that initial project Rick completed for the "S'équiper pour la vie" ("Prepare to Cope") classroom workshop program for the University of Quebec at Montreal, the "Social Studies Short Stories" series, *The Remainders*, *The Outliers*, "Pablo's Story" from *The Most Costly Journey*, *The Scopes Monkey Trial*, "Dragonhelm" and others from *Nature Comics*, "The Secret Life of the Brain," and more. There are downloadable comics by Rick and Steve available at the site, and Eureka can be contacted directly at contact@eurekacomics.com.

7. Editor's note: Veitch does not include the umlaut in Otzi's name in the title or body of his work, so it is only included here when referring to the historical Ötzi.

8. See Jack Kirby, *New Gods* #1 (February 1971), and thereafter in Kirby's momentous Fourth World series.

The Form of the Future

BRANNON COSTELLO / 2023

Transcript of a previously unpublished interview conducted via Zoom on November 3, 2023, with clarifications and edits following via e-mail. Published by permission.

Brannon Costello: You've just brought *Boy Maximortal* to a close this year, and so I wanted to start there. One of the things that struck me across *The Maximortal* and *Boy Maximortal* is that even though you're interested in the transcendence of the superhero archetype as an idea outside of history, your work is also very alive to the consequences of when this archetype gets incarnated in the material realm. These are superhero comics that are very interested in the grotesque and the abject, in the comedy and the horror of the body. This is an interesting kind of contrast to something like, say, *All-Star Superman*, which is interested in similar ideas but in a much more sanitized kind of way. I'm wondering, is this just your Catholic school upbringing that has you thinking about the incarnation in this way? Or are there other sources that inform your emphasis on the grotesque and visceral?

Rick Veitch: Well, in my heart of hearts I'm an underground cartoonist. I was in high school when the first *Zap Comix* started appearing. And more appropriate to what we're talking about was Wonder Warthog, by Gilbert Shelton, which was one of the first twisted superhero comics that was ever done, and that really kind of rang my chimes when I was younger. And then, as I moved into the mainstream, even though I was working for DC and Marvel and other mainstream companies, I was always trying to bring in subversive ideas and push the limits and even to try to reform business practices. So, I kind of felt like I was an underground guy who snuck in there to do his work. That's what comes out of me when I'm free of editorial interference. And it's kind of a ripe fruit ready to be taken because the superhero comics have operated under censorship for so many years that a lot of these ideas just could not even be approached, even though they were obviously built into it—things like

193

194 CONVERSATIONS WITH RICK VEITCH

vigilantism and might makes right and the eroticism of the superhero. When I look at it, I see all those opportunities to explore rather than to hold down, which is what you have to do when you're working in the mainstream.

BC: I'm thinking of those images in *Maximortal* of the superbaby punching his dad in the face as he's walking along, and even the focus on Jerome Spiegal's colitis, the way that his shit is a plot element in the story. In terms of the philosophical ideas you're exploring, is there something about the low and the material and the abject that is of interest to you, that you feel has not been explored in superhero comics?

RV: Mostly it's the transcendent part of it. Most superheroes, especially the modern superheroes, the Marvel superheroes that we see on screen, are just kind of nihilistic. Might makes right, fight-fight-fight. They don't have any higher ideals like Superman originally had when he first arrived on the scene. I think his tagline was "a champion of the weak and oppressed," and superheroes don't champion the weak and oppressed anymore. They battle these abstract monsters. I see that the superhero archetype contains a transcendental aspect or dimension that should be explored, and I don't see many people doing it.

BC: I think that's right. But I'm also interested in the idea that your focus on the transcendent doesn't then move the superhero into the space of pure ideas, right? That there are physical, material consequences when ideas take form on Earth.

RV: I would jump in there and say, you go back to Nietzsche, and he says the Übermensch is this intermediary step between man and God. That's kind of like what the superhero should be, and that includes the transcendental ideas that we think of as God.

BC: When the Maximortal comes to Earth, it's destructive, not because he's evil but because it's such a radical new idea, right? It's inevitable that things are going to get changed and broken.

RV: And he's come in a human form, and he has human foibles, and he's heir to all of that as well. So, that kind of figure is like an intermediary. He's got to resolve the flesh and the spirit.

BC: Looking at *Azoth*, the most recent collection of your dream comics, I was struck by the images of you and the kids coming out of the river mud and by how they reminded me of El Guano, visually at least. Mud and shit aren't the same thing, but I'm interested in that rhyming of images across these different types of work.

RV: It's kind of derived from alchemy. I think one of the famous quotes of Paracelsus is, "Out of the shit, the gold." In other words, the essence of the Divine Spirit is right in front of us, and we don't see it.

From *Boy Maximortal* #4 by Rick Veitch (Sun Comics, 2023). © Rick Veitch.

BC: The way that seeing it, or being open to it, can be transformative, seems like a theme across your work. There's the conclusion of *Boy Maximortal*, where you have various people either joyously or painfully surrendering themselves to incorporation or discorporation into the Maximortal, and then I'm also thinking of *The One* and the way that the people who experience the One have this strange transformation where they lose their eyes because they've been given access to some kind of deeper vision. And the conclusion of *The One* is about how the oneness of the One is different from the oneness of the Other—the idea that the people who joined together in the One are still living their own lives in some way. Obviously, these are very different points in your career, but it seems like, when you're envisioning the ends toward which these archetypes might be leading us, there's a tension

196 CONVERSATIONS WITH RICK VEITCH

between harmony and liberty, or between community and autonomy. *Is that a tension that is of interest to you?*

RV: I guess so; I think what I was driving at in both those instances is what it's like to connect to higher dimensional realities beyond what we think of as time and space. If these higher dimensions exist, and I think modern physics teaches us that they do, then there might be points where we intersect with them, and they're going to be really strange because they've got this extradimensional aspect that we don't perceive. In both of those cases, that's what I'm playing with. In *The One*, what's a higher dimension that the collective aspect of humanity would join? In the case of the Maximortal, it is like a higher dimensional being coming down into our dimension. But as you say, at the end of the book, he reveals the higher dimension that he is to the human beings around him.

BC: Do you imagine that in such a higher dimension there is a space for the individual self, or is this a cosmic sort of oneness, where the individual is just sort of gone?

RV: Well, that's the big mystery, isn't it? I'm playing around with fantasy, so sometimes I'll think of it one way, and I'll create characters that try to explore it that way, and other times I look at it in a different way.

BC: That's fair. At the end of *The One*, there's a suggestion that what's being described is a cycle that repeats itself, of beings coming to an awareness of this kind of higher dimension, this higher consciousness. To what extent do you see those types of cycles as inevitable, and we're just caught in them, and to what extent do we have agency within those cycles?

RV: Well, isn't that one of Nietzsche's other core concepts? Eternal recurrence. I don't know Nietzsche backward and forward, but I'm familiar with that one, and the idea that these things happen over and over and over again. It makes sense in Jungian terms, that we are following the path to understanding the archetypes again and again, and we win it and then we lose it, and we win it and we lose it. Again, this is fantasy; I don't have any answers for anybody other than these imaginative stories that come out of me.

BC: That winning and losing process repeating is something to come back to a little bit later on. While we're on the topic of *Boy Maximortal*, though, I wanted to ask about the depiction of Jack Kirby in the first issue. I was really moved by the depiction of Kirby as someone who's drawing for dear life, translating his PTSD into art in this fevered anguish until the Maximortal shows up. And it made me think about the "New Jack City" issue of *Supreme: The Return* that you did with Alan Moore. Do you feel like the process of drawing like Kirby—I don't want to call it pastiche, because it seems deeper than that—do you feel like, over the years, as you have had opportunities to draw like Kirby, that has given you more insight into his perspective, his philosophy, his ideas?

RV: Oh, yeah. As a kid, I taught myself to draw by copying Jack's panels. It was later, when I went to the Kubert School, where I kind of unlearned it and got educated in the foundational aspects of drawing. But I love working in Jack's style, and when I do it, I will think to myself, *Okay, Jack, I'm your hands, come on*, and I'll try to let that come through the back of my mind, whatever it was that was empowering him. And yes, I think PTSD is one of the main aspects of his life that hasn't been explored yet. If you go on YouTube, there are some interviews with him about his war experiences, and some of it was really harrowing. That scene I drew where he knifes the three Nazis, apparently that really happened to him. It makes him a much more interesting and historically important artist, that he was able to have those experiences on that level and then translate it into comics. It's pretty awesome.

BC: Thinking about that arc from tracing his panels to the work that you have done more recently, is there something that the act of doing that drawing, being his hands, has taught you about Kirby?

RV: Not really. I think it just put me more in tune with what I was already getting. And he's the guy, you know. He really transformed the whole medium, and I followed him from the later Marvel monster mags right through *Fantastic Four* and *Thor* and through *New Gods*, really closely. I hardly ever missed a Kirby issue.

BC: It's been interesting to see, even just in my lifetime, the ups and downs of his stock within fandom. Obviously, Kirby is untouchable now, and he should have always been. But there was a period when people were more dismissive of his contributions.

RV: For me, the peak Jack Kirby is *New Gods*, and you can see he's throwing everything he's got into these Fourth World titles that he's doing, which apparently had problems on the distribution level. There's been some scholarship lately where people are saying that the books were actually wildly popular, but the sales weren't being recorded from the distributors, and that what was happening was, the books were going out the back door to the early comic book dealers. So, Kirby threw everything he had into *New Gods* but was told that it didn't sell. I think it kind of broke his heart a little bit, and the stuff that he follows it with is aimed at a younger crowd. *The Demon* is great and *Kamandi*'s great, but it has not got the depth, the reach, of what he was doing with the New Gods. I think a lot of people don't understand his creative arc through Marvel into DC. They just sort of see the stuff that came after. Visually, the later stuff is great, but it's just not as compelling as his earlier stuff.

BC: In these interviews you've talked a lot about the influence of Kirby and some about Moebius. But as I was rereading the *Question* miniseries you did with Tommy Lee Edwards, it made me wonder about the influence of Steve Ditko. I know you encountered his Marvel work early. But did you follow him as he went into the independent and self-publishing worlds?

RV: Not really, but I definitely followed him during his Marvel era. I didn't pick up his Charlton books, either. They didn't seem as good. But what I dug about him that most people don't really think about was that he used intuition as a superpower. He had done it with Spider-Man and his spider-sense. So, that's what I was trying to do with *The Question*, to bring that intuitive power into the superhero realm.

BC: On a visual level, do you see elements of Ditko that you've incorporated into your style?

RV: Other people do. Alan Moore often says to me, *Man, that's a Ditko panel!* I really liked his early *Amazing Adult Fantasy* stuff, which was very designy. He'd design these incredible splash panels, and I would just marvel over those. And Spider-Man was great. In terms of his art, it's those *Amazing Adult Fantasy* short stories that really turned me on.

BC: Speaking of *The Question* and intuition—that comic has a plot where the villain's plan is to take this fundamental mystical truth of the Chi and then shear away all its spiritual implications in order to turn it into a weapon. This is an idea that recurs across your work. Big Finger in *Army@Love* is like a commercialized, profit-driven version of Mercurius's egg. Both of them are embodiments of the collective unconscious, but one is being used to make ringtones, and one is a connection to the divine or the unconscious. Maybe this goes back to eternal recurrence, the recurrence of this moment of transcendence that gets turned into a commodity. Can you talk a little bit about that in your work?

RV: Well, in our popular culture, there's a really big example, and it goes back to Jack Kirby. He creates the Source. It's his greatest character, the source of everything. Now, George Lucas reads those comics and kind of pilfers that idea, and he turns it into the Force. And you think, oh, yeah, the Source and the Force. But just that little slight change of spelling—instead of a Source, you have a Force, which is now a weapon, something that the ego takes control of. And that's what George Lucas, I think, doesn't understand about what Jack was talking about with the Source. No one controls the Source. The Source feeds us all. So, I think you put your finger on one of the problems of the modern world, which is that we try to take everything and turn it not only into a commodity but into a weapon, and *Star Wars* is a really good example of that.

BC: This comes up in other places in your work even going back to *Swamp Thing*. There's the story where the Sprout gets incarnated as the Wild Thing—the Swamp Thing that is brainless—and the hucksters and salesmen are there to try to turn him into a kind of corporate greenwashing mascot. That felt very prescient.

RV: Well, that's kind of what's always going on when you're working for a mainstream company. The stuff going on behind the scenes drives you nuts. You just want to make your story and be creative, but there are pressures to have characters act in a certain way, and to have certain ideas incorporated into the story line. I can't help myself—I have to react against that in the stories I create. It's the underground part of me, I think.

BC: While we're on *The Question*, can you say a bit about working with Tommy Lee Edwards on that series? Was he someone whom you knew, or did DC just pair you up?

RV: It wasn't DC; it was done through Homage. Jim Lee organized the whole thing. DC gave Homage a list of characters that they didn't know what to do with anymore, and the Question was one of them. And so Jim Lee said, *Hey, run with this. Let's get away from the Ditko thing, try to do something completely new with it.* That's why I went in the urban shaman direction. This ended up being incorporated into what was going to be a Superman crossover that a number of other books were going to be part of, and Jim was going to be the central guy drawing the main Superman part of the series. For some reason, I'm not sure what, that part of it all fell apart, and I think Tommy Lee's and my *Question* was the only part of it that ever got published. That idea of the tower and the Chi and everything, that was going to be part of a much larger story line. To answer the other part of your question, though, I had never met Tommy Lee up to then. We were paired by the company, but it was fantastic working with him. The guy's just got this amazing style, with poetry to it, and the use of color and graphics is just astounding. I just love working with that guy.

BC: Was he working from a full script, or more of a plot?

RV: It was full script. Obviously, we looked at *Strange Sports Stories*, and we did those silhouette captions all the way through it. Those captions are sort of like this other mystical realm that the Question could go in and out of. I thought it worked pretty well.

BC: It's really striking; I think it should be better known among your corporate work, for sure. Since I mentioned Big Finger earlier, I wanted to talk about *Army@Love* a bit. Do I understand correctly that the rights to *Army@Love* have reverted to you?

RV: Yes, that's right.

BC: That's great. Reading it all in one sitting, I was interested in how the scope of the book evolves from those early issues, when it is an almost Chaykinesque near-future sexy political satire, to the second series, when it becomes much more metafictional and metaphysical. You're writing yourself into the book, and the book becomes about the nature of reality. Did you always have this larger arc in mind? Or is this a case of your basic preoccupations asserting themselves as the book went along?

RV: Well, that's always going to happen. The last six-issue story arc was compressed because the book got canceled early on. So, I was expecting another twelve, and I had to compress that down. I'm not sure if I have any answer to why I put myself in it other than just to be a wise guy and to make people laugh a little bit.

BC: As different as the beginning and the end are, they do fit together. One way to read the second series is that it's about the war's transition from being what it is in the first series, a highly mediated but still fundamentally physical war, to literally a war of information about who believes in what reality—which is where we're at now in the real world, as well.

RV: I guess I could feel it coming. That's kind of what we fiction writers do. We're sort of tied to the mast, heading through the storm and reporting back to the people under the deck. As we're heading into the future, I think a lot of us are wondering why we did so many dystopian fantasies back in the eighties, because now we're living it. I see myself as an artist now who, instead of doing dystopian things, needs to do things that provide solutions to the problems of our world, or at least provide a spiritual direction for people to look toward to find meaning in their lives.

BC: Do you think the dystopian fiction creates a context in which the dystopia can happen? Do you feel like the glut of dystopian work in pop culture leads us toward dystopian conclusions in our lives?

RV: It's a good question. At the time we thought we were warning everyone. No one accepted the warning. It's almost like they took it as a template.

BC: On the conclusion of *Army@Love*, I was really struck by where you leave Loman, who ends up being kind of the tragic hero of the series. He saves his reality because he's not as susceptible to media manipulation. He doesn't really care about TV and popular culture; he's this old-school, throwback, criminal operator type. But there's no place for him in this new world. It's not that I expected an upbeat ending! But there seems to be a notion that simply seeing through the facade isn't enough.

RV: Also, I was sort of hoping that someday I would be able to go back. Someone would go to the dump and find Loman and get the thing off him and bring him back into the story, so it's just a transitional thing for him.

BC: Well, that's more hopeful than me just imagining that there's no possible resistance to any of this. Now that *Army@Love* has come back to you, is it something you have any interest in revisiting? Or do you feel like that phase of your work is behind you?

RV: I could revisit it, but it would require a publisher, because it's a full-color book. There is going to be an Italian edition. Cosmo Publishing and I have just signed a contract for that. But the logistics of mounting a full-color book in the direct sales market are more than I want to take on as a self-publisher, so it would have to be something I did with somebody else. But the rights are available, and if any of you publishers out there want to talk to me, give me a ring.

BC: In terms of the information war in *Army@Love*, I was also thinking about *The Big Lie*, not necessarily about the merits of that particular conspiracy theory but just about conspiratorial thinking generally. It seems on the one hand like there's a value in looking for connections and not trusting what you're told, because obviously our leaders lie to us all the time, and there are people working against our interests. And yet how do you balance that with the need to not fall into some of the conspiracy theories that we've seen in the last few years around vaccines, Pizzagate, things like that? Is this an interest of yours, thinking about how to think critically without becoming prey to these types of conspiracy theories?

RV: Absolutely. One of the odd things about conspiracies is that they've been turned into this nutty thing, like with QAnon, and it's used as a political tool to move the masses in a weird way. But if you grew up in the sixties, there was a lot of terrible stuff that happened that there was no explanation for. The Pentagon Papers were a big eye-opener. Those of us who stood against the war [in Vietnam] and challenged the narrative that was being produced by the media and the government about what the war was about were vindicated when the Pentagon Papers were released. Same with the CIA and what the [Senator Frank] Church Committee revealed. So, I think there's value in questioning these big events and how they are presented to us. I don't know why they would have to lie about them, or why they would have to create false narratives about them, but I think they do. But I really don't like the whole QAnon thing and how that's being manipulated by the Trumpians to promote all kinds of crazy stuff. The real events that should be questioned are being devalued.

From *Can't Get No* by Rick Veitch (DC/Vertigo, 2006). © Rick Veitch.

BC: Do you have a set of values or a core idea that keeps you grounded, that allows you to be critical but without going all the way down a QAnon rabbit hole?

RV: What I do is sort of come up with a theory. Like, *I think* this *is happening*. And then I'll start using that idea template against the news and see if there's anything happening, any movements happening that fit in with my idea. If they're not there, then my idea doesn't work. But if my idea is correct, then you'll see it in the moves by the power players. That's not to say that you end up with any concrete answers. You're playing with Silly Putty here. But it's something I do for my own understanding about what's really going on.

BC: *Can't Get No* ends with the protagonist returning to a version of his old life. He's had this transcendent experience, and he comes home and he finds out that his bosses want to use it in an advertising campaign. Do you see this as a kind of tragic conclusion in which the transcendent has been debased? Or is the fact that he had a moment of enlightenment kind of hopeful?

RV: Well, I'm a baby boomer. My generation came into their adulthood being antiwar, proecology, antisexism, proequality—all this great stuff. The boomers were originally very progressive, and that all got turned around. By the time the baby boomers hit their thirties, they're starting to drift toward Reaganism, and they're voting against what they really need. It's just crazy. I think that that's what I'm trying to get at in *Can't Get No*. It's kind of a shadow play of what I witnessed, when my whole generation turned away from making the world a better place and turned to making a buck.

BC: With the 9/11 backdrop for that book—did you see that moment as an opportunity to turn away from that pattern, or . . . ?

RV: I think I was just processing what was going on inside me after that. I think I started it like three or four years after 9/11, and we were all still walking around, going like, *What the fuck?* It knocked the blocks out from under everybody, and as an author I was trying to get to the heart of that through the unconscious. The center part of *Can't Get No* is like a mad nightmare that the character goes through, and none of it was planned. I just worked on it, and it evolved, and it came out of me as a dream, almost.

BC: Was the landscape format in there from the beginning?

RV: Yeah, it was. My pitch to Karen Berger at the time was, let's do something that doesn't have the tactile presence of a comic book. Let's do it in a different size and shape, because we want to change people's heads right from the beginning, from the time they open the first page.

BC: The thing that seems to set him on the path to this nightmare, or this enlightenment, is when he is literally subject to art—he bursts into the girls' art studio and they draw all over him.

RV: And of course, it becomes a design element at that point. No matter what panel he's in and what size he is, you know it's him.

BC: How about the poetic, impressionistic text for *Can't Get No*—were you writing the text as you drew each page, or did you add it after you had contemplated what you had drawn?

RV: I wrote it after the art, working in sections of fifteen pages at a time.

BC: On the topic of 9/11 comics, how did your collaboration with Sergio Aragonés come about for the comic you did for the 9/11 benefit collection?

RV: That was organized by DC. Paul Levitz was the editor, and I was working for DC at the time, so I was included and got to work with Sergio.

BC: Had you written that script and they just assigned it to him, or did you know it was going to be for him?

RV: I didn't know it was going to be for him. I was thinking it was going to go to Leslie Cabarga, but Paul had Sergio lined up, and he thought, *This is good for Sergio*. Sergio called me up as soon as he read it and said, *Yeah, I like this!* It was great. We met early on, I think in 1981 when I went to Lucca, Italy.

BC: On the topic of how your personal interests inevitably come out in your commercial work: I knew that you had done the *Teenage Mutant Ninja Turtles* stories as a kind of rebound after *Swamp Thing*. I had imagined these were generic, paycheck comics. But then I read "The River," and I was struck by how much it resonated with your stories about the history of Bellows Falls—the petroglyphs, the Abenaki people, the sense of growing up in a town that's dying. I'm interested in how all that came out in a Turtles comic.

RV: Well, the first thing is that Northampton, Massachusetts, which is where Peter [Laird] and Kevin [Eastman] lived and where the Turtles were supposed to be, is just down the river from Bellows Falls. So, it was a natural connection to me that there was this river between them, and if the Turtles might go up the river, what would they find? And of course, your upbringing is always going to feed your creative work. It provided an opening there to explore those themes, and I took it. The whole thing ended up being a mess on the business end. Payment didn't come as a regular up-front page rate like I got at DC. Mirage gave you a very small page rate as you delivered the art, but the promise of a back end of 50/50, so that if there were books published or toys made, you would get 50 percent of the profits. So, you're essentially investing in yourself to do these books, which is what I did. I did almost two hundred pages worth of work, and I was getting my 50 percent of things that were being made. And then, all of a sudden, Kevin and Peter just went "Nope!" and reneged on the agreement. It soured everything in my relationship with both those guys, and to this day that stuff has not been reprinted.

BC: Yeah, I can imagine a Bloodsucker action figure, that leech character being a toy down the road.

RV: Or all those weirdos from the issue set in the car dimension. When I designed all that, I was thinking, *Oh boy, I hope all of these are going to be toys!*

BC: That's another case where you're drawing really specifically on something from your biography, which is the Big Daddy Roth contest in *Drag Cartoons* that you entered early on.

RV: Yeah, back in 1963, I got honorable mention, but just having my name in the book was such a trip for me. It definitely pointed the way, like, *Yeah, Rick, that's the way to go!*

BC: In the first Turtles story, the idea of Raphael regressing to this child-like state in this run-down and corrupt town seemed to resonate with stories you've told about people getting trapped by the gravity of Bellows Falls. Was that a conscious thing?

RV: It's part of my DNA. I escaped it, so I'm always going to look back on it as that. Whenever I go to the town, on one hand, I love it. But on the other hand, it's like there are a lot of ghost images or something. Nobody in my hometown believed in art, and I was an artist in my heart of hearts. It was a real struggle for me, and I was very, very fortunate to get out and fulfill my calling.

BC: The splash page of issue #25 isn't a generic, comic book image of a river town. It's so specific and so beautiful. Are those three kids based on anyone in particular?

RV: They're just three characters that came out of me. That whole area of the town where the petroglyphs were was a giant Native burial ground. When the white settlers first arrived, they started making roads, and they were just digging up bodies right and left, so there was a spiritual element to that area that was defiled and lost as the insatiable monster of industrialism moved up through New England. It tore the whole place apart. In historical accounts, the area was described as the most beautiful place in New England. You go down there now, and it looks like a war zone.

BC: A while later, you did the "North by Downeast" story with Eastman. He provided the plot for it, and then you scripted and penciled. Was this after things had gotten strange?

RV: No, I was just finishing that story when things went sour. There was this kind of angry exchange between me and those guys, and they just said, *Finish it, no problem.* But I could never get them to sit down and negotiate a fair buyout.

BC: Maybe this is a good point of transition to talking about collaboration. You won't be surprised that a lot of the interviews in the book focus on your collaboration with Alan Moore, so I wanted to talk about some of some of your other collaborations. Since we were just talking about *Army@Love*, can you say a bit about working with Gary Erskine on that? Were you giving him tight pencils? What was the nature of that collaboration?

RV: I was giving him really tight pencils. He brings a clarity and cleanness to the line that I don't get when I ink my own stuff. I thought it looked really good in terms of a mainstream environment. I love working with him. He's really, really good.

BC: How about the flashback sequences in *Supreme*? There are times when you have different inkers that you're collaborating with, like Bill Wray on the EC issue. Were you recruiting inkers who you thought could give you a certain type of finish for certain types of stories?

RV: No, that would have been Eric Stephenson. He was the editor, and he would look at whatever was going on and go, *Yeah, this guy will be good for this story.* Plus, it was whoever was available at the time.

BC: Were there any of those where you weren't inking yourself that you were particularly happy with?

RV: I liked them all. I thought they were great. I wish they would be able to reprint those. I mean, there's a theme running through my career with all these projects I worked on that can't get back into the marketplace because of bizarre business shenanigans. It begins with *Swamp Thing*, which got derailed. The *Turtles* stuff, the *Supreme* stuff, *1963*.

BC: I don't want to blame you for this, Rick. I don't think it's your fault.

RV: Oh, I don't think it's my fault either, but it's really frustrating. That's when I was in my prime, when I was really kicking. All those projects are somehow blocked by failed personal relationships or business skullduggery.

BC: Well, let's go back for a minute. I know some of your earliest professional work was in the *Sgt. Rock* backups that Joe Kubert arranged for you and the other students. After a while you had credits on stories like "Dead Reckoning" and "Leftenant" written by Robert Kanigher. Did you deal directly with Kanigher? Do you have Kanigher stories?

RV: Kanigher was an amazing cat. The scripts came through Joe, and they were often heavily edited. But Kanigher was teaching at the school in my second year, although I didn't have him as a teacher. He was teaching the new class, but he was around the Kubert School, and as a person he was a lot like Hans von Hammer, this solitary figure that everyone looked at but avoided. You could see what he was doing in "Enemy Ace"; he was kind of exploring that aspect of himself. I was always amazed that Roy Lichtenstein's paintings, most of them, are taken from Kanigher panels, but no one ever talks about that part of it—that he wrote those panels. Somehow Lichtenstein plugged into whatever it was that he was doing. But he seemed to like me. A lot of people see him as standoffish and insulting to others, but he liked me, and he seemed to like my work.

Here's the bizarre story I have of him. The school was in this old mansion, and there was this big foyer that we would all come to in the morning, and we'd be hanging around talking. I just happened to be standing next to him when somebody came in the door and said, "Mort Weisinger died!" And Kanigher's whole body just kind of shook in this weird way. Then he walked up onto the landing of the stairway, and he pretended to have a Shakespearean cloak, and he gave this speech about how he had survived, and Weisinger was dead, so he won. So that's the kind of odd character that he was.

BC: Do you think there is something about his writing that made Lichtenstein interested in those panels? Is there a quality that set his war stories apart from other DC war stories?

RV: Don't forget his romance comics. I think his approach to what made comics of that era work constellated something really pure that Lichtenstein was plugging in to. When I first met him, he told me the story of how he got his first job writing comics. He went into the office to talk to the editor, and the editor said, *Give me a story right now.* And just off the top of his head he imagined a skeleton driving a convertible on fire down a street. He had that kind of imagination on the spot, to come up with some sort of bizarre visual image. And he used a purply prose, but very succinctly. And that really works in comics.

BC: A lot of war stories from that era, going all the way back to EC Comics, often favor an O. Henry–style twist ending. You read these stories growing up, and then you were working in that mode a lot early on. Was that a narrative structure that you found helpful in terms of learning to tell stories? Did you find it confining?

RV: At the time, we always were looking for that "hook." It was like writing a pop song hook that would grab the reader. If you can come up with a twist ending where the reader goes *Whoa!*, then you've got something. That was one of the great things about collaborating with Joe Kubert when he allowed me to write my own war comics. We would sit, and I'd pitch an idea to him, and the two of us would start playing with it. That's when I first really learned the pleasures of collaboration, where two people kind of surrender their egos to the story itself. It's not about who comes up with the idea that gets used. It's that it's the right idea for that story. It's just really pleasurable, and I thank Joe Kubert for providing me with that experience.

BC: On that subject, one of my favorite stories that was reprinted in *BONG!* was "The Brain Zoo," the Steve Bissette collaboration, which is about you and Bissette in a friendly but also vicious competition with each other, each trying to outdo the other. Sometimes it looks like you're helping each other, and sometimes it looks like you're going to murder each other.

RV: Steve is one of the most brilliant artists I've ever met. He was born talented, but he had a tendency to get blocked and be unable to work. He gets stuck and can't face the drawing board. So, "The Brain Zoo" came about as a collaboration that kind of challenged him to get back to the board. It was 1981, 1982, something like that. I did a few panels to get it going, and then gave it to him. You can see he's breaking through whatever had blocked him just with the physical action of the brushes. We worked on "The Brain Zoo" off and on, as needed, probably over three years. Whenever he would get stuck, I would do a few more panels and pass it along, and pretty soon we had like nine pages. We should pick it up again now that we're old men.

From "The Brain Zoo" by Rick Veitch and Stephen R. Bissette, originally published in *The Puma Blues* #20 (Aardvark One International, 1988). © Rick Veitch and S. R. Bissette.

BC: I would read "The Brain Zoo," part 2, for sure. The quality of the collaboration you're describing, does it have a different sort of timbre with Bissette than with other people you've worked with because of your long history?

RV: "The Brain Zoo" is just one aspect of our collaborations. Steve and I had a really great creative collaboration similar to what I was talking about with Joe, except we're both from the underground. If we'd been able to continue to work together, we could have done some real damage, I think, because we both brought out this morbid madness and felt the need to get it down on a page. And we just had a lot of fun the first couple of years we knew each other. Even if we weren't working on comics, we were just throwing creative ideas back and forth about all kinds of stuff. But finally, when we got into the mainstream side of things and it required the discipline of working on production and deadlines, our partnership just was not suited for that.

BC: Another collaboration that I hadn't read until recently but ended up really digging was your work on *Teknophage* with Bryan Talbot. Did you already know Talbot? Had you worked together?

RV: We hadn't worked together, but he had worked with my brother Tom on a project. We met each other at various conventions over the years and were aware each other's work. I always considered Bryan the leading edge of the so-called British Invasion. *Teknophage* was a Neil Gaiman project, and Neil actually worked one-on-one as story editor with me, even though he didn't have to. He had sold this group of characters to Tekno Comix because he needed to buy a house or something. But because he believed in them, he would get on the phone with us and talk us through it, help me do the visual creative work to create the character and go over the scripts and everything. I learned a lot working with Neil that way. That was really great. And then Bryan knocked it out of the park. He was the perfect guy for that particular thing. It all happened when the Soviet Union collapsed, and so it ended up becoming this parable about capitalism devouring communism.

BC: I have thought frequently in this era of billionaire worship about the sequence where the Phage is eating the mayor and the mayor's cheerful about it, because it means he's going to get to be part of the boss's money in some way.

RV: Yeah, and he looks like Karl Marx, too.

BC: Was the theme of capitalism devouring communism something that was baked into Gaiman's concept from the beginning, or is that something that came out of your and Gaiman's and Talbot's collaboration as you were putting the series together?

RV: I think I brought it to the early character development work we did together.

BC: The poet Ed Sanders blurbed *Can't Get No*, and you collaborated with him, too?

RV: Yeah, we collaborated on a book called *Broken Glory*. It's an epic journalistic poem, and I did, I think, 120 illustrations for it. It's a project that Ed had been working on ever since Bobby Kennedy was shot, and he'd amassed this incredible amount of evidence and information about what had gone down. I guess we file this under conspiracy theories, although in the case of Kennedy, we know the LA coroner made it clear that he was shot at close range from behind, even though [Sirhan] Sirhan was like twelve feet in front of him. So, this has never been resolved. To Ed's generation, this was a huge blow, and I think he was really motivated to try to figure out what the hell happened. But he was kind of stuck in terms of how to get the thing done. I pitched the idea of adding illustrations to it, and I did a few as a sample, and he liked that. So, he allowed me to just sort of go through the book and pick out scenes that I thought would work and draw them, and then he arranged them, and we worked together writing the captions on them. It creates a very interesting read. His style of journalistic poetry is awesome.

BC: It's been interesting seeing resonances in work from across your career. There's an early *Sgt. Rock* story you did with Bissette, "The Life and Times of Big Howie," which is narrated from the point of view of a howitzer. And then more recently you did the Joshua Dysart *Unknown Soldier* story that's all from the perspective of an AK-47. Is there anything to that connection?

RV: No, I think that was a Bob Haney script on "Big Howie," but that was Steve and I collaborating on the art. Steve's finishes are so strong that he would end up being the inking guy. It kind of looks like a Bissette comic, but those were more like 50/50 collaborations. The Dysart *Unknown Soldier* story was an amazing piece of writing on his part. I'm really proud of how it came out.

BC: I'm assuming there was a lot of research for that one issue.

RV: Oh yeah, we want to get everything right. That's one of the deals with doing military comics—you've got to get it right. But in this day and age, it's piece of cake because you've got Google Image Search and you can find anything. In the early days you had to go to the library and come back with dozens of books or photocopies, all so that you could get the machinery right.

BC: I know you work on a tablet now. Are you incorporating images and transforming them? Or are you sort of tracing from one to the other and drawing from reference?

RV: I'm working on a Cintiq, a full monitor with the stylus, in Manga Studio. What you can do is, you can find your image. You can bring it in as an underlayer, trace over it, and work it up from there. Photography doesn't quite translate into comics, so you've always got to adjust something. It's really great if you've got to draw something with specific details like a car, but also for emotions. I can be drawing my character, and he or she's got to have a certain extreme emotion. I can find a picture of somebody experiencing that emotion on the internet and bring that in and get the mouth right and the eyes right. You really can communicate not only strong emotions but also subtle emotions as well. It also helps me a lot because I'm not a great figure artist, so if I've got to draw figures doing things, I can find something on the internet to work from. Even superheroes—a lot of times what I'll do is, I'll look at soccer, where bodies are flying around, arms and legs akimbo and stuff. I'll take a soccer player and make that into a really amazing superhero pose you could never conceive of.

BC: There are a number of references across the interviews to a project you were doing with John Totleben that was first called *The Ironic Man* and then became *Hellhead*. Is any of that ever going to see light? I understand John isn't able to finish it.

RV: Yeah, John is legally blind now, so we're not able to finish it. He did about twenty-eight pages of finished art. There's another seven or eight pages of pencils and partially colored art, and I wrote the script for all of that. But it's only like a third of what the whole thing was supposed to be, so it'll never be finished unless they come up with a way to give him new retinas.

BC: It's not something you'd want to finish with someone else, I assume.

RV: I don't think it would work. John's style is so distinctive and so amazing, and in this case he worked in this giant oil-painting scale because we were planning to have it printed as a big tabloid book. It's a damn shame—it's incredible. Someday, somewhere, they'll probably just publish those pages that he did, just for people to look at, but I haven't been able to find anyone yet.

BC: Surely someone will do an *Art of John Totleben* book at some point. There are some interviews in the book about *1963*, but I was wondering if you'd had a chance to read Don Simpson's recent bootleg conclusion to it, *X-Amount of Comics*.

RV: I haven't read it. I've seen a few pages on the internet. It seems like he's not really addressing *1963* in terms of what the story was. It's more like he's working out his own angst about it. I'm happy that he's back drawing because he stopped drawing for years, and that guy should be doing comics if anybody should. So, if he's going to make fun of *1963*, I'm happy.

BC: Yeah, it's a kind of a metastory about the fact that *1963* didn't get a conclusion. I know everyone broke up the characters in different ways, but no plan to use yours in any particular way for anything?

RV: I personally am just done with 1963. I've given up trying to solve that mess. The real issue is the break between Alan and Steve. It's like two people who love each other who divorce, and I'm the monkey in the middle. I love them both, and I did everything I could to bring them back. It just proved impossible, just too much heartache. A few years back, I finally had to let it go. If someone else wants to solve it and bring me a finished deal, I'll say yes or no, but I am not going to lift a finger trying to make it happen.

BC: That seems fair. You had a story in *Sgt. Rock* #316, "Welcome to the Machine," that you did a kind of sequel, or spiritual sequel, for in *Epic Illustrated*, "Ghosts in the Machine." Tell me about the connection between those stories.

RV: It's not an actual sequel, but yeah, I'm mining the same genre of the dystopian robot future. With the *Epic* story I had full-color printing, airbrush, everything to bring to it. Graphically, it's a lot more striking than what I was able to do with the *Sgt. Rock* story. But what was great about the *Sgt. Rock* story is that it was my first script for Joe. When I went to the Kubert School, it was like getting a bachelor's degree. But in the evenings I was working on these stories with Joe, which is like getting a master's at the same time. So— luckiest guy in the world.

BC: I wanted to talk a little about the comics that are collected in *Azoth*. You talk about your discovery of *The Book of Lambspring*, this alchemical text that looks like a comic. This made me wonder, do comics just happen to be the form you work in, and so that's what you pursue your philosophical ideas in? Or is there something about the nature of comics that makes it especially appropriate for these ideas?

RV: Both. I think, when I was growing up, if I had had guidance and education in art, I would have become a fine artist. I got interested in comics because it was a type of art that I could find on my own, and buy with my own money, and work with and teach myself. So, this became my preferred way of communicating to the world. This is what I am. But I've also had these deeper experiences that were kind of profound and life-changing, and I want to express those. If I were a painter I would be doing giant canvases that would express them in some abstract way. But with comics, I can actually take words, and I can take imagery, and I can pull them together to describe these experiences. You're syncing word and image, and that way you're syncing the mind. That's why comics give you that buzz when you read them—when it really works, it's great. It might be the form of the future.

The tragedy of the form is, it's been strangled by the business side of it, especially with superheroes. In the public's eye, comics are superheroes. It's hard for civilians to see beyond that. It can do so much more. A big part of my focus right now is Eureka Comics, which is a company that creates educational textbooks using comics. And I think there are huge possibilities there in terms of teaching kids, and we're just beginning to scratch the surface. As a method to illustrate interior states, can you think of a better one than comics? Film does it, but with comics you can stop and ponder. You see a panel you like that makes a point. You can stop and think about that point for a minute. With film, it goes by, you can't stop it. This is probably best demonstrated with *Rare Bit Fiends*, my dream comic. When I watch [Akira] Kurosawa's film *Dreams*, it's great. It's brilliant. But you can never stop to think about what the symbolism he's showing you might actually mean. And that's so important to dreamwork, deciphering the nature and depth of the symbols and what they might mean personally and collectively.

BC: Yeah, you get to move at your own pace through a comics page. You're getting all the panels at once, but also you have to navigate through them.

RV: It's that temporal thing. You're able to stop and reflect whenever you need to, and that's a really powerful aspect of comics.

BC: You're right that people associate comics with superheroes, even though superheroes are a small fraction of comics that are being sold in the US, because of the big YA market and educational comics as well. But are superheroes holding comics back, or are they just a symptom, and the market itself is the problem?

RV: The publishers are a problem because they've got this history of being awful. What we experienced as we went into the new century was that the publishers went into cahoots with a single distributor that is run by a superhero guy. That's what he loves, that's what his whole life is, so he didn't expand his business to include all these other aspects of what comics could be. In fact, he constricted it and made sure that anything he didn't like didn't really get any traction. So, the whole thing is stunted again. I see the Diamond monopoly as a catastrophe for American comics as big as Dr. Wertham. This is all coming to an end now, but it might be too late, because the infrastructure of selling comics has deteriorated to where there's only like a thousand, twelve hundred stores in the whole country, and those stores cater to people who are buying new omnibus versions of the same comics they bought thirty years ago. Even a new issue of *Batman* might sell forty thousand copies, but with seventeen covers, which means no one's reading those comics. People are putting away seventeen covers. We've got to get back to the point where people are reading this stuff and allow the grassroots to grow it in really new ways. There are really potent things that could be done, but the people who control the business of it have been strangling it.

BC: As someone who grew up buying comics off the spinner rack and then buying them from retail shops, I have an attachment to the floppy, to serialized monthly comics. But is it necessarily bad if that format has run its course, or are we losing something in losing cheaper, shorter comics and only having bookstore comics?

RV: It's not that we're losing anything in terms of the format; it's that the format is being used for a very small spectrum of what it could be. If you want to build readership and get everybody reading comics and interested in comics, you've got to open up that spectrum. That's what we saw in the early eighties when the direct sales market came into bloom. *Elfquest*, *Cerebus*, First Comics, *Turtles*. All this creativity came out of the grassroots of America.

BC: Yeah, at that point comics shops provided a place for the grassroots to get published and be visible. If you were going in to buy *Batman*, you might see *Cerebus* or *Elfquest* or *American Flagg!* and find your way to those types of comics. As the center of comics distribution seems to be moving toward bookstores, can bookstores offer a place for that kind of cross-pollination and discovery?

RV: To get into the bookstores, you've got to work with the big book publishers. There's a whole other monopoly thing happening right now. Simon and Schuster was just bought by some giant hedge fund. When you talk to people who are doing those books, the advances are tiny. You might get $20,000 or $30,000 for a whole graphic novel that takes two years to draw. How does that work? There are a few giant success stories, like *Dog Man* and *Captain Underpants* and *Bone*, but I know there are a lot of struggling graphic novelists out there right now just trying to pay the rent while they've got to fulfill their contracts.

BC: In *Azoth*, you make a distinction between fantasy and imagination that I really liked: "Fantasies all about generating wish fulfillment scenarios for our fears and desires. But imagination tackles reality head on. We use our imaginations to build things, solve problems, make art." I was thinking about this in the context of what imagination means in our current moment. This feels like an obligatory question for 2023. As somebody who's been on the cutting edge of a lot of technological advances in comics, do you have any hope for AI as a meaningful or useful tool, as something other than a grotesque parody of human ingenuity? I'm in the "grotesque parody of human ingenuity" camp, but I'm willing to be persuaded.

RV: Well, I wouldn't mind playing with it, and maybe people wouldn't be offended if someone like me, who has spent their life drawing and writing comics, played with it. I'm sure I could do some cool stuff. I know I've seen some amazing AI art, but I think it has the potential to generate a lot of crap.

The thing that scares me the most is, what kid is going to pick up actual pencils and paper and learn to draw when he can just type a phrase into a computer and get this incredibly finished image? I wonder if the generation now is the last generation of people who will actually make hands-on physical art. But I don't have any solutions for this. It's crazy, and the art part of it is only the small tip of how it's going to direct the media that we're plugged into and how the media each of us gets is going to be personalized in this weird way, even more than that already is. I think there's a lot of danger there.

BC: You mentioned earlier not wanting to do dystopian stories anymore, wanting to do stories that point toward possible ways forward into better futures. What are you working on next?

RV: There will be more Heroica and more *Rare Bit Fiends*. On my drawing board right now, I'm putting together the collected *Boy Maximortal*, doing a new cover and writing a new essay for the back about the nature of superheroes. There'll be more issues of *Rare Bit Fiends*. I think that's the best thing I can offer now, because my own experience with dreamwork really brought me to a point where I found a sort of meaning in life. This is going to sound kind of pompous, but there are times, utilizing simple meditation techniques I've been able to teach myself, when I experience the spirit, what Jack portrayed in the Source. It requires flexing the imagination in a different way, as a kind of a tool to experience this thing that is living in us all. I want to get that story across, because I know a lot of people are walking around going like, *What the fuck, what is this world about?* I think the perception of spirit in matter could help anyone who's lost. I don't know why we're not normally able to perceive it. But it's here, right in front of us, and experiencing it changed my life.

BC: It was the process of many years of dedication to your practice, right? The specific moment that you depict in "The Art of Mercurius" with the candle, that's very deep into your practice of dreamwork and meditation.

RV: The only way it works is, you've got to process all the bullshit in your life, and I think forty years of dreamwork did that for me. It's not that I'm free of all the bullshit; I just sort of digested it. Doing that allows the deepest part of our consciousness to reach out and reveal itself to us. And this is a natural development of aging, which Jung calls the individuation process. I did not understand any of this until it happened to me. I went back and reread Jung, and finally got what his whole take on alchemy was all about. The alchemists weren't changing lead to gold; they were self-hypnotizing so that they could perceive the spirit in matter.

INDEX

ABC A to Z, xxi

Abenaki (Indigenous people), 73, 204–5

Abraxas and the Earthman, xi, xix, xxi, 11, 34, 35, 61, 62, 101–2, 158, 161, 168, 183

Acme Novelty Library, 121

Adobe Illustrator, 115, 169

Adobe InDesign, 168, 180

Adobe Photoshop, 147, 153, 168, 174, 177, 179

Adventures of Unemployed Man, The, xxii

AI, 214–15

airbrush, 11, 13, 37–38, 99, 105, 128, 169, 212

"Alien Comix Presents," xviii

Allagash Incident, The, 166

All-Star Superman, xiv, 193

Amazing Adult Fantasy, 198

Amazon, 114, 132, 135, 156, 177–78, 179, 182, 188

Amazon Kindle, 135–36, 139, 179–80

American Flagg!, 214

America's Best Comics (ABC), xiii, xxi, 55, 57, 128, 131, 140–43, 145, 146–49, 153–55, 158, 162–65, 177

Anderson, Murphy, 121, 125, 176–77

Angel and the Ape, 4

Aquaman, xiii, xxi, 55, 57–58, 63, 103

Arad, Avi, 160

Aragonés, Sergio, xxi, 203–4

Arcade, 102

Archie, 109

Arlington, Gary, 108

Army@Love, xiii, xxi, xxii, 61–69, 113, 158, 165, 198, 199–201, 205

Asherman, Allan, 99

Association for the Study of Dreams, 81

Athanas, Charlie, 191n1

Atom, The, 97

Awesome Entertainment, xx, 57, 128, 131, 141, 148

Azoth, xxiii, 189, 194, 212, 214

Baker, Matt, 151

Barks, Carl, 87

Batman, xii, 25, 28, 32, 53, 57, 104, 109, 130, 142–43, 144, 156, 162, 213, 214

Batman (film), 41

Beano, 108

Beatles, 92, 102–3, 131

Bechdel, Alison, xiii, xxii

Bedlam, xix, 26

Bedrock, 133

Bellows Falls, VT, x, xvii, 70, 85, 89, 92–94, 96, 204–5

Berger, Karen, 5, 6, 16, 18, 21, 40, 64, 131, 164, 203

Bierce, Ambrose, 185

Big Bang, 142

Big Lie, The, xiii, xxii, 201

Big Numbers, 46, 123

Bissette, Stephen R., x, xi, xii, xiii, xiv–xv, xviii, xix, xx, 3, 9, 13–14, 15, 23–24, 26, 34, 37–38, 39, 48–49, 53, 63, 77–78, 80, 87, 92, 98–100, 101, 106–7, 114, 117–19, 121–22, 124–29, 132, 133, 136, 141, 158, 170, 180, 184, 207–9, 210, 212

Bloodsucker, 204

217

218 INDEX

Blueberry, 186

Bode, Mark, 131

Bone, 214

BONG! Comix, xxiii, 62, 207

Book of Lambspring, The, 212

"Bossy," xix

Boy Maximortal, xiv, xxii, xxiii, 132, 180, 185, 190, 193, 195–96, 215

Boys, The, xiv

"Brain Zoo, The," xix, 207–9

Brat Pack, xii, xv, xx, xxi, xxii, 23, 24–26, 28–32, 36, 43, 45–46, 47, 49, 52, 55, 56–57, 58, 60, 61, 63, 69, 104–5, 158, 162, 165, 168

Brat Pack/Maximortal Super Special, xx, xxi, 190

Broken Glory, xxii, 114, 210

Brown, Chester, 125

Bucky, 28

Bulaski, Stephen, 89

Buscema, John, xviii

Bush, George W., xiii

Butch Cassidy and the Sundance Kid, 100

B'Wana Beast, 16, 104

Byrne, John, 4

Cabarga, Leslie, 203

Cabbot: Bloodhunter, xxi

Cages, 46

Campbell, Eddie, 127

cannabis. *See* marijuana

Can't Get No, xiii, xxi, 55, 58–60, 63, 65, 68–69, 70, 158, 178, 180, 184, 202–3, 205

Capital City Distribution, 161

Captain America, 25, 28, 121

Captain Underpants, 214

"Casey Jones: North by Downeast," xx, 205

"Cell Food," xviii

Cerebus, xix, 24, 37, 48, 101, 214

CETA (Comprehensive Employment and Training Act), xviii, 9, 86–87, 100

Charlier, Jean-Michel, 186

Charlton Comics, 97, 198

Chaykin, Howard, 21, 102, 200

Chippy, xii, 25, 29

Cho, Frank, xxi, 147, 151

Cintiq, 138–39, 168–69, 178–79, 210–11

Citizen Kane, 110

Clip Studio Paint, 169, 174. *See also* Manga Studio

Clockwork Orange, A, 110

Cobweb, 57, 146, 150

Cochran, Russ, 110

collaboration, x–xi, xii, 15–16, 26, 37–38, 57, 58, 77, 90, 98, 99–100, 119–24, 128, 132, 145–46, 148, 152, 166, 170, 172–75, 199, 205, 207–10, 212

Columbia University Libraries, xxiii

Comicon.com, xii–xiii, xxi, xxii, 60, 61, 69, 140, 154–55, 159–60, 163, 170, 173

Comics Buyer's Guide, 18, 19, 22, 159

Comics Code, 95, 118, 162

Comics Feature, 133

comics form, 3, 15, 56, 65, 97, 135–36, 139, 143–44, 151–52, 175, 178, 183–84, 198, 203, 212–13

Comics Journal, The, 129, 159

Commander Solo, 129

Congorilla, 4

Conley, Steve, xiv, xxi, xxii, 69, 113–14, 140, 157, 158–59, 160, 165, 166–67, 168, 170, 173–75, 190

"Conquest of the Banana Planet!," xviii–xix

conspiracies, xiii, 201–2, 210

Constantine, John, xix, 4–5, 16, 146

Contract with God, A, 171

Cosmopolitan, 69

Cosmo Publishing, 201

Cozine, Franny, 88

Cracking the Codex, xxiii

Crazymouse, x, xvii, 36, 158

CreateSpace, 114, 177–80

Creative Burnouts, 158

INDEX 219

Creator's Bill of Rights, xix
Creepy, 95–96, 106, 109
Cricket, Jack, 25, 31
Crisis on Infinite Earths, 16, 57
Crumb, Robert, 9, 100, 101–2, 189
Cryptic Cinema, 180
Crypto Zoo, xxi, 81, 91, 162, 168, 189
Crystal Man, 131
Cy-Gor, xxi, 63

Daredevil, 39. See also *What If? Daredevil*
Dark Horse Comics, 148, 154
Dark Knight Returns, The, 15, 32, 57, 104–5
"Day to Remember, A," xix
DC Comics, x, xi–xii, xiii, xviii, xxi, 3, 5–6, 10,
    13–17, 24, 26, 28, 35, 37, 49, 50, 55, 57,
    62, 64, 69, 85, 87, 96, 97, 99, 100, 103,
    106, 118, 125, 130, 133, 140, 143, 144,
    148–49, 151, 154–56, 160, 161, 163, 164,
    172, 176, 193, 197, 199, 203, 204, 206;
    Veitch's disputes with, xx, 7, 17–22, 25,
    32, 36, 40–43, 103, 104, 117–18, 164–65
DC Comics Presents, xix
DeCarlo, Dan, 148
Delano, Jamie, 4–5, 21
Demon, 103, 104, 197
Detective Chimp, 4
Diamond Comic Distributors, 24, 133–34,
    140, 154–56, 159–62, 164, 213
Dick Tracy, 89
Dienethal, Bob, 191n1
digital art, 138–40, 165–70, 177, 178–79, 182
digital publishing, 133–34, 174, 177–82,
    191n1. See also print-on-demand (POD)
direct market, xiv, 37, 42, 55, 61, 62, 101,
    133–34, 154, 159–60, 162, 178, 180, 186,
    188, 201, 214
Disney, Walt, 50, 52
distribution, ix, xiv, 24, 87, 101, 118, 119,
    133–34, 140, 148, 159, 160, 161–62, 171,
    177–78, 197, 213–14
Ditko, Steve, 51, 198, 199

Doctor Blasphemy, 190
Doctor Manhattan, 97
Dog Man, 214
Drag Cartoons, xvii, xx, 92, 204
Dragon, Catherine, 87
"Dragonhelm," 192n6
dreams, ix, xii, xviii, xx, xxi, 47–49, 60,
    70–84, 113, 119, 136, 138, 183, 184–90,
    213, 215. See also *Roarin' Rick's Rare
    Bit Fiends*
Dreams, 189, 213
Dreams of the Rarebit Fiend, 186
Dream Team, The, 60
Dr. Fate, 19
Drucker, Mort, 151
Druillet, Philippe, ix
Dr. Wirtham's Comix and Stories, xviii, 101
Dunbier, Scott, 147, 163
Dylan, Bob, 103, 110
Dynamic Forces, xxii
Dynamite Entertainment, 130
Dysart, Joshua, xxii, 210

Eastman, Kevin, xix, xx, 22, 41, 48, 204, 205
East Village Other, 90
EC Comics, 95–96, 110, 141, 152, 205, 207
Eclipse Comics, xix
educational comics, xiii–xiv, xxii, 114–15,
    157, 158, 170–75, 191nn4–5, 213
Edwards, Tommy Lee, xxi, 198, 199
Eisman, Hy, 9
Eisner, Will, xiii, 57, 58, 110, 141, 143,
    144–45, 146, 148, 149, 150, 153, 156,
    163–64, 170, 171, 174, 175
Elder, Will, 96
Elfquest, 37, 101, 102, 214
El Guano, 50, 194
Eliot, Marc, 52
Enemy Ace, 103, 206
Epic Comics, xi, xix, 12, 14, 34, 37–39, 61,
    62–63, 101, 158. See also Marvel Comics
Epic Illustrated, xi, xviii, xix, xxi, 7, 11–12,

13, 14, 26, 34, 37–39, 77, 101–2, 123, 158, 161–62, 167, 176, 179, 212

Erskine, Gary, xxi, 205

Erwin, Bob, 101n1

Estrada, Rick, 9

Estren, Mark, 105

Eureka Comics, xiv, xxii, xxiii, 113–15, 158, 168, 170–75, 190, 191n5, 192n6, 213

Evanier, Mark, 172

"Everlasting Tag, The," xix

Ewins, Brett, 17

Extreme Studios, xx

Eyes of the Cat, The, 135, 178

Fantastic Four, 87, 121, 132, 197

Feduniewicz, Ken, 9

Feiffer, Jules, 174, 178

Fine, Lou, 174

First Comics, 165, 214

Flash, 17, 87, 96, 97, 104

Flash Gordon, xviii

Fleischer, Dave and Max, 52

Forbidden Book, The, xxi

Fourth World, 17, 90, 106, 108, 192n8, 197. See also *New Gods*

Frazetta, Frank, 86, 96

Freud, Sigmund, 68, 83

From Hell, 46, 118, 127, 149

Fun Home, 188

Fury, 129

Gaiman, Neil, xx, 21, 49, 52, 70, 78, 114, 165, 191n2, 209

Gebbie, Melinda, 57

Geppi, Steve, 160, 162, 213

Gerhard, 78

"Ghosts in the Machine," xix, 212

Gibbons, Dave, xiii, xxi, 57, 120, 121, 125–26, 130, 142–43, 147, 149, 151, 152, 156

G. I. Combat, xi

Gillis, Peter B., 191n1

Giordano, Dick, 9

Giraud, Jean (Moebius), ix, xix, 32, 49, 135, 178, 186, 198

GlaxoSmithKline, 170

Golan, Gan, xxii

Golden Gladiator, 104

Goodwin, Archie, 11–13, 34, 39, 96, 101

Google Image Search, 169, 210

Goosebumps, xix

Gorilla Grodd, 4

Gould, Chester, 89

Green Arrow, 17, 19–21, 25, 28

Green Arrow: The Longbow Hunters, 19

Green Lantern, 87, 97

Greyshirt, xiii, xxi, 55, 57, 131, 141, 143, 144–51, 155, 158, 164, 165; and "How Things Work Out," 57, 145–46

Greyshirt: Indigo Sunset, xiii, xxi, 57, 146–48, 150–53, 156

Grimjack, xix

"Guns of Africa, The," xxii, 210

"Guts," xviii

Haney, Bob, 210

Hawkman, 87, 97

Heartburst, xi, xix, xxii, 11, 62, 158, 161, 167, 168

Heath, Russ, ix, xiii, xxi, 106, 147, 151

Heavy Metal, xi, xviii, 14, 26, 34, 39, 99–100, 101, 102, 176, 184

Hee Hee, xvii

Hellblazer, 4, 17

Hellhead, 36, 53, 211. See also *Ironic Man, The*

Hero Comics, xvii

Heroica. See *King Hell Heroica*

History of Underground Comics, xvii–xviii, 105

Hogan, Peter, xxi

Holland, Abigail (Abby), 5, 6, 16, 17, 22, 146

Homage Studios, 133, 141, 148, 199

Hoover, J. Edgar, 52

Horus, 121, 128

INDEX 221

Hostileman, 178
Hulk, 53, 77
Human Torch, 28
Hypernaut, 129

IDW Publishing, xxii
Image Comics, xiii, xx, xxi, xxii, 42, 47, 49, 51, 62, 63, 118–19, 122, 123–27, 130, 133, 142, 148, 158, 163
Images of Omaha, xx
independent comics, x, xii, xiv, 37, 101, 104–5
Infantino, Carmine, 17, 86, 97
Insect Fear, 105
International Monetary Fund, xxii, 158, 170
Iraq War, xiii, 64, 65, 66, 68
Ironic Man, The, 32, 211
Iron Man, 32, 53
Irons, Greg, xvii, 8, 34

Jaws, 110
Jenkins, Paul, xxi
JLA, xxi
Jodorowsky, Alejandro, 135, 178
Joe Kubert School, x, xi, xviii, 9, 11, 26, 34, 36–37, 39, 72, 86–87, 98, 100–102, 106, 113, 119, 136, 143, 152, 158, 163, 170, 171–72, 186, 191n3, 197, 206, 212
Johnny Beyond, 127
Jonah Hex, xviii, 186
Jones, Jeff, 106
Judge Jury, 31
Jung, Carl, xiii, xviii, 47, 72, 73, 75, 80–81, 184–85, 188, 189, 196, 215
Justice League, 154

Kahn, Jenette, 18–19, 21, 40–41
Kaluta, Michael, 107
Kamandi, 197
Kanigher, Robert, 206–7
Karpinski's Economy Market, 88, 95, 97
Kathman, Bob, 189

Keefe, Kristen, xviii
Kelley, Bill, xviii
Kennedy, John F., 92, 93
Kennedy, Robert F., Sr., xxii, 93, 114, 210
Kid Vicious, 31
King, Martin Luther, Jr., 93
King Hell, xx, xxi, xxii, 7, 11, 13, 23–26, 28, 34, 36, 41, 43, 49, 60, 62, 70, 158, 161, 162, 168
King Hell Heroica, xii, xiii, xiv, xx, xxii, 25, 31–32, 34, 36, 43–44, 47, 48, 49, 54, 56–57, 162, 165, 179, 183, 188, 190, 215
King Rad, 31
Kirby, Jack, ix, x, xxi, 8–9, 17, 23, 36, 51, 86, 90, 95, 97, 105, 106, 109, 110–11, 112, 119, 132, 136, 144, 153, 184, 186, 192n8, 196–98
Kitchen, Denis, xx
Kitchen Sink Press, xviii, xx, 49, 117
Klein, Todd, 141, 163
Krenkel, Roy, 96
Kubert, Joe, x, 9, 10, 37, 56, 86–87, 98, 106, 110, 111–13, 136, 151, 152, 163, 169, 170, 171–72, 191n3, 206, 207, 209, 212. *See also* Joe Kubert School
Kubrick, Stanley, 110
Kugler, Jimmy, 158
Kujava, Sam, 9
Kurosawa, Akira, 82, 189, 213
Kurtzman, Harvey, 96

Laird, Peter, xix, 22, 41, 111, 204
"Landmass," xix
Last Gasp, xvii, 9, 86, 144, 175–76
Last Temptation of Christ, The, 18–19
League of Extraordinary Gentlemen, 142, 164
Lee, Jim, xiii, 118, 126–29, 132, 133, 148, 162–64, 199
Lee, Stan, xviii, 109, 122
Leone, Sergio, 185
Les Humanoïdes, 135, 178
Leszczak, Cindy, xviii, xix, 102, 110–11

222 INDEX

Let's Explore Your Mind, 186
Levitz, Paul, 18, 130, 140, 154–55, 164, 203
Lichtenstein, Roy, 151–52, 206–7
Liefeld, Rob, xx, 126, 133, 162–63
Light and Darkness War, The, 7
"Li'l Tiny Comics," xviii, 178
"Little Annie Fanny," 96
Little Lulu, 87
Lloyd, David, xiii, xxi, 147, 151
Loman, 200–201
Love & Rockets, 46
"Love Doesn't Last Forever," xix, 12, 13
Lucas, George, 198
Luna, 31

MAD Magazine, 88, 95, 96, 100
Magazineland USA, 172, 191n3
Manga Studio, 168, 169, 210–11
marijuana, 93, 117, 151, 166, 182
Marvel Cinematic Universe, xiv, 194
Marvel Comics, xi, xiii, xviii, xix, xxi, 10–11,
    14, 19–20, 21, 24, 32, 34, 37–39, 41–42,
    49, 51, 53, 70, 85, 86, 87, 88, 92, 96, 99,
    100, 101–2, 103, 106, 108, 117–18, 122,
    125, 132, 141, 143, 154–56, 159–60, 161,
    176, 193, 197–98. *See also* Epic Comics
Marvel Graphic Novel, xi, xix, 11
Marvelman, 13, 142. See also *Miracleman*
Marx, Karl, 209
Masereel, Frans, 178
Mavrides, Paul, 131
Maximortal, The, xii, xx, 36, 43–46, 47, 48,
    49–52, 56–57, 58, 60, 61, 63, 104, 132,
    156, 158, 162, 165, 168, 182, 189–90,
    193–94, 196
Maximum Press, xxi
McCartney, Paul, 82, 189
McCay, Winsor, xii, 186
McCloud, Scott, xix, xx, 47–48, 78, 177
McFarlane, Todd, 118, 126, 133
McGraw-Hill Education, xxii, xxiii, 113, 115,
    158, 170, 173, 174, 191n5
Meadows Bee, xxii

Mercurius, 188, 198
Metal Hurlant, xi
Midnight Mink, xii, 25, 29
Mighty Crusaders, The, xix
Military Times, 66
Miller, Frank, 21, 39, 41, 57, 101, 102,
    130, 142
Miracleman, xi, xix, 14, 15, 32, 33, 39. *See
    also* Marvelman
Mirage Studios, 23, 204–5
"Mirror of Love, The," xix
Moby-Dick, xi, 34
Mod Gorilla Boss, 4
"Momma's Bwah," xviii
"Monkey See," xviii, 63
*Moon and Serpent Bumper Book of Magic,
    The*, xxiii
Moon Goddess, 31
Moore, Alan, xi, xiii, xix, xx, xxi, xxiii, 3–4,
    7, 13, 14–16, 33, 34–36, 39, 41, 48,
    49, 53, 57, 60, 70, 77, 96–97, 98, 103,
    117, 119–33, 141–43, 145–50, 153–56,
    163–65, 196, 198, 205, 212
Moore, Leah, 130
Moore, Steve, xxiii, 154
Most Costly Journey, The, xxiii, 192n6
"Mr. Bigfoot Goes to Washington," xxi
Mr. Scarlet, 28
Murphy, Stephen, 24
Mystery Incorporated, 121–24

National Lampoon, 106
Native Americans, 83. *See also* Abenaki
    (Indigenous people)
Nature Comics, xxii, 172, 192n6
Neal, Cliff, 101
Nepal: Into and Out of the Grey, xxii, 170
New Gods, 106, 192n8, 197
"New Jack City," xxi, 196
Newsarama, 160
Next Planet Over, 160
Nexus, xix, 14
Nietzsche, Friedrich, 92, 194, 196

9/11, xiii, 70, 203–4
9–11, xxi, 203–4
1941: The Illustrated Story, xviii, 99–100, 158, 176
1963, xiii, xx, 47, 49, 53, 54, 61, 63, 117–34, 141, 142, 144, 146, 158, 163, 165, 176–77, 206, 211–12
1963½, 131–32
N-Man, 129
Northampton, MA, xix, 204
Novick, Irv, 151

"Old Magik," xvii
Once Upon a Time in the West, 185
One, The, xi, xii, xix, xx, xxii, 11–13, 16, 23, 32, 34, 38, 39, 61, 70, 77, 102, 158, 165, 168, 169, 195–96
"One Suffers to Provide for the Family," xxiii
Orb, 101
Origen, Erich, xxii
Otzi, xiv, xxii, 136, 180, 181, 182–83, 190, 192n7
Our Army at War, xiii, 64, 87, 165
Outliers, The, xxii, 192n6

"Pablo's Story," 192n6
Panel Vision, xiv, xxii, xxiii, 132, 135–39, 156, 178–86, 190
Paracelsus, 194
Passport: A Guide to Life, 115
PBS, xxi, xxii, 158, 172
Pentagon Papers, 93, 201
Pepoy, Andrew, 147, 153
Perlmutter, Ike, 160
Persepolis, 188
Pini, Wendy and Richard, 51, 102
Pinky, 28
Plot, The, 153
Pocket Universe, xx, xxiii, 162, 168, 189
Preney Print and Litho, 176
"Prepare to Cope," xxii, 192n6
print-on-demand (POD), xxii, 135, 157, 158, 175, 177–83, 185, 186, 188–89, 190

Pro, The, 57
ProCreate, 182
Promethea, 57, 149
PS: The Preventive Maintenance Monthly, 143, 171
Puma Blues, The, xix, 24, 208

Question, The, xiii, xxi, 17, 158, 198–99

Rabid Eye, xx, 168, 189
Rankin/Bass, 14
Raspler, Dan, 58, 164
Rat, 90
Rat Fink, 92
Raw, 57
Raymond, Roy, 104
Reagan, Ronald, 13, 192n5, 203
Realist, The, 90
Redemption, xxii, 136, 138, 183–85
Reisman, David, 189
Remainders, The, xxii, 192n6
"Reversible Man, The," 149–50
Revisioning Food, Farm, and Forest, xxii
Richards, Keith, 82, 189
Richards, Reed, 131
Richards, Ted, 105
Riesman, Josephine, xv
"River, The." See *Teenage Mutant Ninja Turtles*
Roarin' Rick's Rare Bit Fiends, ix, x, xii, xiv, xx, xxii, xxiii, 47–49, 58, 61, 63, 70, 73, 78–81, 91, 113, 132, 158, 162, 166, 180, 182, 184–89, 190, 213, 215
Robin, xii, 25, 28
Rodriguez, Manuel ("Spain"), x, 105
Rolling Stone, xvii, 105, 110
Rolling Stones, 103
Roth, Big Daddy, 92, 204
Rushdie, Salman, 18

Saenz, Mike, 165, 191n1
Saga of the Swamp Thing. See *Swamp Thing*
Sanders, Bernie, 107

224 INDEX

Sanders, Ed, xxii, 70, 114, 210

Sandman, 49

Satanic Verses, The, 18

Saturday Night Live, 106

"Scenes from the Nativity," xix

School of Visual Arts, 9

Schumacher, Joe, 49–50

Scout, xix, 14

"Secret Life of the Brain, The," xxi, 172

Secret Origins, xix

Secrets of the Comics, 109

self-publishing, ix, x, xii, xiv, xix, xx, 23–24, 41, 49, 51, 60, 62, 63, 70, 78–79, 157, 158–64, 176–78, 198, 201

Sentry, xxi

Severin, John, ix, xxi, 147, 151, 152

Severin, Marie, 100

Sgt. Rock, xi, xiii, xviii, 10, 158, 206, 210, 212

Shadow, The, 106

Shadowhawk, 127

Sharon Tate: A Life, xxii

Shatter, 165, 166, 191n1

Shelton, Gilbert, 9, 133

"Shiny Beast," xix

Shiny Beasts, xxi, 62, 161, 168

"Shipmates," xix

Shuster, Joe, 45, 50–51, 119

sidekicks, xxii, 24, 25, 28–31, 36, 104

Siegel, Jerry, 45, 50–51, 96, 119

Sienkiewicz, Bill, 123

Silver Surfer, xviii

Sim, Dave, xix, 23–24, 48, 51, 78, 80, 101–2, 160–61

Simon, Joe, 186, 214

Simon and Schuster, 214

Simpson, Don, 125, 126, 211

Sinnott, Joe, 109

Sirhan, Sirhan, 210

Six Feet Under, 65

Skull, 105

Slow Death Zero, xxiii

Smith, Jeff, 51

Sojourn, 152

"Solar Plexus," xviii

"Song for Saigon Sally, A," xviii

Sopranos, The, 65

"Sounds in the Silence," xxii

Sparky the Firedog, 172

Sparta Printing Company, 172

Spawn, 127

Speedy, 25, 28

SpiderBaby Graphix, 24, 26

Spider-Man, 87, 122, 127, 144, 156, 198

Spiegal, Jerry, 49–52, 194

Spiegelman, Art, 101–2

Spielberg, Steven, xviii, 99–100

Spirit, xiii, 54, 57, 141, 143, 144–45, 150, 163–64, 174

Spirits of Independence, 158–62

Spirit World, 186

Splash, xxi, 55, 60, 140–41, 154–55, 159–60, 177

Spotted Stone, The, xxii, 136, 143, 178, 180–82, 183, 184, 186, 190

Sprouse, Chris, 163

Sprout, 16, 199

Stanley, John, 87

Star Wars, x, xviii, 106, 198

Stephenson, Eric, 163, 205

Stine, R. L., xix

Stop Project 2025, xxiii

Strange, Adam, 15, 17

Strange Sports Stories, 199

Strange World of Your Dreams, The, 186

Streetwise, xxi

"Subtleman," xxi

Sun Comics, xvii, xxii, 114, 157–58, 163, 175, 178, 180

Super Catchy, xxii, 114, 136, 178–80, 186

superheroes, ix, x, xi, xii, xiv, 13, 14–15, 20, 24–26, 28–33, 34, 36, 39, 43–46, 47, 48, 49–54, 55, 56–57, 70, 95–97, 105, 143, 144, 163, 165, 179, 183, 193–94, 211, 212–13, 215

INDEX **225**

Superman, 4, 25, 31, 43, 45, 47, 50–51, 52, 87, 96–97, 109, 122–23, 130–31, 141, 142–43, 144, 156, 163, 194, 199

Supreme, xiii, xx, 57, 96–97, 131, 141–42, 158, 162–63, 165

Supreme: The Return, xxi, 196, 205–6

Swamp Thing, x, xi–xii, xix, xx, 3–6, 7, 13–19, 21–22, 24, 25, 27, 32, 34, 35–36, 39–41, 50, 53, 61, 62, 70, 77, 103–4, 106–7, 108, 118, 119, 130–31, 142, 146, 149, 158, 164–65, 190, 199, 204, 206; "Gargles in the Rat Race Choir," 17; "The Jungle Line," xix; "The Morning of the Magician," xx, 7, 17–19, 21, 32, 36, 40–41, 164; "My Blue Heaven," 15, 146; "The Secret Life of Plants," 17

Swan, Curt, 96, 141, 163

Taboo, xx, 127, 159, 166

Talbot, Bryan, xx, 209

Tantrum, 178

Tarzan, 96

Taylor, Jeremy, 81

Teenage Mutant Ninja Turtles, xx, 7, 22–23, 34, 41, 51, 158, 204–5, 206, 214

Teen Angels and New Mutants, xv

Tekno Comix, xx, 209

Teknophage, xx, 158, 209

"Tell-Tale Fart, The," xviii

Thompson, Don, 22

Thor, 121, 197

ThunderCats, 14

Timespirits, xix

"Tiny Dancer," xxiii

Titano, 4

Tomahawk, 40

Tombstone Hand, xiv, xxiii, 136–38, 185–86

Tomorrow Stories, xiii, xxi, 146–47, 153, 177

Tomorrow Syndicate, 121, 125–26, 131

Tom Strong, 57, 131, 142, 154

Tom Veitch Magazine, xvii

Top Shelf, xxiii

Top Ten, 57

Toro, 28

Toth, Alex, 99–100

Totleben, John, x, xi, xviii, xix, 3, 9, 14, 15, 32, 34, 36, 39, 53, 77, 87, 106–7, 125, 136, 211

"Touch of Vinyl, A," xx, 166

Toy Biz, 160

Trashman, 105

Treasure Chest, 85, 109

True-Man, 31–32, 43, 49–51. See also *Boy Maximortal*; *Maximortal, The*

True-Man: The Maximortal, xxiii

Truman, Tim, 9

Tundra Publishing, xx, 36, 41, 45, 49, 62–63, 117, 158

Turner, Ron, 9, 175

24-Hour Comic Challenge, xx, 78

Two-Fisted Zombies, x, xvii, 8, 9, 34, 36–37, 86, 89–90, 93, 100–101, 105–6, 110, 158, 169, 175

2001: A Space Odyssey, 110

Uncle Scrooge, 87

underground comics, ix, x, xvii, xviii, xxiii, 7–9, 34, 36–37, 45, 55, 70, 86, 90, 100–102, 103, 105–6, 108, 131, 144, 158, 165, 176, 184, 193, 209

"Underpass," xxi

Understanding Comics, 47

Universal monsters, 92

University of Quebec, xxii, 114–15, 158, 170–73, 192n6

University of Vermont, x, xvii, 158

Unknown Quantities, xxi

Unknown Soldier, xxii, 210

USA (character), 121

Valentino, Jim, 117, 118–19, 121, 124, 126–29

Valiant, 108

Veitch, Ezra, xviii, 22, 115, 174–75

Veitch, Kirby, xx, 57, 110, 115, 132, 174–75

226 INDEX

Veitch, Margaret, xvii, xxi, 90, 93
Veitch, Rick: childhood, 36, 47, 54, 71–72, 85–86, 87–89, 92–98, 132, 158, 204–5, 212; style, ix, xi, 8–9, 38–39, 86, 110, 115, 136, 139, 147, 163, 168–70, 197, 198, 205
Veitch, Robert, xvii, 90, 93
Veitch, Tom, x, xvii, xxiii, 7, 8, 9, 34, 36, 71, 72, 73, 74–75, 90, 92, 98, 108, 175–76, 209
Vermont, x, xiii, xvii, xviii, xxii, xxiii, 8, 9, 70, 71, 72, 86, 90, 93–94, 98, 100, 102, 107–8, 117, 166, 176, 177. *See also* Bellows Falls, VT
Vermont Cynic, xvii
Vermont Folklife, xxiii, 85
Vertigo Comics, xiii, xxi, 55, 58, 60, 61, 62, 63, 66, 144, 158
V for Vendetta, 20–21, 149, 164
Vietnam War, 90, 93, 201
Vogue Italia, 69

Wallace, Sidney, 50–52
war comics, ix, xiii, 10, 61, 64–68, 151–52, 165, 206–7, 210, 212
Ward, Lynd, 178
Warhol, Andy, 152
Warner Bros., 19, 41, 66, 149, 191n4
WaRP Graphics, 51
Warren Publishing, 99
Warrior, 13, 32
"War Wind," xix
Watchmen, 15, 32, 57, 104–5, 118, 119, 130, 149, 163, 164
Webtoon, 140
Wein, Len, 35, 107
Weiner, Jack, 159, 165–66
Weirdo, 102
Weisinger, Mort, 141, 163, 206
"Welcome to the Machine," xviii, 212
Welles, Orson, 110
Wertham, Fredric, 95, 104, 162, 213

westerns, 104, 152, 185–86
What If? Daredevil, xxi, 158
Wheeler, Doug, 22
"White House Horror, The," xviii
Who Farms?, xxiii
Wiggam, Albert Edward, 186
Wild Boy, 29–30
WildStorm Productions, xiii, 130, 163, 164
Williams, Chester, 5, 22
Williamson, Al, xviii, 23
Wilson, S. Clay, 105
Wired, 158, 168, 172
Witchblade, xxi
WNET, xxii, 62
Wonder Warthog, 193
Wonder Woman, 143
Wood, Wallace, 153, 174
Woodring, Jim, xii, 49
Workman, John, 125
World Bank, 115
World Color Press, 191n3
Wray, Bill, 205
Wrightson, Bernie, 35, 106, 107

X-Amount of Comics, 211
X-Men, 46, 122

Yeates, Tom, x, xviii, 3, 9, 87, 136

Zap Comix, xvii, 8, 108, 131, 193
Zograf, Aleksandar, 189
Zot!, 47
Zulli, Michael, 7, 24, 36, 40

ABOUT THE EDITOR

Brannon Costello is the James F. Cassidy Professor of English and Barbara Womack Alumni Professor at Louisiana State University, where he teaches and writes about southern studies, comics studies, and the intersections of those fields. His books include *Neon Visions: The Comics of Howard Chaykin*, winner of the Comics Studies Society's inaugural Charles Hatfield Prize, and the coedited volumes *The Other 1980s: Reframing Comics' Crucial Decade* and *Comics and the U.S. South.*

Printed in the United States
by Baker & Taylor Publisher Services